Flares and Graces... & Carnaby Street

MARTHA BERTRAND

authorHOUSE®

AuthorHouse™ UK
1663 Liberty Drive
Bloomington, IN 47403 USA
www.authorhouse.co.uk
Phone: 0800.197.4150

Published by AuthorHouse 12/19/2017

ISBN: 978-1-5462-8620-2 (sc)
ISBN: 978-1-5462-8621-9 (hc)
ISBN: 978-1-5462-8619-6 (e)

Library of Congress Control Number: 2017919100

Print information available on the last page.

This book is dedicated

-   To all the very dear friends who helped make my teenage years
    some of the most exciting time of my life thanks to their loyalty,
    their solidarity, their generosity of heart and their irrepressible
    sense of humour.
-   To the very few teachers who had the courage to stand by me.

Very special thanks to

- My husband for his unwavering support.
- Two exceptional and outstanding friends to whom I shall be eternally grateful for helping me reach a higher intellectual level.

Chapter 1

Napoleon's greatest misfortune was not to have been a little upstart from Corsica but to have had for enemies both Field Marshall Wellington and Rear Admiral Lord Horatio Nelson. He was doomed from the start.

My greatest misfortune was not to have been a lost child from Vietnam but to have fallen at the hands of the two most ruthless sisters of the Order of Charity: Sister Marie-Catherine and Sister Eugène-Marie. Abandoned at birth and incarcerated in a ghastly orphanage, I appeared to be doomed too... until fate intervened.

Lulled into an uneasy sleep on the train journey to Paris, I closed my eyes and, with my nostrils still twitching with the smell of hot hay and sea spray, I saw myself back at Sangatte. The coolness of the North Sea breeze swept my forehead as I looked out to the sea, at the mystical horizon that was now coming closer to me. I saw our little silhouettes walking in a neat crocodile file ambling through the main street of the village, gamboling in the fields or jumping in the sand-dunes. We were singing. Now, we were giggling as we saw nature exactly as it was with its funny noises, its pungent smells and its delicate pastel colours clashing with the stark black and white coats of cows mooching. A familiar tune started ringing in my head. With the supervisors nowhere to be seen, Maryse and the rest of our gang began dancing, holding hands while singing: *"Donne-moi ta main, et prends la mienne..."* Then, slowly, Maryse's hand slipped away from mine and the circle we had formed opened and started moving away. All I could see now were my friends' smiles and their hands waving goodbye as they disappeared into a nebulous mist of a past that was already fading away, fast.

At that moment, the strident sound of a whistle woke me up with a start. The train stopped and a voice crackled through a loud hailer: "Gare du Nord! Terminus!" We had arrived in Paris. I should have been excited but instead I felt lost, nervous and scared.

The City of Lights looked rather dark with its rows of grey buildings covered in grime. The bustling streets smelt of hot sticky tar and the ground shook every time a metro roared below ground, puffing clouds of hot fumes through the grids of large air vents suspended from the pavement. I had not as yet read Victor Hugo's '*Les Misérables*' but I had seen the film, shot in black and white to enhance the misery of life back then and as the godmother led me through the same streets with half of the buildings propped up by giant wooden trestles, I began to wonder whether I was about to become one of the '*misérables*' too. The thick wooden beams looked just like the barricades from where I had watched young Gavroche waving the Tricolore flag while shouting '*Liberté, Egalité, Fraternité!*' before being mowed down by a royalist bullet.

About half-way up a narrow street, the godmother pushed me through the small opening of a crumbling building supported by yet more wooden trestles. On the other side of it, I emerged into a cramped courtyard stinking of the acidic stench of stale urine which burnt my throat, garroted my senses and made my eyes water. The godmother noticed my reaction but chose to ignore it. Instead, she jerked her head towards a row of green doors lined up against the wall and pointed:

"If you need the toilets, that's where they are".

As we climbed a dark and dank narrow staircase that spiraled towards a small lugubrious landing on the first floor, I became more and more convinced that this was indeed Victor Hugo's notorious slums. The more I observed the insalubrious surroundings, the more I shivered with excitement at the thought that fresh riots were bound to burst to eradicate once and for all the exploitation of the *condition humaine* of the much put-upon French *citoyens*.

On the first floor, the godmother stopped outside a door half hidden in a dark recess, shook her Hermes handbag while mumbling that she could never find her keys, and led me into her domain. The minute I stepped in,

I froze in dismay. Still dressed in her pink Chanel suit with its matching salmon pink frills playfully tickling her chin, the woman's designer clothes were a far cry from the grotty little bed-sit which she called 'home'. The cramped room was taken up by a double bed on one side and an upright piano, a wardrobe and an armchair on the other. A large rug festooned with bare patches covered most of the old moth-eaten and flee-ridden carpet underneath. The shaded light pierced through a set of tall double windows from where I would soon while away the hours watching cars and passers-by below. To the right of the small entrance lay a small kitchenette with a sink which had cold *and* hot running water, the godmother would proudly declare. Underneath the sink, a small array of pots and pans lay hidden behind a grubby curtain, and among this lot, she retrieved a large plastic bucket which she placed in front of me.

"If you need to pee during the night, you'll have to use this!"

I looked aghast, shocked by the squalid conditions of her decrepit abode in which she proudly stored her pristine and elegant Chanel suit and Hermes handbag. She even boasted to living in relative luxury since she had a highly prized commodity: a telephone.

"See," she grinned proudly, brandishing the receiver and waving it towards me as if I had never seen a telephone before, "not many people have a telephone, so compared to others, I'm quite rich."

To my unsophisticated perception of worldly things, this was the first indication that it was possible to be poor and a snob at the same time.

All I could do was to snigger under my breath while wondering if, in Maryse's expert opinion, the godmother would qualify as a witch, but witches have crooked teeth, warts on their noses and do not wear expensive clothes. In every respect, the godmother failed the test for she had a smooth complexion, two perfect rows of sparkling white teeth and a bouncy mane of black hair which she swept capriciously over her small delicate shoulders. No, I concluded with bold confidence, she was definitely not a witch.

Paris in August resembles a vanity fair teeming with curious onlookers, ambling with their noses constantly sweeping the air. This particular type of people was new to me. I learnt later that they were called 'tourists' and, during the summer months, they took over the city while the Parisians themselves fled in drove to their country residences until well into September.

While touring the main sights of Paris, the godmother kept looking at me with a queer eye. It was not so much the interminable queues, the stifling heat or the racket that excited tourists created wherever they went which bothered her. Far from it for she soon made it clear to me that she would have preferred to be walking next to a sweet-looking precious little poppet blessed with an angel face rather than next to a provincial urchin, sporting cropped dark hair and staring back at her through prescription lenses.

"Pleeease! Don't wear your glasses when you're out with me." She would insist with a barely disguised air of disdain. "I'm used to being surrounded by beautiful girls. You don't need glasses anyway."

Her capricious stance did not bother me too much. Cheered on by the hustle and bustle of a city on holiday, I followed her around the popular sights of the capital and the banks of the river Seine where she declared dreamily in a whisper smouldering with desire: "this has to be the most romantic place on earth". Then, turning her head towards the primitive urchin standing next to her, she glared at me, turned up her nose, and moved on without saying another word. Wondering where that 'romantic place' was, I scowled at the murky waters, searching the fast flowing current frothing with polluted scum. Not that it mattered too much to me for I much preferred to take in the aesthetic beauty and historical significance of grandiose buildings and pompous monuments which I could only admire through a myopic haze.

Alas for the godmother, fate had the knack to show her wrong and just after she had been extolling the romantic beauty of the river, further along under one of the ancient stone bridges of Paris, we came upon an unsightly makeshift camp tended by the three scruffiest individuals I had ever seen, swilling wine from a plastic bottle and hailing each other in the rudest terms. The godmother immediately grabbed my arm and muttered under her breath: "close your ears!" while dragging me firmly towards a flight of steps.

"These," she said, with an air of profound disgust, "are the famous '*clochards de Paris*'. Don't you ever go anywhere near them. Those tramps are full of nits and fleas and they smell."

As we hurried away from the primitive encampment, one of the tramps got up, opened his ragged coat and started to dangle something below his belt.

"*Eh, les belles!*" He shouted. "Come and have a look at…"

"Oh my God!" The godmother exclaimed in complete shock.

I did not even have time to see what it was the tramp was showing off as the godmother pushed me in front of her and used her body to shield me from the censored scene. I do not know why she was so worried because I was not wearing my glasses anyway.

Another group of people had also attracted my attention but for rather different reasons. I had seen them punching tickets or sweeping the platforms in the metro; I had watched them clean the streets, pick up litter and, with grace, humility and perfect manners, greet the odd passer-by, always smiling and sometimes even singing. What did intrigue me about this particular group was the fact that they were all black. I had never seen so many black people before but unlike the notorious lay-about tramps, they had taken their righteous place in society, not begging, not scrounging, just starting off, like me, from the bottom rug of the social ladder. Watching them labouring on to keep our beautiful city clean made me realise that no matter where one starts in life, one should always proceed with the utmost dignity.

As for the godmother, she continued to observe me from the end of her nose, still wondering how on earth she had ended up with the ugliest of all ugly ducklings.

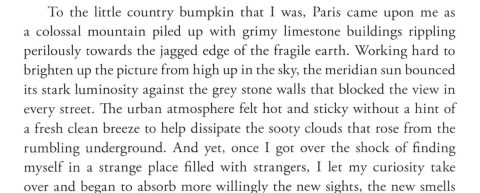

To the little country bumpkin that I was, Paris came upon me as a colossal mountain piled up with grimy limestone buildings rippling perilously towards the jagged edge of the fragile earth. Working hard to brighten up the picture from high up in the sky, the meridian sun bounced its stark luminosity against the grey stone walls that blocked the view in every street. The urban atmosphere felt hot and sticky without a hint of a fresh clean breeze to help dissipate the sooty clouds that rose from the rumbling underground. And yet, once I got over the shock of finding myself in a strange place filled with strangers, I let my curiosity take over and began to absorb more willingly the new sights, the new smells and the unfamiliar natter of people going about their everyday business while chatting animatedly. But the sight I least expected to see was that of children laughing freely and playing carefree in the streets. This baffled me, mesmerized me even and gave me hopes that perhaps, despite all my misgivings and forebodings, I might have landed in the right place after all.

Compared to the regimented routine I had been accustomed to, the godmother's way of life was somewhat unhurried, unstructured and pretty much idle. In the morning, under strict orders to stay in bed for as long as she did, I was forced to stare at the ceiling, at the damp patches and crumbling walls for hours on end until Madame deigned arise, which usually happened at around midday. On more than one occasion, I feared I was about to faint with hunger as I waited in vain to be fed.

Then after a week or so of my arrival, she started to leave the bedsit, sometimes during the day but mostly at night when I would be left alone with, for company, the screams of squabbling neighbours and the creaking of the old rumbling building shaken by the occasional car bobbing along the cobblestones. Thankfully, there was a small black and white television perched on the wall at the foot of the bed and its constant droning noise helped me forget that I was alone in a strange place where I knew not a single soul. Often, when the godmother was out yet again on some mysterious errand, I would hang out at the window, stare at the scene below and dream of Sangatte. Sometimes, I would close my eyes to leap back into the world I had left behind: the sandy beaches with its gigantic white cliffs, the little boats trudging along the waves, the fields that smelt of freshly churned up earth and ripe barley, and best of all... the cows, the big fat smelly cows with their doey eyes and their irresistible habit to smooch one another with those tender loving strokes they lavished on each other using their heads and their necks. I could even hear Maryse drop a casual remark mixed with her special brand of humour which never failed to have us both in stitches.

Back inside the grotty bed-sit in Paris, when the traffic faded away and the room became too quiet, I sat myself at the piano and began to tinkle the ivory keys at random until I discovered the musical scales that we had so earnestly sang in class under the guidance of the man's voice on the radio. With my fingers tentatively trying out every key, I was soon able to play the little ditty *'Au clair de la lune'*.

Being left alone at night, however, was the most frightening thing of all. I had never been left completely on my own before and I was scared. Several times, I caught myself staring at the worn curtains half expecting them to twitch. Monsters come out at night, Maryse had warned, but the curtains remained still and I invariably fell asleep with all the lights on and the television crackling and hissing at my feet after Roy Rogers had ridden into the sunset, bucking his horse, swinging his lasso above his head and singing his farewell tune that still rings inside my head... in French.

Unfortunately, my nightmares gradually began to return, more vivid and more terrifying for this time, I was no longer a hapless observer of blurred scenes where men in uniform fought and died, I had now become one of them. As an officer serving in the French army, I was poring over a map and plotting our next strategic move when the enemy burst into our headquarters and shot everyone in the room. Then, I was a floor manager in a large factory that was bombed and the roof collapsed over me, crushing me to death. Other heroic dreams followed and repeatedly, I saw myself involved in relentless battles which I fought over and over again alongside other courageous soldiers in the company of whom I always died.

"You move a lot at night," the godmother moaned, "can't you lie further towards the wall? I need my sleep and I can't sleep with you tossing and turning all night long."

What was I supposed to do? How could I possibly lie still in a strange bed when I was desperately trying to escape my enemies?

Chapter 2

Sometime towards the end of August, the godmother took me for a stroll on the *Champs Elysées*. As soon as we emerged from the metro, I was ineluctably pulled by the momentum of a slow moving crowd. I had never seen so many people ambling along in two synchronized flows that resembled the rolling waves of the sea. I felt so small that, unable to keep my head above the crowd, I feared drowning in this totally alien world. However, driven by an insatiable curiosity, I began to look around. Ignoring the enormous imposing shadow of the *Arc de Triomphe*, I stared with wide open eyes at the whole spectrum of human eccentricities parading, unabashed, in bright multicoloured clothes. In the distance, I even saw the incredible silhouette of a man - I think - perched on a pair of platform boots and wearing skin-tight yellow trousers, a white jacket and a large leather cap that was dipped over his right eye. His neck was wrapped up in a long silk scarf and the hand that held his handbag over his delicate shoulder had large rings on each finger, and that was not all… I swear he was wearing make-up. Unable to avert my eyes away from this extraordinary creature, I ogled at the alien, mouth baying. As his androgynous body whisked passed us, he glowered at me and squeaked: "*Et alors*?!" Then, with his middle finger, he flicked his blonde fringe, re-adjusted his cap and carried on walking, wriggling his pert little bottom all the way. I stopped to look at him for a few more seconds, in awe of this most flamboyant character. Not knowing what to think, I just smiled in wonder. Then, further along the avenue, I spotted a man wearing a pleated skirt, a small black jacket and thick cream socks. As the godmother and I continued to saunter along the famous avenue, more colourful citizens emerged from the homogeneous crowd, teasing my eyes and my sense of wonder. The avenue itself was bordered with magnificent trees, and alongside them lines of shops that looked so chic and so elegant that I felt nervous just walking past them as they spewed out their rich bountiful displays fanned out behind sparkling glass walls. Suddenly, the godmother's voice interrupted my thoughts. I had almost forgotten she was walking right beside me.

"It's the largest avenue in the world, and at Christmas, all the trees are covered with thousands of lights" she effused with childish wonder.

After we had passed the George V café, we turned into a side street. She was taking me to the F.O.E.F.I. (*Fédération des Oeuvres de l'Enfance Française d'Indochine*), the organisation in charge of looking after all the Vietnamese orphans in France. We climbed the stone staircase to the first floor and entered a dark antechamber where we were welcomed by a middle-aged woman.

"*Entrez, entrez*," she invited with a big smile.

The godmother stepped in feeling all jittery. Her head began to twitch nervously and her hands fumbled with the frills of her blouse and the buckles of her handbag. I followed closely behind, inspecting the surroundings and the faces behind the desks.

There were four desks in the main office, one in each corner of the room. We were led towards the furthest on the right-hand side where an imposing lady sat with a fixed smile. An aura of warmth and gentleness exuded from her, even if her heavily pasted face made her features look artificial, still and rigid. Instead of eyebrows, she had two neat penciled lines drawn above the eyes just like actresses I had seen in American films. The nameplate on her desk read: *Madame Graffeuil*.

"So," she said, extending a warm and welcoming hand, "you are… Martha Bertrand. Welcome to Paris." Then, after a short pause which allowed her to look me up and down, she asked as a matter of course: "Are you doing well at school?"

I looked at her blankly, not knowing what to reply. Did she not know? Had no one told her? Realising that she would not be able to strike a dialogue just yet, she pointed at the desk opposite hers.

"Let me introduce you to Madame Chauvineau, the social worker who will be responsible for your welfare."

I turned around and, in complete contrast with Madame Graffeuil, I caught sight of a woman with cold eyes and a frozen smile. As she scrutinized my face, the woman pulled her cardigan tightly around her middle-aged frame, bristled in her seat and looked as if she was preparing herself to confront a new enemy. Ready to meet my new foe on her own battleground, I returned her sustained glare and greeted:

"*Bonjour madame.*"

The soft and gentle voice of Madame Graffeuil aborted the first lightening charge.

"You'd better go and see her so that she can give you all the details of your new school, and when I hear about your school reports, I hope to hear only good things."

"*Oui, madame. Merci, madame.*"

I shuffled across to the other desk and stood rigidly with my hands tightly tucked behind my back. I was ready to go to battle… and so was she. Madame Chauvineau began to talk to the godmother as if I was not there.

"Now, the name of the school is '*Ecole des Bernardins*', a nice little boarding-school in the Latin Quarters.

Sandwiched between the *Boulevard Saint Germain* at one end and the river Seine at the other with, just beyond it, the spires of *Notre Dame de Paris* jabbing the sky, the school was surrounded by giant wooden trestles and if I had wanted final confirmation that this was indeed Victor Hugo's Paris, all I had to do was to walk to the end of the street and gaze at the magnificent, imposing shadow of the most famous cathedral in the world.

I entered the dark narrow corridor that led to the courtyard. Suddenly, I heard the patter of light footsteps and the sound of someone panting heavily. Then, something landed on my chest and I screamed.

"Dick! Come here, Dick! Now, sit! Sit! You're frightening the poor girl!" a female voice shouted. As the voice came closer, a nun appeared, wrestling with a young black Labrador. The dog barked excitedly.

"He's quite harmless and I can assure you, he won't bite, will you Dick? Now, sit, there's a good boy. You must be Martha Bertrand. Do you like dogs?" She said all in one breath.

"I don't know…" I replied nervously.

"Go on, you can stroke him. You need to show that you're not afraid."

But I was afraid. The dog, barking wildly and drooling at the mouth with excitement looked like an enraged beast. How could I not be afraid?

"Now," Sister Geneviève continued. "I'll give you a guided tour to show you where everything is so that you won't feel lost on your first day here."

Gathering her robes around her, the nun led us towards a wooden staircase and took us to the top floor of the main building where the dormitory was situated. It was a huge room with fifty beds or more, all lined up in rectilinear rows, their metal frame forming an iron grid over the parquet floor. What a ghastly place, I thought. At least at the orphanage, the dormitory was partitioned into smaller dorms.

Before leaving the vast dormitory, the nun took us to the washroom and pointed at two small cubicles.

"And next to the toilets, you've got the bidets… *pour la petite toilette*," she added almost in a whisper.

I had never heard of a '*bidet*' before and could not quite work out what they were for. However, the godmother had warned me not to ask any questions, for fear of showing my ignorance and my complete lack of sophistication. She had already sampled the depth of my ignorance when once, as we were standing in a queue, I asked quite innocently: "Who's Johnny Haliday?" She had looked aghast and shocked, which made her head twitch with embarrassment. She glanced at the blank faces of the people in the queue, and I could almost read the words forming on her bright pink lips: "she's not my daughter. In fact, we're not related at all!". Indeed, to her, the question was as embarrassing as going to Memphis and asking loudly: "Who's Elvis?" From then on, she had formed an unequivocal opinion of my little self: this street urchin was quite simply dense, primitive and ignorant to the point of being retarded, a condition she could just about tolerate as long as no one equated my poor cerebral powers with her own.

On the first floor of the building, we passed Napoleon scurrying nervously along the skirting boards.

"That's the boarding house's cat. He's supposed to catch mice but I'm afraid he's not much of a mouser. I think he's more afraid of the mice than they are of him." Sister Geneviève chuckled.

I looked at the scraggly little thing and felt no immediate urge to cuddle it.

"Then here," Sister Geneviève continued, showing a room laid out just like a classroom, "we have the study room, this is where you'll do your homework with all the other girls… Now, I can't show you the actual classrooms – they're over there – as the building is locked up, but don't worry, you can't get lost, it's only a small school."

———————⁂———————

On the first day at my new boarding school, I felt nervous, awkward and, just like the godmother had remarked, a bit of a peasant for I had been led to believe that only rich people lived in Paris. I thus expected to be crushed by an overwhelming parade of highly sophisticated girls with elaborate bows in their perfectly coiffed ringlets and with their noses turned up so high in the air that they would not even notice me.

As the evening beckoned, we gathered in the study and to my surprise, I saw a line of perfectly normal girls gradually file into the room. What a relief. And just like at the orphanage, there were some neat-looking girls and some grubby ones except that here, the contrast was even more startling as there was no uniform to conceal the difference in clothes. I scanned the faces eager to see who might become a potential ally. Alas at first glance, none appealed to me.

At school, a lively parade of highly manicured teachers took it in turn to sit at the teacher's desk and I watched in awe how Madame Lefevre, the heavily pregnant English teacher, manoeuvered her bump around the desk and how Madame Valois, the slim, petite Maths teacher, clacked her mini stiletto heels on the floorboard. We giggled in our sleeves every time Madame Delagrange, the History and Geography teacher, deposited her large heavy breast – one at a time if you please – on the desk at the beginning of each lesson. The atmosphere was decidedly very different here. The teachers seemed more relaxed, friendlier though somewhat aloof as they peered condescendingly at us from their elevated desk.

Since we were allowed to choose where to sit, I feathered my nest right at the back of the class and, hiding behind big Delphine's broad back, I let myself sink into a soft cocoon of blissful ignorance where no one would resent me for being a smart ass. My mind was made up. I would daydream away my teenage years, dangle as I pleased my spindly little legs, still too short to touch the floor, and giggle to my heart's content through the jocular mood of innocuous pedagogues who wanted to make their lives as easy as I wanted mine. The back of the class would from this day on become my very own private domain, out of bound and out of reach from the vitriolic remarks of resentful adults. This, I decreed with determination and aplomb, was going to be the Big Easy... Then, the headmistress walked in.

Mademoiselle Germaine was the only spinster among all our teachers and when I first saw her, I could not help exclaim in my cuffed hands:

"Oh my God! She's got a wart!"

But her wart was neither on her nose, nor on her chin. It was situated right there, on the left-hand side of her upper lip. You just could not miss it. However, I decided, she was not a witch; she looked far too sophisticated for that. Her auburn hair streaked with filaments of grey was pulled back in a tight bun, as was the fashion in those days, and her wide well-defined lips were always painted with the same red brick lipstick. To us, she looked tall and slim, and moved about with an overflowing abundance of physical and intellectual vigour which terrified us. When she occasionally lost her cool because we could not remember how to spell a word or we failed to regurgitate the twelve verses of a complicated poem full of alexandrines, she would pace frantically *l'estrade* - the wooden steps in front of the blackboard - and chant:

"*Il faut rabacher*! *Rabacher*!... until you know it by heart."

Drill, drill. Everything had to be drilled and hammered into our little brains. That was her uncompromising way, but, catching sight of our terrified faces, she would instantly calm down.

"I know it's hard, but it's the only way you're going to learn!"

And learn we certainly did, by force, by rote and by threats of thick volumes of '*travail supplémentaire*' if we did not fulfill her exact expectations.

Despite the fact that all of us were absolutely terrified of her, we could not help but admire her. She possessed an inexhaustible knowledge of Literature, vocabulary and grammar. To top this, she taught us the Classics as well as Mathematics to the upper classes. In every respect, she was the equivalent of the 18th Century's universal man except that this was the 20th Century and she was a woman. For the first time in my life, I was in complete awe of an adult, totally captivated by her cerebral powers and hypnotic charm and charisma.

She only once allowed herself to show her softer side and that was the day she brought in her beloved dog, a huge German shepherd called Prima. We never did find out why on that day she brought Prima into school but it completely changed my perception of her. I was still terrified of her like everyone else but gradually, though shy to admit it, I was beginning to like her.

So far, life in my new boarding school had been rather uneventful. With no close ally with whom to lark about, my only crime to date had been to be hopelessly inept at sewing, a fact that Sister Agnès found very peculiar, at odds with her firmly set views that all girls should be obedient, subservient and good at sewing. However, she liked to call a spade a spade, regarding the use of euphemisms as a waste of words which could easily lead to misunderstandings. And so it was that one day I found her waiting for me at the top of the stairs, legs akimbo – I know because I could see her small feet sticking out from beneath her voluminous robes - and fists firmly dug into her hips. What had I done this time? I stared back trying to guess the origin of the storm that was about to explode.

"Martha Bertrand!" She whistled through her teeth. "I've never known a girl so bad at sewing. Either you need new glasses or you need to see a psychiatrist."

Hugely relieved that my crime was nothing worse than a minor deficiency in the art of sewing, I smiled at her directness and walked on.

There was something else I was about to learn about myself. Nadine was a senior girl and during our ushered conversations stolen in private moments, she tried to explain to me the origin of life. To tell the truth, I did not understand one iota of what she was trying to tell me for this was a topic I had never pondered over. The words 'mother' and 'father' had never entered my vocabulary and Sister Eugene-Marie had told me outright that my parents simply 'did not exist'. Needless to say, what Nadine was about to reveal shook me to the core.

"Of course you've got a mother and a father!" She spurted out. "You need a man and a woman to produce a child. You don't just appear on earth."

My jaw hit the floor.

"What!? You mean… I have a mother… and a father... like everyone else?"

"Of course you have! It's not because you don't know who they are that they don't exist."

I was stunned. I was not issued from celestial dust after all. In one fell swoop, I had been reduced to the low level of a right proper little earthling. How could it be? *Me*, Martha Bertrand?

Once I had recovered from the shock, life resumed its dull ordinariness. The school work I produced was mediocre to say the least and I was perfectly happy with that. Never again would I ever let anyone think that I might be smarter than I let on.

In the narrow entrance of the school, high up on the wall, featured a *'tableau d'honneur'*, a kind of merit board where pupils with marks averaging 13 or above out of 20 were listed. My name never managed to make it on the merit board although at the beginning I came very close, in fact a bit too close for comfort. As I was inspecting the names at the end of another mildly productive week, a girl pointed at the board and said:

"Your name should be up there."

I looked at her flabbergasted. With the mediocre marks I had been getting, how could she tell? What surprised me more was the fact that it was a girl in my class who made the remark and not one of my teachers. Did anybody care?

Being Martha Bertrand, it was never too long before I got into trouble but this time, it was quite unintentional.

Sister Marguerite was the nun in charge of teaching us religious instruction. She was kind and gentle and seemed to have a genuine fondness for us girls. Approaching the Easter holidays, the notes for our homework concerned, quite appropriately, the crucifixion. Having decided a while ago that I would have as little to do as possible with religion - and here, with no threats of public condemnation and soul bashing, it was a rather easy thing to do - I did not bother to even look at the printed sheet we were asked to learn by heart. Anyhow, the end of term test came. Sister Marguerite negotiated perfectly the tight angle of the teacher's desk, gathering her voluminous robe around her chair with expert hands, and sat down looking at us with her usual warm and friendly smile. As soon as the question sheets were distributed, the test began in earnest. With all the religious knowledge that had been drummed up into my head, I diligently proceeded to waffle my way through all the questions until I came to a particular one: "after he had been entombed, how did Jesus rise again?" I scowled. How? Well, I was not sure. Was it mentioned in the homework? I did not know. As I raised my head to try and retrieve some long forgotten knowledge buried in a distant memory, I felt the full weight of Sister Marguerite's glare fall upon me. I panicked. If she saw me idle, she would immediately suspect, correctly, that I had not done my homework so I picked up my pen again and wrote the first thing that came into my head.

'Jesus', I began, 'did not die on the cross. Because of the heavy loss of blood he sustained, He was in a lethargic state and the perfumes and scents in the tomb revived Him.' I looked at my answer mightily pleased with myself. It was, after all, a perfectly logical explanation.

Alas, a few days later, hell fell upon my head.

"How dare you say that Jesus did not die on the cross!" Sister Marguerite scolded. "How much more suffering do you think He had to bear to prove that He was the Son of God? Was it not enough that he gave his very last drop of blood on the cross to save people like you? I am shocked by your ignorance and I shall have to report the matter to the Headmistress."

And while she wailed in the name of God and Jesus, I stood rigid by my desk, disappointed that she had failed to appreciate the good use of vocabulary. After all, how many girls were familiar with the word 'lethargic'?

Back at the boarding house, Sister Agnes was waiting for me. The way she stood at the top of the stairs with her eyes darting killer flashes of lightning did not bode well.

"I can't believe you wrote this!" She remonstrated. "Quite apart from anything else, it is blasphemous, pure blasphemer! No one has ever written anything as odious as this! You're going to need to repent, girl, because if you don't, it's hell for you, you can be sure of it. And the first thing you're going to do, my girl, is to go to confession. Then, I'm putting you in quarantine to give you time to reflect on your thoughts and more importantly on your faith. For a start, each Thursday afternoon, you're going to learn by heart five pages of the Bible. That should help you redeem yourself in the eyes of God… if He'll ever forgive you!"

I stood in front of her quite incapable of understanding what all the fuss was about. It was a perfectly logical answer, I wanted to explain, but I knew she would not listen. As far as she was concerned, I was well beyond redemption.

In class, I had expected a similar wrath from the headmistress and when Mademoiselle Germaine entered the classroom, the usual silence that followed froze us solid in our seats. As she passed my desk, she glowered at me. I looked sheepishly back at her. Then she shook her head and muttered with a cynical smile: "well, Martha Bertrand, I don't know…" and said no more. I stared at her in sheer disbelief. Was that it? Was she not going to condemn me, curse me and send me to hell like everyone else?

───────────※───────────

It was around this time that music began to filter into my life. Back at the orphanage, there had been very little of it, some fragments of popular waltzes by Strauss, the odd song from Disney films and Sister Sourire's international hit 'Dominique' of which we knew all the lyrics by heart. Here in Paris, I discovered France Gall, the cutest girl I had ever seen, still in her teens, and right now she was at the top of the chart with *'Les Sucettes'* (lollipops), a melodious little ditty written by the unkempt, unshaven and chain-smoking crooner Serge Gainsbourg. I loved that little ditty and sang it all the time in my squeaky girly voice and so did France Gall until Gainsbourg quizzed her about the song. Did she understand the meaning behind the lyrics? Of course she did not. Years before the fourteen year old Vanessa Paradis charmed the world with her sweet little song 'Joe le Taxi', France Gall was the most adorable, innocent and cutest poppet to grace the charts, blessed as she was with the purest mind God could have bestowed on her. How could she possibly have guessed the perverted twist Gainsbourg had given to the lyrics? When he told her, the poor girl was so shocked, so mortified and so crushed by shame that she refused to leave her apartment for several weeks afterwards and point blank refused to perform that song ever again.

───────────※───────────

Sometime during that first term, the godmother announced that we would soon be moving to a new abode called '*un appartement*', in the chic district of the XVIIème *Arrondissement*. For our inspection tour, we walked a short distance down the *Avenue de la Grande Armée*, turned into a side street and passed a small square where a modern apartment block stood. In complete contrast to the godmother's bedsit, this building glowed with freshness set off by the vibrant green of perfectly manicured lawns. Rather excitedly, we made our way towards the glass doors, greeted the concierge and took the lift to the sixth floor. I walked with my nose up in the air, absorbing the bright light, the wide space and the clean air. This was more like the Paris I had expected, the City of Lights people always talked about.

The apartment looked grand and spacious, and so bright with all the rooms facing south. Best of all, it had proper rooms: a kitchen, a living-room, a small lounge, a bedroom, a bathroom… and an inside toilet. Now, that really was the height of luxury. What's more, I would be able to have my own bed in the shape of a nice springy divan set up in the small lounge next to the bedroom.

To help her adjust to this new life of luxury, the godmother had drafted in the services of a maid. Her name was Conchita. With her big chest suspended high on her large frame, she looked quite maternal and wholesome and I could easily imagine her going about her daily chores with half a dozen snotty little kids tugging at her long black skirts. However she did not last long. I do not know why though I suspected that with me around, the godmother no longer needed a maid.

Anyhow, we settled graciously in our new abode and life resumed its ordinariness, with the godmother idling her time away and I wondering what my next adventure would be. Then, inspired by nostalgic memories of exotic landscapes, paddy fields and aromatic spices, the godmother resumed her favourite activity which was to sketch colourful patches of her lost paradise on big silk canvas tightly clamped on gilded frames.

The godmother lived alone; that fact was plain to me. However, she had a large posse of woman friends, most of whom dated back from Vietnam. Together, they would reminisce about their school days, the tricks they played on the nuns and the handsome French soldiers they wooed. They nattered away in Vietnamese and laughed a lot, leaving me to observe silently the similarity of their exotic features, the long dark hair, the beautiful almond eyes, the porcelain skin and the sparkling white smiles that creased their smooth faces with laughing lines. The godmother was particularly fond of Sonia, the wife of the Ambassador of an ex-French colony somewhere in the north west of Africa. Virginie's ebony features were stunning, especially when she wore her brightly coloured *boubou* with matching head-dress. In those days, telephone calls were charged per call and not per minute which allowed the women to gossip for hours, usually at night and in bed. When Sonia was not busy accompanying her husband on some ambassadorial duty, she would turn up at the apartment with her two toddlers in tow. Sometimes, her husband would come too. He was a remarkable male specimen, very tall, extremely well-built and delectably handsome. Unfortunately, I could never follow an entire conversation with him – usually revolving around politics, corruption among government officials, the best Mercedes series or the best way to serve his favourite scotch - because his speech was marked by the thickest African accent I had ever heard. Years later, when I was a fully fledged adolescent and had acquired a suitable degree of sophistication, he invited me for a drink at his posh hotel where he was staying on business and as I sat down, he introduced me to his colleague: "this is Mr ..., the Foreign Affairs Minister". Goodness, I thought. Here I am, mixing with the cream of African society. Me! Martha Bertrand, the little snot from that ghastly orphanage.

I do not know whether the ugly duckling had suitably transformed into a swan yet but the godmother would soon let me know. Amidst her glamorous posse of friends, as far as her artist eye could fathom, I stood out like an eyesore and she was determined to do something about it. She dragged me to the hairdresser's to have my hair permed in order to make me look older and more sophisticated and less like that peasant girl from the North as she kept reminding me. I ended up with an elaborate bouffant mop that bobbed around my head like a loose turban. It was useless. Whatever means she used, in her eyes I remained the steadfast ugly duckling that had landed on her patch and blotted the perfect tableau of her life. And boy, didn't I know it! Many times she made it blatantly clear that she did not want me around, accusing me of cramping her style and impeding on her private life. I used to listen to her rants wanting to point out that: 'by the way, I never asked to come here; besides, I am away at boarding school during the week'.

Did she ever show any genuine interest in me? Not one bit. Not once did she enquire about my past, my friends or my life at the orphanage. Not once was she interested in finding out how I might feel, having been uprooted from the only world I knew, because if she had, I would have told her that I missed my gang and yes, I missed the orphanage.

This aloof attitude verging on disdain led me to the inevitable question: why on earth did she take me out of the orphanage? So I began to probe her.

"Are you really my godmother?"

She took affront.

"Of course I am. Why else do you think I'm putting up with you?"

"How did you become my godmother then?"

"Well, when you were found on the steps of the Red Cross Hospital in Danang…"

"I was found on the steps of the Red Cross Hospital?" I eagerly interrupted.

"Yes you were, but don't interrupt. Anyway, it was Sister Therese who found you and you know what nuns are like. They have you baptized before you can say 'amen', just in case anything happens to you. They do that to all abandoned children…"

"Okay I get that, but how ***did you*** get to be my godmother?" I interrupted again.

"Well, next door to the hospital, there was a primary school and the nuns always went there to ask who would like to be godmother to a new orphan. Now, I was an assistant there with my friend Adèle. Sister Thérèse asked Adèle first but she was not interested. I don't know why because you were a cute little baby. I remember saying to her: "how can you say no. Look, she's beautiful and she's got green eyes".

"Green eyes? I don't have green eyes. Are you sure you've got the right orphan?" I asked wistfully.

"You may not have green eyes now, but you did when you were a baby."

"But how can you be sure it's me?"

"Oh, I know… I just know."

In months to come, she would often mention her friend 'Adèle'. At first, I remained totally indifferent to her remarks. After all, I had never met the woman, and quite frankly, I was not interested. However, every now and again, she would use early reminiscences of Vietnam to drop a few more hints about 'Adèle' so much so that I began to suspect that there might more to the elusive Adèle than she was prepared to admit but finding herself bound by a vow of silence, she could reveal no more.

Chapter 3

It was now May 68. The weather was hot and the atmosphere stifling. There was not even the usual fresh breeze that swept away the last remnant of pink blossom fallen from the cherry trees. Behind the scenes, the rumblings of a political storm were beginning to ripple throughout the city. The newspapers splashed on their front pages close-up pictures of union leaders shouting rallying cries for a general strike. Students everywhere were deliberating over the merits of a communist regime, and how to drop out of a ruthless society that sent its young men to pointless wars. To the sound of popular music, led by the Beatles – **who?** I remember asking - they pledged to make love and not war, and founded their own utopia based on free love, peace and harmony which they acted out in makeshift communes where the notion of sharing extended far beyond the bounds of morality. But in the whimsical wind of change of the Sixties', who cared?

The students of Nanterre University were the first to walk out. Keen to be seen at the forefront of any revolutionary movement, those of *La Sorbonne* soon followed. They met up in the Latin Quarters with the intention to start a peaceful demonstration to protest against a system that was too rigid, too elitist and too orderly. It was a time when romantic ideas overruled the dogmatic regime. The age-old motto of the king's army, *Les Mousquetaires – Chacun pour soi et Dieu pour tous* (Each for himself and God for all) – was now viewed as a self-centered, self-serving and arrogant slogan, and was rejected outright. No more 'each for himself'. We are all in it together; brothers as we are, we shall love as one, be as one and share as one. That's our new motto. And as the intellectual youth of the day, swayed by idealistic notions that had first been thrashed out in compulsory Philosophy classes, embraced wholeheartedly the ideals of communism, the authorities swiftly moved in. The resulting clashes turned the Latin Quarters into a war zone. News reporters rushed to the area and chronicled the events with rolls of films full of atrocities from both sides: students were seen attacking the police force with cobblestones and *'cocktail Molokov'*, a homemade incendiary devise using glass bottles and burning fuel. One student was even filmed throwing several *'cocktail Molokov'* into a wheelbarrow before pushing it towards a thick cordon of policemen. The authorities responded by beating up the protesters ruthlessly and mercilessly. During that fateful week of May 68, all the papers gleefully splashed on the front pages the bloodied faces and battered bodies of all those who had been caught in a modern revolution. As in all wars, any sense of human dignity and decency promptly disappeared and those not directly involved in the confrontations were avidly poring over newspapers' picture diaries which revealed, blow by blow, all the horrors of citizens at war. Bizarrely, what shocked many people most was to see water canons being used to disperse the warring factions. If it was perfectly acceptable to clean the streets of Paris with powerful water jets whooshed down the gutters, it was less so to watch the very same tactic used on humans, a rather demeaning and humiliating technique that reduced men and women to the level of street litter. With these shocking pictures being blasted into the quiet realm of every French citizen's lounge, no one could remain indifferent to the unfolding drama. The peaceful and romantic idyll that had started it all, that of a society made of equals united as one, lay in tatters and all that remained were violent and ugly scenes captured on celluloid for posterity. The President, General De Gaulle, at first remained firm and inflexible in his stance; but by the end of that eventful week, he began to relent. The fact that he did not intervene earlier would turn out to be his downfall and after seeing this catastrophic display of his own beloved country at war, of his loyal citizens fighting each other, and of the pride of France being crushed by a stubborn corps of revolutionaries, he was left with no other option but to resign.

However, for us girls sequestered within the impenetrable walls of the boarding school situated just a cobblestone's throw away from the *Boulevard Saint Germain*, the revolution had only just begun. With politics banned from French schools, most of us had no idea of what was going on. Unwitting witnesses of a social revolution, all we cared about was whether the school was going to close or not.

Monday morning came.

"Do I have to go to school?" I asked the godmother, somewhat nervous.

"Why?" She reacted, seemingly surprised that I should even asked such a question. "Did the headmistress say there was no school?"

"No."

"In that case you have to go to school or I'll be in trouble if you don't go."

"But there's a war on."

"Don't exaggerate. You always exaggerate. You must have picked up that bad habit at the orphanage."

Early that morning, I emerged from the metro station, and there they were: dozens of dark blue police coaches lining the right-hand side of the *Boulevard Saint Germain*, their windshields and side windows covered with protective iron grids. I felt nervous and scared but at the same time excited. I had not long left the orphanage but already I found myself caught up in the middle of a real revolution. If only my gang could be with me to share the excitement… but I was all alone, so I walked at a brisk pace on the other side of the boulevard averting my eyes well away from the instruments of war.

Two days later, a daygirl burst into the playground all flustered.

"They're coming!" she shouted, red in the face.

"Who?"

"The riots! They've stormed *La Sorbonne* and now, they're coming this way!"

"Oh no! What are we going to do?" A girl shrieked.

"Great!" Another girl exclaimed. "They'll have to close the school now. No grammar lesson today! Yippee!"

The long awaited revolution had finally reached the threshold of our school, not that it bothered Mlle Germaine.

"No," she declared firmly. "We have a duty, a duty to ourselves and a duty to the school. This is our chance to show that we are brave, that we have courage and fortitude and you will prove it by coming to school!"

As her words thundered above our heads, an alarming clamour rumbled a few meters away from the school's front door.

The rioters had now reached the top of the *Boulevard Saint Germain*, and as we sat rigidly at our desks, in tense suspense, we could hear loud cries of war and pain rise up from the streets. We jumped, startled, in our seats as another glass wall of a nearby café exploded under the impact of several cobblestones. Hundreds of CRS officers, the most feared police force in the country, had been drafted in the capital and they were throwing tear gas bombs to try and control the rioters. Worried parents rushed to the school to take away their girls. Victor Hugo had fled the country when things got too hot but we, under the unflinching command of Mlle Germaine, would have to sit it out.

At night, the riots continued. From the dormitory situated on the top floor, we could see nothing but we could hear the police sirens, screams, the defiant chants shouted with anger and force, and the deafening fracas of shattering glass and exploding cars. As darkness fell, we crowded around the tall windows to stare with wonder at the sky redden by the jumping flames of several bonfires that the rioters had lit on top of makeshift barricades.

The following days, frantic parents phoned to demand that the school be closed for the duration of the riots but Mother Superior refused to give in to their demands on the ground that it was not her school, therefore not for her to decide. As for Mlle Germaine, she also refused on the ground that we had to battle it out for the sake of our future. Parents were not impressed. Of course they cared about their daughters' education but they cared even more about their safety and they swiftly took them away while we, boarders, had to brave the heat, the noise and the tear gas as we sat at our desks choking in the heat and with our eyes stinging and streaming.

"Mademoiselle, can we at least open one window please?"

"You know very well we can't. It's going to be far worse if we open the windows. So, you'll just have to be brave and just like many of our great philosophers and poets, show some stoicism in the face of adversity. Just think of Verlaine who wrote some of his best poems while he was in prison."

And when she ran out of solid arguments, she would always rely on her favourite phrase: 'do yourself proud and do it for the Honour and Glory!'

I did not hear the rest of her speech for I was stuck on one word: stoicism. This was another new word and I quickly made a mental note of it. During my two years at the school, I never ceased to admire Mademoiselle Germaine for she always came up with some magical words with mysterious meanings that never failed to excite my intellectual curiosity. And with a revolution being played out on our doorstep, life could not have been more exciting. Paris had indeed become a fantasy land with all kinds of words swirling around my head and brave Gavroche gesticulating in the middle of my dreams.

Chapter 4

If Mademoiselle Germaine felt unable to close her school, the local authority did it on her behalf and shortly after witnessing my first revolution, we all packed our bags and left for good.

That summer, I was sent to a holiday camp in a small Savoyard village in the French Alps called Berneix. Up until now, the only hills I had ever seen were the slag heaps of coal mines that cluttered and darkened the featureless landscape of Northern France. But these were not hills, they were mountains, so big and so tall that the rectilinear horizon I had observed at the far end of the sea did not exist at all here and instead all I could see was a series of jagged peaks, some covered in snow, stretching high up in the sky. I stared at the mountains overwhelmed by their magnitude, their solid mass and by the array of colours I had never seen before: the stark grey of the bare rock interspersed between splashes of vibrant green from the fresh pastures and mountain pines, the rustic brown of wooden chalets peppered with multicolour patches from flowers growing in wooden tubs suspended from windows and balconies. The sight of this vast magnificence was like an awakening. I was seeing **beauty** for the very first time, the kind of beauty that connected you spiritually with nature.

The camp was mixed which made me rather nervous. Not since my nursery school days had I been in the company of boys and right now, tittering on the threshold of their teenage years, they looked big, imposing and in complete command of their senses. At first, I felt totally intimidated by their masculine presence and kept well away from them.

The camp was run by a husband and wife team supported by a handful of hippy students who, armed with guitars, helped out with the daily activities. Making friends was easy especially as there was a whole bunch of us, Vietnamese orphans, who had been drafted from all over France. I did not know any of them but we clicked straight away. The conversation always begun by enquiring which boarding school/orphanage we were at before moving on swiftly to the funnies: the tricks, the pranks and the naughties we had all been up to. At this stage, I contented myself to listening to the other girls' misdemeanours for I had never laughed so much. By comparison, my own life seemed rather dull despite having lived through my very first revolution, a topic in which nobody was interested and nobody cared.

In amongst the girls, however, I spotted one named Marie-France. What attracted me to her was the fact that she laughed a lot. Actually, she laughed all the time. She would point at something, at someone or simply in the distance and burst out laughing. In fact, there was very little on this earth that did not make her laugh. Our favourite pastime was word games and if she was stuck for a word, she did not hesitate to make up one.

"*Merdouille!*" She once trumpeted.

"*Merdouille?*" I looked dubiously at her. "That word doesn't exist."

"Yes, yes!" she insisted before dissolving in laughter. "It is a proper word."

Every now and again, my new gang of friends turned their attention to the boys, although they did not seem all that taken by them. Boys... I had never been that close to boys before and observed them like a naturalist observes a new species. They appeared very different from us girls in character, in demeanour and in the way they felt superior to us. But apart from this, they looked perfectly normal to me, although I could not quite work out why they should feel so superior to us.

The girls at my table had noticed that the most personable group sat at a table not far from ours. The leader was a boy called Alain. He was blonde, tanned and handsome, and oozed self-confidence from every pore. He was arguably the most popular boy in the whole camp. But I was not interested in him. No, my eyes had rested on his right-hand man for, in my pubescent considered opinion, he was by far the most handsome specimen I had ever seen. Tall for his age and athletic in shape, he had the most gorgeous mop of blond hair that rested lazily on his square shoulders. Mademoiselle Germaine had taught us all about Greek gods, so I knew exactly what they looked like. Sitting two tables away from me in the crowded refectory, he was listening passively to Alain. His name was Sébastien. His smooth slightly sun-tanned skin glowed with the first adolescent hues. I made up my mind on the spot. I did not care that I might be the ugliest of all ugly ducklings, I was determined to pair up with him. After all, the director of the camp had described me as 'enigmatic', a word I did not fully understand but which sounded good.

That evening, I scribbled a quick note on a torn piece of paper and I asked Nicole, a girl at our table, to pass it on to him. From afar, I watched him intently, waiting for his reaction. He probably had no idea who I was and upon finding out, he would probably laugh and throw my note away with the rest of the rubbish. Nevertheless, I watched him like a hawk. After reading my note, he looked aghast. Used to moving in the shadow of his ever-popular friend, he seemed quite shocked that anybody should have noticed him. A few minutes later, he returned the note to Nicole who handed it back to me. I opened it eagerly. On it, Sébastien had written: *meet you after supper*. What! He actually wants to meet me, **me**, Martha Bertrand, the ugliest of all ugly ducklings! I whispered the news to the other girls.

"Oh my God!" Marie-France exclaimed. "You've bagged the best one!"

"Have I?" I questioned. "I thought Alain was."

"No, he's too full of himself. Sébastien is much nicer. But how did you manage to get him?"

"I just wrote him a note."

From then on, I played cool. I took my glasses off, flicked capriciously my growing fringe, and wrote '*billets doux*' to my intended which I passed from girl to boy at meal times. Living in a blurred dimension next to my sweetheart, I lost myself in his beautiful blue eyes, in such close-up that his smooth olive skin was almost touching mine. We held hands and when we happened to be standing still, I rested my head on his swelled-up chest and listened to his heart. During walks in the mountains, he remained with his tight cluster of friends but every now and again, he would look behind to steal a glance from my adoring eyes.

During the rare moments we enjoyed together, Sébastien would look at me and simply smile, a glorious happy smile that allowed our mutual fondness for each other to grow and flourish without being hindered by a string of clumsy words.

Then, one day, he whispered in my ear:

"I would like to kiss you…"

I looked at him rather coyly. A kiss seemed the natural progression in any romantic adventure but for me it was a huge deal. Before Sébastien, no one had ever held me tight, murmured gentle words in my ears or even kissed me. I panicked. I had no idea what I was supposed to do. Just in case I made a complete fool of myself, I decided that the utmost privacy was required.

"All right…" I finally conceded, "but not in front of everybody."

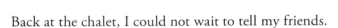

Back at the chalet, I could not wait to tell my friends.

"Did you close your eyes?" Marie-France enquired all excited.

"Why? I wanted to see his face. He's so gorgeous!"

"But you're supposed to close your eyes," Gisèle butted in. "It's more romantic."

Our little tryst did not go by unnoticed. Everyone seemed to follow our every move with keen interest. Even the director of the camp could not help comment: "you make a very glamorous couple".

At the end of the holiday, we promised to see each other again and exchanged addresses. DecipheringSébastien's address, I saw that he lived far away, in that thick concrete jungle that extended south in the suburb of Paris. I knew instantly that we were not likely to meet again, but ever? That, I did not know.

On the platform of Gare de Lyon, we stood awkwardly, not knowing what to say to each other. The word 'love' had never entered our vocabulary. As far as we were concerned, it was a word only used by grown-ups. Only *they* could fully understand it. Besides, it sounded far too complicated. But the whole experience had been the beginning of the awakening of my senses, an exciting adventure that we had lived together, forever imprinted in our hearts.

My thoughts cut short, I heard him say goodbye and I watched him disappear in the distance with his tall and slim mother carrying his suitcase. He turned around one more time and waved. I waved back and smiled, one last coquettish smile. When he eventually disappeared out of sight, a rush of strange feelings made me feel forlorn, sad and rather queasy.

We did write to each other but after his second letter, suspecting that we would probably never see each other again, I lost interest.

Behind me, Marie-France was trying to get my attention.

"If you want to see him again, you could always ask to go back to Berneix."

"Yes…" I replied dreamily. "I can't wait for the next holiday." Then I turned to my friend. "Where are you going now?"

"To *la fédé*."

"I'd come with you if it wasn't for my suitcase, it's so heavy. Do you know where you're going for your next holiday?"

"Probably skiing…" Marie-France replied on an indifferent tone.

"Skiing!" I exclaimed. "I'd love to go skiing. What do you have to do to go skiing?"

"Just ask."

"Ask whom?"

"Your social worker. Which one is yours?"

"Mme Chauvineau."

"Oh, bad luck! Mine is Mademoiselle Cany… She's really nice"

"Can I come to *la fédé* with you?"

"I thought you didn't want to lug your suitcase around."

"I know but I want to go skiing… I really hope Mme Chauvineau is going to be in."

"Come on, then," Marie-France said, chivvying me along. "Let's go and see."

When we entered the lounge of *rue Washington*, my friend introduced me to other girls and immediately joined into the joking and bantering. I pricked up my ears as some of the girls were speaking in Vietnamese. As the banter and laughter grew louder, a buxom woman with her head wrapped up in loose streaks of grey hair suddenly burst into the room and scolded:

"I don't want to hear that tongue of savages again! I only want to hear French spoken, and French only, understood?!"

"Yes, Mademoiselle Blanchard." The girls chorused.

Then, as soon as the door was closed, the girls resumed their chatter in Vietnamese, but quieter this time.

"Who was that?" I asked Marie-France. "Is she one of the social workers?"

"No, she's just a general helper."

"And what was that accent? That was some accent!"

"She's from Belgium, from the Walloon side. She's actually really nice and very funny. We're always winding her up, especially with her accent, but she doesn't seem to mind."

Eventually, Mademoiselle Blanchard returned to say that Mme Chauvineau was ready to see me. As usual, the social worker was clad in her aged-old twin set though without the pearls. Requiring a quick answer, I came straight to the point.

"I want to go skiing at Christmas with…"

Immediately, the social worker interrupted me.

"*I want* won't get you anywhere. I'd be more inclined to listen if you said: *I would like.*"

I stole a quick glance at Marie-France who was now standing in front of Mlle Cany's desk.

"I would like to go skiing at Christmas…" I reiterated on a more diplomatic tone; then pointing at my friend I added "With Marie-France."

Mme Chauvineau glowered at my friend with a suspicious look and hailed at her colleague:

"What kind of girl is she?" She enquired with Mlle Cany.

The popular spinster *d'un certain âge* smiled at Marie-France, then looked at Mme Chauvineau and declared:

"She's actually nice, very nice indeed and very well behaved. She's a good example, not likely to lead anyone astray."

"I'm glad to hear that." Mme Chauvineau surmised while writing something down. "All right, then. I'll think about it."

"When will I know?"

"Your godmother will let you know."

Soon after, Marie-France and I left *rue Washington* together.

Chapter 5

With the holiday over, it was now time to pay a visit to my next school. I could not wait for the new term to begin, mainly to escape the harassing godmother. Her persistent nagging had become intolerable. "Don't wear your glasses! Especially in front of my friends. You're such an embarrassment!" Then one day, on the spur of the moment, she decided to go and see the latest James Bond movies '*You Only Live Twice*'. As we stepped onto the pavement after the film, she effused about Sean Connery and compared herself favourably to the leading actress.

"That was great! That was really good fun! Did you enjoy it?"

"No." I exhaled in frustration.

"Why?" She asked surprised. "Don't you like James Bond?"

"I couldn't see anything." I replied petulantly.

"Why? Where are your glasses?"

"I left them at the apartment because you told me not to wear them."

"Pity. You missed a really good film."

Her nagging covered everything from the way I looked to the way I did anything.

"God you are slow! Why do you have to be so slow? And don't use your left hand, it's the hand of the devil; use your right hand! And say 'yes Godmother', 'no Godmother', 'thank you Godmother'".

If I accidentally broke a glass or a piece of crockery, I had to write hundreds of lines pledging that 'I must be careful not to break anything'. On the occasions she cooked something I did not like – which happened frequently as I was not yet familiar with Vietnamese cuisine, especially with the pungent fish sauce – she would barrack me with instances of her miserable life back in Vietnam. Her every sentence always began with '***During the war***, we didn't have this... we didn't have that... and we certainly didn't have the other…'. The worse meal she ever served was a foul fish soup complete with a whole fish head floating and seemingly smiling at me through the gloopy liquid. I had had to ingest some pretty vile stuff in the past but no one was going to force me to consume that revolting soup. I would rather starve. And I did. Thank goodness there was another place to where I could escape.

'Louis XIV lived near my school'. Yes, I was going to be a neighbour of the Sun King, only separated by three centuries or so, but that did not bother me. I wanted to become as sophisticated as his retinue of countesses and marquises and with the boarding school so close to Versailles, I was bound to pick up a hint or two. Unfortunately, the school was not exactly in Versailles itself but… close enough. More to the point, how was I going to find my new school?

"You'll find it easily," Mme Chauvineau explained, "As you leave the station, you turn right and you'll soon see it, it's right by the railway track, so you can't miss it."

Despite my poor sense of directions and the boarding house being concealed by tall concrete walls, I found it easily and entered through the large green gate which opened onto a vast playground with an enormous pear tree in the middle of it.

I crossed the playground, small suitcase in hand, feeling nervous, gauche and out of sorts. As I stepped inside the main entrance hall, I jumped as two girls burst out of a room on the right hand side and chased each other up the stairs laughing and screaming. That was a good sign. Seconds later, a woman appeared in the door frame and shouted.

"Not so noisy girls! And don't run up the stairs, you're going to break a leg!"

I stood in the hall, absorbing the joyous atmosphere and the happy vibes that permeated throughout the building. I knew straight away that I was going to be happy here.

The young woman spotted me.

"Ah, you must be a new girl. What's your name?"

"Martha Bertrand."

"Ah yes. You're joining the seniors. I am Mademoiselle Jocelyne and I look after the seniors."

"*Bonjour, mademoiselle.*" I greeted timidly.

"I'll get one of the girls to show you around."

At the sound of hurried footsteps, Mlle Jocelyne turned her head around and hailed a girl.

"Ah! Marceline, could you come here please? I'd like you to show Martha around."

"*Oui, mademoiselle.*" The girl replied obligingly.

"Take her to the dormitory first so she doesn't have to lug her suitcase around."

The building was solid, airy and rather ordinary looking but I was totally overwhelmed by the size of it. Each room looked enormous. There was even a vast area next to the refectory called '*la salle de détente*' where we could simply sit, chat and relax.

Situated on the top floor, the dormitory was nothing like those I had stayed in before. This one numbered a series of small cubicles clustered all along the walls with the washroom tucked away at the far end of it. Furnished with a single bed and a bed-side table, it was almost like having one's own bedroom, except that instead of a door, it had just a plain curtain to provide a modicum of privacy. Modicum or not, I rejoiced, I had never had my own room.

Next, Marceline took me to the study room on the middle floor. Again, it was a huge room, bright and airy. What a contrast it was after my previous school where the building was so small and cramped that you could pass it not realizing there was a school there, and even greater with the orphanage where the main room served as a refectory, playroom and study.

When I eventually met the girls at supper time, around thirty of them, they turned out to be the friendliest and most exuberant bunch I had ever come across. During the animated chatter among the tables, I discovered that two of them would be in my class. Marianne was tall, lanky and so uncoordinated that we could not help but laugh at her utter clumsiness. She appeared mature beyond her years giving the impression that she was more sophisticated than the rest of us. Mathilde, however, was more like me: petite, dark and outgoing. But she was a dark horse, pretending to be frivolous and silly, but all the while carefully concealing her more serious and mature side. As I would find out later, she was also intelligent and extremely shrewd. The three of us became firm friends and practically inseparable. Both Mathilde and Marianne taught me how to play card games. Later, Marianne taught us how to play poker. From then on, none of us three were ever seen without a pack of cards tucked away in our pockets. Mlle Jocelyne followed our developing friendship with keen interest and promptly nicknamed us 'the casino'. Well before Dallas and Dynasty hit our TV screens, she drew a lot of pleasure watching us laugh, scream, fall out and get back together again. And whenever she bumped into one of us, she would invariably say:

"When I see one, I always see the three of you."

Two other girls stood out on that first evening. One was Josephine, a large chubby girl who was perfectly happy within her own skin. It was her mother who insisted that she be put on a diet. Here, food was brought to the tables in separate dishes and we were left to help ourselves, except for Josephine who had her own individual dishes brought to her: usually boiled carrots or some other bland vegetable accompanied by boiled chicken breast. However, it was not in Josephine's nature to watch us feast on shepherd's pies or pasta bakes, so she would wolf down her meager rations and then dig into the main dishes with unrestrained vigour. Her nickname was 'Balloo' after the loveable bear of the Jungle Book. She loved her association with Balloo the bear, knew the song '*Bear Necessities*' by heart and often mimicked the dance moves while singing at the top of her voice. And of course we would all join in clapping our hands as she swayed her large derriere from side to side. Sorties to the local swimming-pool were always huge fun with Josephine as she insisted that everybody watched to see how much volume of water she could displace in one single jump.

Another girl who drew my attention was 'Bunny', predictably nicknamed so because of her buckteeth, although her caring nature made her look more like a mother hen than a fluffy bunny. Tall, skinny and very sporty, a bit of a tomboy really, she did not care two hoots what she looked like. All she cared about was her love of horses despite the fact that she had never been near one in real life.

The school itself, primarily a day school, was tucked away on the other side of the main building. By comparison to the boarding house, it looked rather dingy and had a neglected look about it. The classrooms were superimposed in two neat rows with a concrete balcony running along the first floor.

The headmistress was a rather tall and lively nun called Sister Marie-Madeleine, affectionately known as 'Maddo' behind her back. The first affable nun I had ever come across, she was blessed with a happy disposition and, for all her sins, taught us German. Her knowledge of the language was somewhat rudimentary but she belonged to the ancient school of thoughts which boldly claimed that if one could read one could teach, no matter how limited one's knowledge of the subject was. Her forte in the German language was her masterful pronunciation of the syllable '*ch*' which she used to impress us by racking her throat, hence producing a guttural roar that came out from the back of her throat, spraying the front row with a shower of spit. When the sun shone, you could actually see a cloud of spray hit the unfortunate girls sitting on the front row which never failed to set us off in fits of laughter. What was even more remarkable about Sister Marie-Madeleine was the fact that she liked to boast to anyone who cared to listen that the school had just spent the best part of £3000 on a brand new science laboratory. How privileged we were to enjoy such modern facilities, she would serenade over and over again. The only problem was that she was so scared that anything might go bump or even explode in her cherished laboratory that no experiments were ever to take place there. In the end, it was just used as another classroom. We even had our music lessons in between the Bunsen burners. How privileged was that?!

Returning from a weekend, Marianne had brought back some matches to be used as stakes for our poker games. The three of us had become so addicted to our card games that we played at every opportunity, even during lessons. Our Maths teacher, Madame Croissant (yes, that was her real name!), was universally disliked and we thought nothing of continuing our poker game during her lessons. Unfortunately for me, she caught me red handed flashing a royal flush to Mathilde when I should have been grappling with some unfathomable mathematical equation. For my crime, she suspended me for a day. The godmother was baffled.

"What's that you've done again?... Play poker during Maths lessons?...

Using matchsticks? There's no harm in that, as long as you didn't use proper money." She declared, confounded.

"You don't understand." I tried to explain. "To the nuns, it's a perverted game, a devil's game. First, Satan steals your money, next he steals your soul. In the eyes of the nuns and my teachers, only bad people play poker."

"Only if they play for real money." She quipped. "Right, well… What am I going to do with you then?…"

After a thoughtful pause, she asked: "Do you fancy going ice-skating?"

On Thursdays, traditionally a no-school day, the highly-strung supervisor, Mlle Jocelyne, would sometimes take us to nearby woods and parks for some restorative walks. It was thence under the glorious mantel of flamboyant autumnal colours that I first discovered the vast symmetrical gardens of Versailles. Standing on the well-trodden central path while staring at the magnificent palace commanding the breathtaking views stretching as far as the wooded hills in the distance, I imagined Marie-Antoinette and her royal posse of sycophantic ladies-in-waiting sauntering along the tree-lined avenues. Escaping momentarily the pressures of court life, they acted out the roles of humble shepherdesses, though when summoned by a footman for afternoon tea, they glided gracefully to have tea and cakes served on silver platters by an army of servants dressed in full livery under the solid roof of a wooden pavilion that was bigger than a mansion. Digesting these historical facts with glee, I could easily empathize with Marie-Antoinette for, by sheer coincidence, this too was my idea of being poor, unsophisticated and close to nature.

In the grounds of Versailles, I discovered a different aspect of nature. The trees, the sky, the air: everything looked so fresh, so bright and so enchanting. Sébastien may have faded away in the midst of time but he had left me with a romantic glow that mingled with the poetic hues of vibrant autumn leaves. While at the orphanage, I had only ever experienced three emotions: fear, utter boredom and frustration. Here, I was besieged by a surge of unfamiliar feelings and emotions which I did not understand and which left me thoroughly confused, though deliciously so. I did try to analyze and dissect each emotion but to no avail because, in these early days of the awakening of the soul, I was still at too primitive a stage to realize that what I was trying to do was to separate the elusive and untouchable colours of the rainbow.

Living in a daydream of sheer bliss, I decided that I wanted to live in the same style as the poets I had encountered in Literature which was not difficult since like me they tended to be penniless, ill-disciplined and with a penchant to fritter their time away. Forlorn and crushed by unrequited love, through their poems they decried the tragedy of a life without love and a soul without passion. And in the same manner I had seen my favourite poets pictured in textbooks, I took to striking poses, sitting pensively on a bench like I had seen Chateaubriand sit with his head resting on his fist, staring at the choppy seas of his beloved Brittany, his loose locks of hair swept wildly by the North Atlantic wind. More and more, I wanted to savour these precious moments alone. I walked along paths '*en solitaire*' like Rousseau, pondering over a poetic idyll which I could not as yet define. And while I studied the tragic passions of the likes of Rimbaud, Verlaine and that unfortunate young André de Chénier who, having barely reached manhood, managed to scribble down a few soulful verses before being driven to the guillotine, I continued my own personal struggle to try and understand what was happening to me. Then one day, it hit me... maybe I was growing up... ***really?***

Chapter 6

At Christmas, I returned to Berneix. First I had to go to *rue Washington* to meet up with my Vietnamese friends. I was beginning to get to know more and more of them and as we squeezed on the soft sofa and deep armchairs of the waiting room, we caught up with each other's news and gossip. Before long, the room resounded with loud chatter, cries of joy and excitement and, as always, laughter.

We travelled by night to the ski resort. The steam train hurtled through the frozen landscape as we slept, our bodies slumped over each other wrapped up in our brand-new anoraks.

When I woke up, it was daylight. The windows were all steamed up. I wiped the steam off with my sleeve and stuck my nose against the glass. The train chugged along, carving a neat charcoal line through the snowy mountains. I barely recognized the landscape. Everywhere was white, icy white.

When the snow fell, it was silent, totally silent. I watched in awe large snowflakes floating weightlessly as if they were white down falling from angels' wings, skimming passed our cold cheeks and melting softly on our lips.

In the evening, the warm yellow glow diffused from the chalets mingled with the multicolour lights of Christmas decorations twinkling with joy and happiness in the darkest of night. Inside the chalet, the director and his wife had place the Christmas tree right next to the snow-covered window panes. At this moment, nothing and no one else mattered. I was too busy absorbing the fairy tale atmosphere of this special moment:

the cosy wooden chalet with the heartwarming scent of wood burning and crackling in the fireplace. Everywhere I looked, I saw only happy faces with red noses and rosy cheeks. Outside, the shadow of enchanted mountains moved slowly under the moonlight. It was magical, purely magical and to this day, nowhere in the world has had such a profound effect on me than that of seeing alpine villages twinkling at the foot of mountains covered in snow. Somehow, I knew instinctively that this kind of love would never die.

On the first morning at the ski shop, we were made to stand up very straight, arm outstretched high above our heads in order to measure the length of the skis. No carvers existed back then, just heavy wooden planks clumped inside metal braces. There were no automatic bindings either, just a strap made of steel fixed around the leather boots and tightened by a metal clip which had to be pushed down onto the ski. The main safety feature was a leather strap attached to the ankles. This was meant to stop the skis from hurtling down the mountain should you lose one or both in a fall. A loose ski has the potential to kill. What nobody realized at the time was that if you fell with your skis still firmly attached to your ankles, you ended up black and blue as they repeatedly clobbered you senseless while you rolled out of control down the mountain. Thankfully, with the arrival of automatic bindings, that safety feature was soon replaced by breaks fixed to the base of the bindings. No more black eyes or cut cheeks leaving a red trail of blood on the pure white snow.

Our ski instructor was a dashing medical student called Jean-Michel. Tall, dark and extremely handsome, he was the dream instructor. At first, he did not quite know how to handle our exuberant bunch and as he did his best to demonstrate the advanced technique of the snow plough, one by one we tumbled down the slope screaming and laughing before finally coming to rest in a heap… between his legs. At this point, I was firmly clamped onto his left leg while Marie-France had anchored herself onto his right leg. Jean-Michel rolled his eyes and shook his head.

"What happened? I showed you what to do." He said, mildly frustrated.

But of course, we had not listened. We just wanted to experience the exhilarating sensation of speed, sliding out of control using our skis like sledges.

"Yes, but you didn't tell us how to stop!" Marie-France retorted in between hiccups of laughter.

We did eventually master the snow plough and Jean-Michel, patient as he was, moved on to teach us the stem. After a few days, he seemed more than satisfied with our progress and declared - rather prematurely we thought - that we were ready to take our test.

"Test? What test?"

"The test to get your first star."

"Star?"

"Yes 'star'. Let me explain. Stars are awarded according to your level of skiing. To gain your first star, all you have to do is ski a little slalom in snow plough. That's all. It's really not difficult."

"A slalom!" Several voices chorused in panic.

"Don't worry. You can do it… all of you." He asserted looking directly at each one of us in the eyes. "Come on, let's go and practise."

Shaking with nerves at the prospect of this unexpected challenge, Marie-Celeste grumbled under her breath.

"I'm gonna fall… I know I'm gonna fall."

I had never had so much fun in my life. From then on, nothing could dampen my enthusiasm or eagerness to return to the slopes day after day, not even the sore legs or sore muscles, the chaffing caused by the wet leather rubbing against my tender ankles, the frozen hands inside wet gloves and frozen feet inside wet boots or the biting cold cutting through my thin anorak during the occasional blizzard. It was cold, freezing cold but God it was fun.

What was most frustrating, however, was that technologically speaking, our skis were no more than a pair of wooden planks. Carbon fibre had not yet been used en masse to create a smooth base smothered in wax to allow the skis to run freely. As a result, clump of snow used to accumulate under the skis, making it difficult to work on one's own technique, a term Jean-Michel never ceased to use to remind us: "***La technique!*** Concentrate on your technique!". Indeed, like Toni Sailer, the most handsome ski racer beautifully demonstrated even better than Jean-Claude Killy, skiing was all about style and elegance, with the occasional stop to rest tired muscles and admire the stunning scenery.

Eventually, *la technique* won and most of us did gain our first star with the result that Jean-Michel rose even higher in our esteem. He was now hinting that I should try for my second star.

"Oh no." I said quite firmly. "I'm too nervous and I don't think I'm good enough."

"Of course you are. You're the best in the group."

It was nice of him to say so but there was no way I was going to indulge in anything more taxing than swinging my hips in the snow plough position all the way down a blue run. Besides, after the austere years spent at the orphanage, I was not interested in the rigorous discipline of training, I just wanted to have fun.

The next time we went skiing, Bernard, our new instructor, was not as considerate – or as handsome for that matter. After a short test to assess our technical skills, I was separated from Marie-France and placed in a higher group. This was an ominous start. By day two, our group was taken to the top of a black run. Nobody had alerted me to this and the sheer sight of a vertical wall opening out onto a white abyss made me take such a sharp intake of breath that my lungs nearly froze on the spot. I shuffled gingerly towards the edge, petrified. I had only just mastered the stem. I was not ready for this. My legs turned to jelly and forced me to sit down in the snow. Had Marie-France been with me, she would have egged me on and together we might have attempted the steep slope, no doubt screaming and laughing all the way. But without her cheerful support, no amount of coaxing could budge me from my cold spot.

"Come on, you can do it." Bernard chivied on a tone betraying a hint of impatience.

"I'm not moving." I decreed bluntly, refusing to move an inch.

"You're going to be the last one down."

"I don't care."

"It's going to get dark soon."

My eyes fixed on the 'precipice', I crossed my arms and shook my head.

At this moment, the engine of a snow plough roared up the slope. Its orange light flashed intermittently in the semi-darkness like a beacon of hope. Bernard seized his chance and made a quick dash towards it. Soon after, I watched the driver make a call on his radio and moments later, the rescue services arrived on the scene.

"No," I overheard Bernard explain. "She hasn't broken anything. She's just tired."

Very gently, the rescuers bundled me on a stretcher and wrapped me up from head to toe like a papoose. As one of the rescuers set off dragging the stretcher behind him, I could see nothing but I could feel the breakneck speed of the rescuer racing down the slopes as my body ploughed mercilessly through every snow trough and mogul. The descent seemed to take hours. Far from being a pleasant leisurely slide in a reclined position, Nero's style, I could feel all my organs being tossed about. If my body had so far escaped unscathed, I was convinced that by the end of this run, all my bones would be shattered and ground as if they had been put through a bone crusher. The experience turned out to be so painful that in future, should I be confronted with another black run, I made the firm decision that I would rather slide down, on my bottom if need be, rather than call upon the rescue services ever again.

When I finally arrived back at the chalet, I felt a huge sense of relief. Stepping across the rustic threshold was like being wrapped up in a comfort blanket which I figuratively pulled tightly around my shivering body while I savoured the sight of a roaring fire and the delicious smell of hot chocolate served with brioche.

From then on, I lived for the holidays. Every Christmas and Easter holidays, our exuberant crowd invaded the Alps and screamed down the slopes of Berneix, Praz-sur-Arly, Alpe d'Huez, La Foux d'Allos, Tigne, and reverberated inside the youth hostel of 'La Moubra' in Crans Montana, the only place where our laughter and screams were surpassed by a bunch of over-excited American kids.

I did eventually muster enough courage to go down a black run and…
I did get my second star.

Chapter 7

Returning to school, the contrast could not have been starker. I lost complete interest in the learning process which left me uninspired, unchallenged and unimpressed by lessons where the sole object was to regurgitate pages learnt by heart, by teachers as old and rancid as Cleopatra's milk, by music lessons taken in a science lab where the Bunsen burners had never been turned on and where not a single musical note had ever been played. What's more, I resented a regime that seemed determined to crush my natural effervescence and free spirit. I wanted to break free from that regimented hell, to be left alone to nurture those wonderful feelings I had experienced in an idyllic world miles away from school. Most of all, I wanted to do something a great deal more exciting than spending my days sitting in class bored out of my mind, sighing heavily and counting the days to the next holiday.

Then I discovered books. In the main study of the boarding house, I had seen a shelf with a dozen of books or so but having never had free access to books, I somehow believed that I was not allowed to touch them. As far as I was aware, books were the preserve of classrooms, bookshops and private libraries. It would be years still before I discovered that public libraries existed. Right now though, I did not know that I could take a book from that shelf and read it. It was Martine, an avid reader herself, who directed me towards the small 'library' and told me to pick a book. I stared at the bookshelf blankly. Which one was I supposed to choose when I had no idea what I was looking at? In the end, Martine chose one for me, '*The Prince and the Pauper*'. I was hooked instantly.

Through books, I was able to cultivate my fascination for words, especially the obscure ones and those most difficult to spell. I read them out loud and discovered that each had a tone, a distinctive rhythm, and when written in lines of matching syllables, they created a melodic sound that cascaded in a soft murmur of sublime sentiments, gentle and mild like whispers, occasionally punched by the odd harsh line that sprung out like a pugilistic blow. I could no longer think of words without putting them into rhymes. Verses had become to words what lyrics were to music and I hailed myself as a new literary composer blessed with the magical gift of freeing haunted souls through the mellifluous flow of verses and poems.

When the summer holidays came, with the usual crowd of Vietnamese friends, I was sent to a small *pension familiale* by the seaside in Berck-sur-Mer on the Opal Coast. Our group consisted purely of us lot: *les Eurasiennes*. Being in their company was always a wholesome experience often filled with laughter.

In Berck-sur-Mer, it is not so much the golden sand of endless beaches that I remember fondly but the gradual introduction of a new kind of music that permeated slowly into my life and which began to punctuate its most glorious moments. Too shy at first to go to the local disco with the other girls, I preferred to stay behind in the bedroom, surrounded by bunk beds, in order to lose myself in the new sound of ballads and pop music played on a small portable player that Monique, the girl with the most striking looks in our group, had brought with her. Some evenings, walking along the promenade or standing by the white parapet, I watched the sunset sink imperviously into the untroubled waters with 'The Sound of Silence' ringing inside my head whose notes synchronized softly with the slow melodious rhythm of the waves. Back at the *pension familiale*, I carried on dreaming to the sound of the Bee Gees's 'I Started a Joke', Otis Reading's 'Sitting on the Dock of the Bay' and Nina Simone's 'Ain't got no, I've Got Life'.

In the town center, however, I was beginning to sense a ripple of excitement. I did not know what but something big was about to happen. It was July 1969. Newspapers had got hold of the story. Before Mission Control had even started the count down, the front pages discoursed of nothing else except to extol the selfless courage of the astronauts about to land on the Moon.

In the *pension familiale*, a black and white television was brought into the small lounge area. The moon landing, we had been informed, would take place quite late at night, and I dithered whether I should tuck myself in bed with a good book listening to music or try to stay awake and witness an extraordinary moment during which half of the world would be glued to their television set, determined to witness the momentous event. My curiosity got the better of me. For once, I decided to join in.

At around ten o'clock that night, the lady in charge of the *pension familiale* switched on the television. We returned to the hostel in dribs and drabs after our evening walk along the promenade. The room gradually filled with every stranger and their dog from the street, all eagerly waiting to witness this extraordinary feat of technical engineering and we, the residents, had to shuffle our seats nearer the screen to secure a better view. At about eleven o'clock at night, the commentator on the screen disappeared to make way to fuzzy pictures crackling with awe and wonder. His voice soon rose into a crescendo as he launched himself into a passionate soliloquy while he described the progress of the astronauts; and we joined in his excitement as we watched, mouths baying, Neil Armstrong bounced a few times on the crusty shell of the moon closely followed by his colleague, Buzz Aldrin. The astronauts had brought with them an American flag and the two of them bounced further away in search of the perfect spot where to plant the flag that now stood as rigid as if it were made of starch. Then, the commentator, his voice crackling with emotion, translated that famous phrase: *That's one small step for man; one giant leap for mankind.*

To this day, the debate remains open whether Armstrong said: '*for man*' or '*for **a** man*'. Nevertheless, whichever phrase he used did not diminish the immense pride felt by all the scientists and engineers at Mission Control for in that one brief moment in time and in the sub-conscious of most people around the world, Planet Earth had suddenly become 'America'.

Chapter 8

When I returned to Paris, I felt somewhat different, not because I had witnessed the landing on the moon or been to my very first disco, but because I had discovered a kind of music that at last appealed to me. Up until then, I had only heard of Johnny Haliday, Claude François, Françoise Hardy, the diminutive crooner Charles Aznavour, and the little sparrow of Paris 'Edith Piaf' whose music, in the exuberant and colourful era of the 60s', sounded slow, mournful, and rather depressing. Hence, the first thing I did was to go and buy my very first record. It was Simon & Garfunkel's 'The Sound of Silence' with on the B side 'I Am a Rock'.

Back at the boarding house, our 'casino' was soon reunited amid shrieks of excitement. I was beyond excited.

"Listen to this." Bunny said, sliding a record out of its sleeve.

"Who's this?" I enquired.

"What do you mean 'Who's this?'. It's Elvis, of course. The King of Rock."

"Never heard of him." I retorted flatly.

"What?! You've never heard of Elvis? Where have you been?"

I knew exactly where I had been which is why my knowledge of music did not stretch very far.

Being of a rather exuberant nature, it was never long before I got into trouble again. And so it was that one lunch time, as we tucked into our sausages and mash, on the spur of the moment, I decided to give an impromptu lesson on the male anatomy using my sausage as a teaching prop. Not that I was interested in sex. At this stage, I was pretty much ignorant of all matters regarding sex. What's more, our Biology textbooks did not contain anything at all regarding the human reproductive system so I had absolutely no idea of what I was talking about which is probably why the girls found my little spontaneous lecture irresistibly funny. And as I went at length to describe the rough composition of a sausage, we choked on our mash potato with screams of laughter. We must have looked like these women who go to see the Chippendales simply to have a good laugh. Suddenly, my friends' peals of laughter stopped… very abruptly. I did not know why but behind me I heard someone take a sharp intake of breath. I turned around and came face to face with the nun. She had that look of horror on her face that freezes all ability to speak. She was red, bright red. I could see her racking her brain to come up with some suitable adjectives to describe the most wayward girl she had ever had the misfortune to clap her eyes on. She was incandescent.

The end result was that I was put in quarantine for a month to give me time to reflect on my pervert behaviour.

Despite this, I was having the time of my life, not once bothering to think about my schoolwork, the approaching exams or indeed my future. *Future*? *What* future? Being firmly anchored in the present, I had no time to think about a realm that might not even exist. My whole attitude towards my studies mirrored that of the proverbial cicada of La Fontaine's fable, choosing to lead a dissipated life and sing my way through the academic years. When the exams finally came, I barely twitched with nerve, so confident I was about my innate ability and natural flair. In the past, everything had come so easily to me that I was under the impression that all I needed to do to pass an exam was to write my name at the top of the page. How difficult was that? I sneered. In our little trio, only Martine had had the foresight to realize that her future was more important than a game of poker. The end result was inevitable. Both Marie-Paule and I failed abysmally. I could not believe it. *Me*, Martha Bertrand suffering from intellectual deficiency? I was in such a state of shock that I felt physically sick. The whole episode left me profoundly humiliated, mortified, mortally wounded with my pride and self-esteem crushed to the core. What made it worse was that the blow came without warning. Not a single adult had taken me to one side to warn me that if I continued to waste my time I would fail. Not one teacher showed enough care or concern to stretch out their hand to stop me from falling. In a flash, I saw that elusive future disappear down a bottomless pit. Back in the classroom, I could almost hear Mme Croissant, glad to get her own back on an unruly pupil, sneer under her breath: 'that'll teach her'. And it certainly did. Suddenly, I was faced with a stark reality. I was treading the path of life alone. Nobody would ever be there to hold my hand to keep me on the right track and if I fell, nobody would be there to pick me up. It was a harsh and painful lesson but one that would change my outlook on life for ever.

If my self-inflicted failure left me shaken to the core, it left the godmother completely cold.

"It's not your fault," came her verdict. "I mean… the stress of it all… you probably got too nervous, so it's not your fault really." And this was coming from a woman who was in the habit of blaming me for all her ills and own failings. I was dumbfounded.

What was going to happen now? I made my way to *rue Washington*.

Mme Chauvineau greeted me coldly and launched herself into one of her endless lectures. There was nothing I could do to stop the flow of peregrinations… except yawn.

"Now, you look at me!" She berated. "And don't you dare yawn when I'm talking to you! Are you listening to me, now? And don't you look at me with that arrogant air… You've already wasted two years of your time; I won't let you waste mine as well! I'm in a good mind to send you to work in a shoe shop on the Champs Elysées. As a matter of fact, Nicole NGérarden already works there. She loves it so I'm sure you'd get to love it too!" She decreed.

I looked at her in horror. I liked shoes, but not that much.

Mme Graffeuil, who had caught the tail end of the conversation, called out to me.

"How old are you, Martha?"

"Fifteen." I mumbled sheepishly.

"Well, she's still young," she said, speaking to Mme Chauvineau. Then, she looked me up and down and added: "you're an intelligent enough girl. I think we should give you a second chance, don't you, Mme Chauvineau?"

The social worker bristled in her seat and replied with a crooked smile:

"Perhaps… although I don't think she deserves it."

Madame Graffeuil ignored her last comment and turned back towards me.

"Very well, then. We'll give you a second chance. You're going to repeat your year."

"They don't want her back." Mme Chauvineau snapped.

"Never mind, we'll just have to find her a new school, preferably in Paris; it'll be easier to keep an eye on her." Then, she turned to me and asked: "What languages are you learning at school?"

"English and German."

"Well, Madame Chauvineau. We'll send her to Germany and England over the summer to help her brush up on her languages. That will be a start."

I looked at her with a beaming smile. Then, Madame Graffeuil called me over and took both my hands.

"Now," she said in a very soft voice, gently squeezing my hands, "you promise you're going to work really hard from now on..."

I nodded my head vigorously, several times.

"...You're a very clever girl, so I know you can do it."

I left *rue Washington* with my head in the clouds. England... Germany... I had never been abroad before.

Chapter 9

A group of young adolescents met at the '*gare de l'Est*', en route to Frankfurt. None of my Vietnamese friends were there. Was this some kind of punishment?

During the journey, once the initial introductions were made, we compared how much pocket money we all had, scrutinized the German banknotes and practised our pronunciation of the words *deutschmarks* and *pfennig*.

As the train approached the border, German customs officers boarded the train and asked for our passports or identity cards. I produced my brand new identity card. Afterwards, instead of putting it safely away, I held it in my hand and stared at it for a while for I had discovered a new piece of information that no one had thought necessary to divulge. On my way to get my identity card back in Paris, I had been given my birth certificate. Having never seen an official document before, I studied it avidly, wondering what the black print would reveal about me. Sure enough, there on the dotted line, next to the rubric: mother's name, I stumbled upon a name… a Vietnamese name. This really shocked me. For the first time ever, I began to question the circumstances of my birth as faithfully related by the godmother. If I had been abandoned on the steps of the Red Cross Hospital in Danang, as the godmother had categorically declared, how did the officials know my mother's name? Had she left a hastily scribbled note on top of her little bundle before abandoning it? Had she left her address too, by any chance? This did not make sense. I kept churning inside my head all the various hints that the godmother had dropped, how she claimed to know my real birth date. I had once tried to clear up the mystery and the confusing hints the godmother kept dropping, by confronting her with my suspicions.

"Is Adèle my mother?"

The godmother panicked. She muttered and stuttered for a few seconds before answering in a rather aggressive manner.

"Of course not. You're completely mad. Where did you get that idea from? You really need to see a psychiatrist."

The force of her reaction took me aback and puzzled me even more. Then, before I could say anything, she added:

"…Anyway, the only person who knows anything about you is Sister Ange who worked at the Red Cross Hospital… But she's dead now."

Hence, having safely buried the truth inside the dead nun's coffin, the mystery remained, though I could not help wonder. Why did she keep banging on about her friend Adèle? Why was she so keen for us to meet? Adèle was clearly not interested and neither was I. And why, when she had relayed my prickly suspicions to Adèle, the woman had exclaimed: "you must have told her something…"? Why then was she panicking at the thought that I had taken in every word she had let slip, believing I was too dense or too dim to even remember them, let alone understand their true significance? However, the very fact that I was asking questions made her realise that in future she ought to be more careful, that an unguarded word or comment might be regurgitated at any time. So she clammed up. The little mystery would never be solved and the little family secret never revealed, but somehow, it was too late. I did not know much but that was enough for me. Rather satisfied with my little detective work, I was now ready to stow away my identity card and carry on pretending that I knew absolutely nothing. Besides, I had managed perfectly well on my own so far… well almost… and at this stage of my life when I yearned for independence and freedom, the last thing I wanted was to be lumbered with parents who might turn out to be as willful, petulant, obstinate and belligerent as me.

Our destination was Heidelberg, the picturesque Bavarian town that stands astride the Neckar river. We were taken to the local 'Gymnasium' where our host families were waiting to welcome us. The organizer had already briefed us on our respective families.

"You, Martha," she had said, "you'll be staying with the F. family. The lady is the head teacher of the school."

Lucky me, I thought. But things never work out the way they should. After all the families had gone, I was left standing alone in the playground with the organizer fretting beside me.

"We've got a problem," she finally admitted, "Frau F. cannot have you after all. Something's come up. I've got to find you another family. She suggested this name which is Renée's family. I need to ring them to see if they can take an extra student."

Upon which, she disappeared inside the building, clutching her clipboard tightly against her chest.

At the end of the school day, the organizer called one of the German students and exchanged a few words. I stood next to them, unable to understand a word of the brief exchange. Finally, the organizer turned to me and said:

"This is Trudi. You're going to stay with her family for the next three weeks, but for the last week of July, you'll have to move to the youth hostel here in town because they can't keep you for the whole month, will that be all right?"

What could I say?

"You're actually better off this way," she continued, "because you won't be on your own, you'll be there with Renée… You've already metRenée, haven't you?"

"Yes, we were in the same compartment on the train."

"Good!" She exclaimed with distinct relief. "Well, I'm glad we're all sorted. Don't look so worried, I'm sure you'll be fine. I don't know what Trudi's French is like but she speaks English fluently, so if you're stuck, you can always try your English with her."

Well, if the organizer was worried about Trudi's French, she had clearly not been briefed on the extremely poor standard of my English or German. In my own defense though, all I could say was that the use of foreign languages had never been called for in a game of poker. However, keen to make a good impression and knowing that my knowledge of German was less than rudimentary, I decided to greet Trudi in my broken English. As I wrestled to string a few tortured words in a flat French accent devoid of any cumbersome diphthongs, Trudi interrupted me and asked:

"Could you speak in English, please?"

I froze mid-sentence. Could she not tell I was speaking in English? What was I supposed to say now? Noting my discomfiture, she added:

"Never mind. Come with me. We need to wait outside the school gates; my brother is going to pick us up."

"Your brother… has a car?"

"Oh yes. He's much older than me."

After twenty minutes pacing the pavement, Trudi began to curse loudly.

'Come on Johan! Where are you?"

Then she turned to me and said:

"My brother's always late! He's so annoying."

Unable to reply in words, I nodded in sympathy. It suited me, really, to be waiting around for I was able to enjoy the hustle and bustle of a new city, to admire the old stone bridge stretching over the river Neckar and the old castle perched high up on a hill which, according toTrudi, had been destroyed by the French under King Louis XIV. I was busy absorbing the full romantic atmosphere of the old town when a small cream Mercedes convertible pulled up.

"Ah, at last! Here he is! There's my brother!" Trudi hailed, pointing at a sports car. The young blond man behind the wheel hailed something back to his sister and the two exchanged a few words in a way only siblings do. Then, we hurriedly jumped into the car with suitcase, schoolbag and all.

Outside town, the car meandered on a small country road that contorted in perilous hair-pin bends as we rose higher and higher in the Bavarian hills.

"This is part of the Black Forest," Johan pointed out.

Unable to communicate with words, I responded with a smile. The air was warm and smelt of fresh pine, and in between the leaves, the sun scurried mischievously between the branches, splashing blinding flashes of sunrays on a smile I simply could not erase. Ready to fly in a delectable dream, I reclined myself against the back seat, threw my head back to loosen my long hair, closed my eyes and savoured the balmy atmosphere of a hot summer's day, smiling to the heavens and imagining myself being a famous movie star with Steve McQueen right next to me driving the car.

Half an hour later, we arrived in a tiny picturesque village with a name that sounded like a Christmas greeting. Soon after we passed the road sign, the car stopped. When I looked around, my eyes arrested on a low stone building tucked against the dark side of the hill with next to it a huge barn. I sighed with disappointment: trust me to end up on a farm, I thought. With my nose right up in the air, I sampled the subdued atmosphere and noted that the place did not reek of the usual pungent smell normally associated with cows and pigs. In fact, the barn I had spotted turned out to be the stables for the family's horses. Where on earth had I landed? I grabbed my small suitcase and followed Trudi and her brother towards a small side-door which led into a dark vestibule. Not long after we had arrived, a petite woman, the lady of the house switched the lights on before greeting us in German first, then in English. I returned a shy '*Guten Tag*'. Renée was already there and greeted me in French.

The house was made up of two cottages which had been linked together. Sofia, Trudi's mother, took us to the first floor of the annex and opened a latched door to let Renée and I inside the guest bedroom. "Wow!" I could not help exclaim. I had never seen anything so pretty, so quaint and so cosy. And the beds: they were carved into the wood paneling and covered with thick continental duvets, gingham pink, to match the curtains. The whole room exuded of rustic charm and pure serenity. I instantly fell in love with it.

Renée had already picked the bed closest to the window.

"Come and have a look at the view!" She beckoned.

From the top of the hill, the house overlooked the whole valley with its wooded flanks splayed with small patches of green fields. Rousseau would have been enchanted by this place and it was most probably a bucolic landscape similar to this one which inspired Beethoven to decry his mortal love and passion through his immortal symphonies.

Later, as I stood by the panoramic windows of the lounge, I contemplated the stunning view remembering that not so long ago, my playground had been a plain paved yard in the middle of an austere building buried in an industrial jungle. Now, I was feasting my eyes on the green pastures of forests and hills, breathing a fresh and clean air carrying with it occasional whiffs of fresh earth, damp leaves and pine needles. And best of all, my playground was now an orchard full of apple trees, cherry trees and some kind of bush I had never seen before. I peered dubiously at its furry little fruit and asked: "*Was ist das?*", hoping that this time Trudi would understand me. She did and replied in kind. I stared at her blankly, desperately trying to decipher the string of words that had come out too fast for me to understand. She laughed and reverted back to English.

"Come on," Trudi urged with a little chuckle, "try it, it's nice."

Reluctantly, I put the gooseberry in my mouth and grimaced in disgust before spitting it out.

Instantly, both Trudi and Renée burst out laughing.

"I love them when they're sharp like that." Trudi chortled.

We continued to walk down the path until we reached the flat area which was mostly taken up by a swimming pool. Next to it, I noticed a strange little wooden hut.

"*Qu'est-ce que c'est?*" I quizzed Renée.

"*Je n'sais pas.*" She admitted. "Ask her."

"**You** ask her," I insisted. "Your German is better than mine."

"Well, there's your chance to improve yours, then." She quipped.

I suppose she had a point so I turned towards Trudi and pointed at the hut.

"*Was ist das?*" I asked, bracing myself for the torrent of foreign words that was about to hit me.

"Have a look." Trudi invited, speaking automatically in English.

What a relief. Without further ado, Renée and I peered inside. I hazarded a guess.

"It looks like a changing room."

"You could be right." She replied, seemingly none the wiser.

"Is it a changing room?" I finally asked Trudi.

"No," she replied with a bemused smile, "it's a sauna."

"A sauna?" I parroted. "What's a sauna?"

The structure was so alien to me that, even after an elaborate explanation given in a mixture of English, French and German, I still did not understand what it was. Far from being put out by my total ignorance of worldly things, I surveyed with a twinkle in my eye the garden and the orchard; I looked back dreamily towards the house, picturing in my mind the lounge with its cosy log fire which filled the place with a smoky, homely aroma that made me feel all warm inside. I then diverted my gaze back towards the distant corners of the valley to absorb the splendid view, the vast open space, the muted light and the suffused atmosphere that pleased my eyes and filled my heart with promises of joy and happiness. Even more so than when I first discovered the Alps, it felt good to be somewhere new and be able to feel at one with nature. In this brief enchanted moment, something inside me told me that everything was going to be all right but how could I trust a gut feeling I barely recognized?

<hr/>

At five o'clock, we retreated to the lounge where Sofia had brought some plates of cold meat and slices of rye bread. I picked sparingly at the unfamiliar food, preferring to save my appetite for dinner.

By seven o'clock, I still could not hear the familiar clatter of pots and pans coming from the kitchen, which was situated just across the lounge. I kept looking at the clock every five minutes, wondering when we would eventually eat. By half past the hour, I was in such a state of hunger that my stomach began to churn roars of protest but everyone in the room seemed totally oblivious to the time, wholly absorbed as they were in a popular programme they were watching on the television, the first colour television I had ever seen, **with** remote control, if you please. I leant towards Renée and whispered:

"When are we going to eat?"

"We have eaten." She whispered back, putting strong emphasis on the auxiliary verb '**have**'. Instantly, my stomach hit the floor.

"Have we?" I whined in panic. "When?" I tried to remember, feeling hungrier than ever.

"At five o'clock."

"But I thought that was afternoon tea."

"No, that was our supper."

"*Mince alors*, if I had known I'd have eaten more. I'm starving!"

"Too bad. You're going to have to wait until breakfast for your next meal."

"Oh no, what am I going to do? I'm so hungry."

"You could always ask for something to eat."

"Oh no, I'm not begging for food, not me." I replied, throwing my head back with pride. I felt enough of a peasant as it was. I sat back in the sofa clutching my stomach, and tried to forget any thought of hunger by watching what appeared to be a family sitcom. Do they not have any nibbles, I suddenly thought? At that moment, Johan got up, asked a question in German and disappeared through to the kitchen.

"*Ja, Ja!*" I wanted to shout. "Whatever it is, I'll have some."

He came back with crisps and peanuts which I devoured, still pretending to be totally captivated by an incomprehensible sitcom unravelling in front of my starving eyes.

The principal lounge was mainly used in the evening to watch television. For any other time, we, youngsters, were able to relax in Johan's and Trudi's own sitting room furnished in the ultra-modern style of the day, with a deep pile cream-coloured carpet stretching from wall to wall, white cubic-form furniture that slotted neatly all along the walls and around it, a white leather sofa stowed away at a right angle. The stereo unit was encased in the fitted shelves that adorned the longest wall with the speakers concealed high up around the ceiling. In the large drawers underneath the record player, an impressive collection of records were arranged in neat rows. Trudi took some out.

"That's my brother's favourite group." She said, showing me a record sleeve with no picture on it. I looked at it and asked pointing at the name printed in large black letters:

"How do you say that word?"

"Bea-tles… The Beatles. You haven't heard of them before?"

"No," I replied, cringing at my ignorance.

Trudi chuckled.

"They're quite famous, you know, and very popular here in Germany. I'll put it on for you; I'm sure you'll like them. Come on, let's dance!"

The harmonious vibrations of songs like '*She loves you*', '*I want to hold your hand*', '*From me to you*' and others by the same group resounded in my head and seemed to unlock a secret door that, when open, whooshed out a flood of delectable sensations that rushed through my entire body and made my hair stand up at the back of my neck. I was entranced, totally captivated by a musical trend that would become my favourite for years to come. Surrounded by heavenly music, stunning beauty and gentle folks who communicated without ever raising their voices, I underwent a complete metamorphosis. For the first time, I felt free to loosen up, relax and chill out knowing that I would not be instantly punished if I spoke, laughed or sang out loud while shuffling my feet on the soft carpet. Here, in the beautiful corner of a foreign land, I was slowly being reborn.

Then, in a moment lost in deep reverie, Johan walked in. He looked at me as if he had stumbled over something unexpected and studied my glowing features with an enigmatic smile. In that very brief instant, something happened, something awesome and powerful which hit me like a bolt of lightning. I stared back at him, awestruck and unable to speak. He muttered something in German... or was it in English? I could not tell for my head was swooning with a swirl of new emotions that I found quite impossible to understand or control. Looking at Johan's smile was like watching the sun throw flashes of lights on the darkest of hills. I was stunned by its devastating effects and... blinded by colours I had never noticed before.

From then on, every time Johan appeared, in the lounge, in the garden or in the car after school, my heart jumped and I became all flustered. Each time he came close to me, unable to cope with the sudden surge of emotions, I froze on the spot. If for some reason, he could not come to collect us after school, I felt devastated and crushed to the core as if the whole of the heavens had rolled up into one large black cloud to come crashing upon my head. When he appeared in a room when I did not expect him, my face lit up as if a spotlight had just been switched on. When he sat in the lounge watching television, I stole furtive glances to study his face, his eyes, his nose, his hair, and when he spoke I observed the way his lips moved, how they caressed the rounded vowels of words cascading in an enchanted stream. I was spellbound, totally enthralled by his whole being.

In the confines of this close family unit, I lived an idyll surrounded by gentle people who accepted me just the way I was, even if holding a conversation with me proved impossible simply because I did not understand half of what was going on. I was no longer seen as a troublesome teenager but as a young girl blossoming more and more after each dawn.

Unfortunately, I did not know how to respond to the sudden attention bestowed on me, especially by Johan's father who never lost an opportunity to tease me. Sitting on the armrest of his armchair, I looked at him defiantly with a cheeky grin. I wanted to respond to his banter but the language barrier shut me dead, so I punched him instead, gently though, to the amusement of all the others in the room. In retaliation, *Herr N.* nudged me back and I fell into his lap. Straight away, he enwrapped me with his strong arms as if he expected me to fight back, but far from protesting, I stayed put, enjoying for the first time in my life the incredible warmth of strong protective arms.

This was not just a different country, this was a new world where human beings were allowed to evolve naturally, to laugh and be happy. This was too new for me, too intense and… quite simply wonderful. I tried in vain to stem the relentless flow of powerful emotions that had taken hold of me. Feeling at a complete loss, the only way I could regain control of myself was by trying to look cool, detached and unaffected, but… how could I when I felt the happiest I had ever been in my life? It was no use. I surrendered, vanquished by the most delicious sensation caused by the most divine human being. Why should I fight it, anyway? It was sheer bliss, pure heavenly bliss.

Sunday lunch was always taken at one of the local restaurants. In the afternoon, we would lounge and play by the pool. It was in one such afternoon that *Herr N.* approached me and asked:

"Haben Sie etwas dagegen wenn ich nackt herimlaufe?"

As usual when I did not understand, I looked at him and smiled sweetly, hoping that he had not just told me that the dog had died or something equally dreadful. However, the next thing I knew, he was… well… peeling off all his clothes right there by the swimming pool. Shocked, I watched him remove his swimming trunks and discard them with careless abandon on the terrace. Aghast, I rushed to Renée's side.

"Oh my God!" I blurted in my cupped hands. "He's taken all his clothes off!"

"Of course he has." She laughed. "That's just what he asked you."

"Oh?… Did he?"

"Don't panic. It's quite customary here in Germany."

"Is it?" I replied, stuttering with embarrassment and wondering whether this would be an opportune moment to retreat inside the sauna and find out once and for all what that little hut really was.

"Don't go in there," Renée warned, having seemingly read my thoughts, "or you'll have to take off your clothes as well."

"Oh really? Is that what you're supposed to do? Well, I'm not going in there then."

"Yes, you just watch. *Herr N.* is going to go for a swim and then, he'll go inside the sauna. You wait and see."

I stood by the pool wondering what to do next. I looked at Johan then at his friend Michael to study their reactions. Then my gaze shifted towards Trudi. None of them reacted. Just as Renée had predicted, after swimming a few lengths, *Herr N.* disappeared inside the little hut. Moments later, my attention was drawn back towards the pool where Michael was trying to push Johan into the water. Then, spotting me standing idle, he came and chased after me. I squealed in anticipation and quickly ran back towards the house.

Days later, when Michael returned, he scooped me in his arms and threatened to throw me in the pool fully dressed, stopping on the way to pick a few cherries which he playfully dropped on my chest.

Overwhelmed by all this attention, I feared I was about to hyperventilate unless I shared the emotional overload with someone.

Alas, Renée was too busy studying to improve her German while Claudia was away in her own little den to enjoy a few moments of privacy.

What was I supposed to do? The mere mention of Johan's name was enough to produce a frisson of delight. It was heaven… and torture at the same time. What was I supposed to do except swoon in a delectable silence and smile inanely every time Johan invaded my thoughts, which was all the time since I could not stop thinking about him?

From then on, the television, even in colour with its own remote control, and every other material object looked rather mundane and insignificant. It was as if I had been struck by a bolt of sublimity that opened my eyes to the wonders of this world. I retreated in a secret haven of sheer bliss where the scent of love heightened the sweet smells of the countryside and made the colours of the trees, the leaves and the sky sparkle with a fresh luminosity that startled my dreamy eyes. Standing at the top of the valley, I united my spirit with nature's brash beauty where the golden filaments of love were interwoven into each bud, each flower, each particle of the universe stretching all the way to the stars above. Like Rousseau had done before me, I imagined myself walking along the solitary path of love, dreaming of eternal passions while suspended in an ethereal dimension where spirits and souls were united by one wondrous love… and that love was not called God, but Johan.

Alas, after three weeks of living in this exquisite paradise, it was time to leave.

Clouds gathered and the rain fell hard on the steps of the patio. Dressed in a beige Mac, Johan suddenly appeared at the patio doors. He had come to say goodbye. I got up to shake his hand, but as I stood in front of him, neither of us moved and for a few seconds, we simply stared at each other. Finally, and very timidly, I raised my hand and just about managed to articulate: *Auf viedersehen*. But instead of shaking my hand, Johan took it to pull me closer to him and kissed my forehead. Then he muttered in English:

"I hope to see you again. *Au revoir*."

Without looking back, he grabbed a large umbrella and left.

As I watched him walk hurriedly through the rain, everything around me seemed to disappear. I stood in the middle of the lounge, paralysed by a pain I had never experienced before. Victor Hugo's poignant poem: '*Il pleut sur la ville comme il pleut dans mon coeur…*' ('it rains on the town like it rains in my heart…') was nowhere near powerful enough to describe the agony I felt at that moment. Perhaps Thomas Hardy had some measure of it when he declared: 'it never rains, it pours', because right now, it was not raining in my heart, it was absolutely pouring.

Herr. N. tried to warm up the glum atmosphere with some cheerful words which, as usual, I did not understand. He took my suitcase and pretended to throw it in the large boot of the Mercedes. I forced a smile and, without uttering a single word, settled myself in the passenger seat.

As the car meandered around a countryside I had come to know so well, Herr. N. tried again to lift my mood, but too busy to control the pain that was wrenching my insides, I could not respond. Clenching my teeth and my fists, I turned my head towards the window and watched the scenery which so far I had only seen in brilliant sunshine. Alas, the trees, with their leaves weighed down by the heavy rain, had lost their stunning luminosity, that vibrant green that not so long ago had startled my dreamy eyes.

Having experienced the happiest days of my life, I never knew that a sublime moment in time would make it so painful to say goodbye.

Chapter 10

Back in Paris, I rushed to *rue Washington* with the firm intention of asking Mme Chauvineau to send me back to Germany. For once, I was prepared to swallow my pride and lower my self-esteem to plead, beg, implore, even beseech on bended knees the woman I detested in order to have my wish granted.

I climbed the marble staircase to the first floor, rang the bell and waited with some trepidation. When the door opened, I made straight for Mme Chauvineau's desk, ready to grovel and beg.

"Perhaps," she replied ogling me with a peculiar eye. She had sensed something different about me, though she could not make out what. She bristled in her seat to give herself time to study me more closely.

"Well you know, once you've passed your German exam," she eventually conceded, "you might not need to anymore."

"But I want to," I insisted. "I want to carry on with German. I made lots of progress and… and… and... I want to be an interpreter."

"Anyway," she replied, "it's too early to decide. It's a whole year away and you might have changed your mind by then."

"No I won't. I know I won't." I re-affirmed as if taking a pledge.

"As I said, we shall see. We've got other things to talk about; your trip to England for a start. Here are the instructions and your pocket money; there's four pounds here and make sure you don't lose it because that's all you're getting. You'll meet the other girls at Orly Airport and you'll fly to London. There, you'll be met by Madame Solange Miller who's the lady in charge of the students exchange organisation. She'll tell you which family to go to. Luckily, she's French so you'll have no problems of communication."

A few days later, I met up with the other girls, *les Eurasiennes*. Straight away, I recognised a few girls I had met on previous holidays but to my great disappointment, Marie-France was not there.

"Do you know where you're going?" I asked Françoise.

"Yes, I'm going back to Ringwood like last year."

"I'm going there too," Dominique butted in. "To the same family."

"Oh? You can choose where you want to go?" I queried full of hope, noting that if they were allowed to choose to return to their favourite places, then perhaps I too would be able to return to Germany.

"I'm going to Bracknell." Jacqueline declared with a beaming smile. "I love my family there, they're ever so nice."

At that point, all the girls began to discuss the various merits of their respective host families and since all of them seemed perfectly satisfied with their lot, I began to look forward to this new adventure.

In London, a coach awaited us outside the airport. However, rather than being herded in the same direction as the other girls, I was given different instructions. I was to go to the station and take a train to Cambridge. There I was to take another train that would take me to Bury-St-Edmunds. Just before leaving, the organiser thrust a piece of paper in my hand with the name and address of my host family.

"They're very nice," she declared. "They've been hosting foreign students for years so you'll be fine with them." Then, addressing the whole group, she reiterated one particular advice.

"And remember, do not let the families use you to baby-sit. You're paying to stay with them so do not allow them to use you, all right? Have a nice holiday everyone."

Upon these words, she took her leave. Having made my way to the station, I sat on my own on the train, feeling totally deserted and panicking at the thought that if anyone talked to me I would not be able to understand. What if I miss the connection and end up in the middle of nowhere? What if I get lost? No, you couldn't get lost, the organiser had assured me, just show the piece of paper to the taxi driver who'll be waiting for you at the station. What if the taxi driver did not turn up? What if he had forgotten to come and collect me? What was I going to do then? Amid this dark cloud of frightful thoughts, I stared at the rolling landscape fearing the worst.

At Cambridge station, I showed my piece of paper to the station guard with the hope that it would be enough for him to put me on the right train. With a friendly gesture, he guided me towards the correct platform speaking jovially while I smiled back, unable to share with him his good humour.

For us, French natives, the pronunciation of the letters '*th*' is a real tongue twister which tends to skid perilously between the sounds 'z', 'sh' and 't'. So, when we reached the right platform, I articulated several 'thank you', concentrating hard on pronouncing the '*th*' correctly so that it did not sound as if I was saying '*sank you*' or worse even '*shank you*'. The station guard chuckled, patted me on the back and hailed '*Bon voyage!*'.

When I finally reached my destination, to my great relief the taxi driver was there waiting for me. I showed him my piece of paper. He nodded, uttered a few words and opened the car door for me. A few minutes later, we arrived in a village so small and so isolated that I thought I had reached the end of the world.

The taxi driver pulled up outside a large bungalow standing on its own, slightly uphill. There did not seem to be a house number so the driver told me to wait in the taxi while he went and checked. He rang the bell and waited. Nothing happened. He rang the bell again and waited. From the car, I watched him peer through the windows, walk around the house, peer through another window and ring the bell once more. I began to grow anxious as I listened to the meter ticking away. I only had four pounds in my pocket and was more worried about not having enough money to pay my fare than finding myself alone in the middle of nowhere.

After several minutes of waiting in vain, the taxi driver returned shaking his head.

"There's nobody there, love." He stated quite plainly. Then he looked at the piece of paper again. "It is the right address... Well, I can't be waiting all day. I'll take you to the vicarage. Maybe they'll know where the people are."

He pulled outside an old stone house. We hurriedly climbed the few stone steps that led to the front door. An elderly gentleman opened the door.

"Yes?"

The taxi driver greeted the vicar and explained the situation. At hearing this, the vicar exclaimed:

"But they're not here! They're on holiday… in Scotland I think. I've got their holiday address somewhere…"

"Can I leave her with you, then? Got to go you see…"

"Well, I suppose you'll have to…"

Then the taxi driver turned towards me.

"I'll fetch your suitcase," he said flying down the steps. When he returned, he deposited my suitcase in front of the door and said:

"That'll be four pounds and ten."

I was not sure what he meant by 'ten', whether it was shillings or pence, but it did not matter anyway. I only had four pounds.

"Oh well," he said, shrugging his shoulders, "that'll do." Then, he ran down the steps of the vicarage and hailed "Thanks, Vicar, cheers!"

Soon after, the vicar's wife appeared at the door and invited me in.

"Do come in, dear. Leave your case here in the hall. We'll go and wait in the lounge." She said with a friendly smile.

She opened a door on the right.

"Would you like a cup of tea?" She offered kindly.

"Yes, please" I replied, suddenly feeling thirsty.

While she was away in the kitchen and her husband was busy rummaging through some papers in the hall, I looked around the room.

The walls were clad with wood-panelling which gave the room a somewhat gloomy atmosphere despite the brilliant sunshine outside. I had just time to notice that the upholstery of the sofa and armchairs matched the pattern of the curtains before the vicar's wife returned with the tea tray.

"Milk in your tea?"

"No thank you."

"Sugar?"

"Yes, please."

"Do help yourself to some biscuits. So…" she resumed, clutching her hands together. "You're on holiday."

After talking for a few minutes without getting much response from me, the lady eventually realised that I did not understand much else beyond her welcoming words. So, displaying a discernable amount of optimism, considering the tricky circumstances, she ceased talking, pointed at her husband and, making a concerted effort to detach every syllable, she said:

"My husband knows where Mr and Mrs Taylor are and as soon as he finds their holiday address, he's going to ring them, so you'll be fine." Then, she added: "They're on holiday… in Scotland…"

Suddenly, her husband exclaimed with glee:

"There it is! I've found their address, Hilda. I'll go and phone them right away."

Upon these words, he stomped out of the room and dashed to the telephone in the hall. A few minutes later, he returned into the lounge. Addressing his wife, he gave her the gist of the conversation, then sank himself into one of the comfortable armchairs and mumbled to his wife:

"They're not happy… I don't think this was planned… rather an inconvenience having to cut short one's holiday." Then, looking at me, he said:

"They're travelling back from Scotland, so they'll be here sometime this evening. You don't mind waiting here until then, do you?"

Late that evening, a man came to the door.

"Good evening, Vicar." I heard.

"Good evening, Mr Taylor. I'm really sorry about all this. How was the journey?"

"Faster than I care to mention."

"Well, here she is," the vicar said, pushing me towards the door as if trying to hurry the proceedings. "Goodbye and good luck!"

Mr Taylor and I got into the car and waved to the vicar. Shortly after, we were back outside the bungalow. Mrs Taylor opened the front door, greeted me curtly and showed me to her daughter's bedroom. By then, I was so tired that I did not even try to understand what she was telling me; I just nodded my head knowingly a few times, hoping it would be in the right places, returned her sharp 'good night', and collapsed on the bed.

The following morning, I came downstairs to find two young children sitting at the breakfast table. Not knowing what kind of reception I would get, I greeted timidly:

"Good morning."

The children returned the greeting cheerfully, then carried on munching their cereals.

"Good morning. Did you sleep well?" The mother said in a nicer manner than I expected.

"Yes, thank you."

"Help yourself to some breakfast. There are toasts and cereals, just help yourself." She repeated.

Later that morning, Mrs Taylor got on the phone. Although I was not able to understand every word of the conversation, the brisk tone she used was enough to indicate that she was busy giving a piece of her mind to the organiser. If she had known the word 'omni shamble', she would not have hesitated to use it liberally to describe the chaotic state of the organisation.

Having ended the telephone conversation abruptly, she came into the lounge where I was sitting on the floor listening to the little boy explaining some game to me.

"Well," she started, hitting herself firmly in the side with her fists. "I've told her what I think of her organisation. I had told her I did not want any foreign student this summer and I've told her again. I don't want any student ever again. Anyway, it's not your fault but you can't stay here for the whole month. I can only have you for two weeks. After that, I've told your leader you'll have to go…" Here she paused to catch her breath. "The taxi must have cost you dear, how much was it?"

"Four pounds."

"Four pounds! That's a fortune! You probably don't have any money left."

"No."

"Right, well, since it was not your fault, I'll give your money back, but don't worry, I have every intention of getting it back from the organiser. After all, you're her responsibility. She shouldn't have sent you here in the first place, especially as I had written to her specifically to say that we didn't want any more students. Anyway, now that you're here, I hope you enjoy your stay."

Upon which, she left the room. Seconds later, she was back.

"By the way," she said, "have you got the receipt for the taxi?"

"Yes, it's in my bedroom."

"It's not your bedroom," she spat back; "it's my daughter's bedroom! Now, could you go and fetch it for me, please."

I stole upstairs as quickly as I could and returned with the solicited piece of paper. As abruptly as she had burst into the room, she left once more.

Her son and I looked at each other.

"What's your name?" I finally asked, trying to placate the ruffled atmosphere.

"Derek. What's yours?"

"Martha."

"OK," he continued unfazed by the flustered mood of his mother, "this is how you play this game."

The remainder of the fortnight passed without any major incident. To tell the truth, I was bored out of my mind. The house was in the middle of nowhere; the father was out all day working and the mother was always doing some housework, cleaning and ironing which left me with the daughter aged nine and the son aged seven for company, not exactly the kind of companions I was looking for. I mean, did they know how to play poker, for example? Lost in the middle of birds that were singing and watching the nests they were making, I spent most of my time daydreaming, writing letters and poring over elegiac couplets I had freshly composed, inspired by the sight of a farmer on his tractor, cows ambling nonchalantly in the fields and the musty smell of the earth that rose from the rich ground each time it rained.

One late afternoon, however, as I was relaxing in the bath after a spot of sunbathing, I heard Mrs Taylor rush up the stairs. Soon after, she pounded on the bathroom door.

"Martha! Martha!" She shouted. "The window cleaner! The window cleaner!"

Startled, I sat up in the bath frantically looking everywhere for something called 'window cleaner'.

"Martha!" She shouted with some anguish. "Open the door! The window cleaner's here!"

Shouting words in a foreign language does not make it easier to understand and only causes panic and confusion. I was now studying every bottle that stood on the window ledge trying to find this 'window cleaner'. Suddenly, I saw a ladder being propped against the window and instantly the meaning of the phrase became clear to me. To my horror, I spotted my bath towel at the other end of the bathroom. It was too late to get it so I grabbed the small hand towel by the wash-basin and placed it in front of me. Then dripping wet, I walked sideways so that my back would face the wall rather than the window, and unlocked the door. Immediately, Mrs Taylor burst into the bathroom, rushed to the window and shut the curtains.

"The window cleaner!" She repeated, pointing at the window.

'I know, I understand,' I wanted to reply, but then she looked at me and smiled.

"Well, I see I was just in time!"

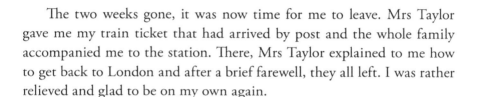

The two weeks gone, it was now time for me to leave. Mrs Taylor gave me my train ticket that had arrived by post and the whole family accompanied me to the station. There, Mrs Taylor explained to me how to get back to London and after a brief farewell, they all left. I was rather relieved and glad to be on my own again.

In London, the organiser was waiting for me. She did not say very much and took me straight to Ilford, an area of London where people wore black suits or black dresses and where boys and men wore on their heads black round hats with long tightly braided tresses dangling from underneath the rims. Ogling them with a queer eye, I wondered what type of cast system or religious order they belonged to.

We arrived outside a small terraced house where a heavily pregnant woman with a toddler clamped on her leg opened the door.

"Hello, Mrs S…, this is Martha who's going to stay with you for the next two weeks."

"Ok, come in, come in." She said with a very pronounced foreign accent.

We walked into the small cramped lounge which I surveyed with dismay. Then, the organiser left.

The woman turned to me and said:

"Me, I show you bedroom. Yes, you take suitcase upstairs now."

The staircase was so narrow that I had to climb the steps sideways to allow enough room to squeeze myself and the suitcase along the tight passage.

I gauged from the onset that we would have problems of communication. The hostess's spoken English was little better than mine and delivered in a tortuous accent that I found impossible to understand. Inevitably, after a frustrating weekend of wrestling hands and words together, the woman began to lose patience. The final straw came when she asked me to look after her little boy while she went out on some errant. Remembering the instructions we had been given upon our arrival, I shook my head and said:

"No baby-sitting."

"No baby-sitting? No good to me!" She declared rather miffed.

The very same day, she was on the phone to the organiser. After a brief exchange, she returned to the lounge, pointed an accusatory finger at me and said:

"You not being nice to my little boy. You go away."

So off I went again. This time, I was carted off to a fast growing town called Bracknell.

"You'll like it here." The organiser reassured me. "Besides, some of your friends are staying with families not far from here, so you'll be able to meet up and socialise. I bet you can't wait to be able to speak French again."

I was in no mood to reply. What I really wanted to do though was to give her a piece of my mind, tell her that her organisation was a complete shamble, that she had been totally irresponsible to send me on a wild goose chase in a place on my own where nobody was expecting me. Anything could have happened to me but she did not seem to be at all concerned, and never once apologized for the terrible ordeal she had put me through. By now, I could feel this thunderous cloud growing inside my head, rumbling and roaring and ready to burst, but I could not let it go because I knew that if I did, I would be in trouble again. So, I simmered down, let her take me to my new destination, to stay with yet another host family and deal with whatever new situation would arise. And arise, they certainly did.

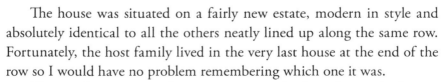

The house was situated on a fairly new estate, modern in style and absolutely identical to all the others neatly lined up along the same row. Fortunately, the host family lived in the very last house at the end of the row so I would have no problem remembering which one it was.

The couple, in my rough estimation, were both in their early thirties and had a young daughter. The woman reminded me of models I had seen on posters and in magazines. She was tall, slim and highly manicured. By sheer contrast, when her husband came home, late that evening, dressed in some kind of greasy overall, he looked unkempt, bedraggled and reeked of beer, but, and that was probably something that his wife did not want to see, he had a bright spark twinkling in his eyes.

Finding a stranger in his house, he threw a cursory glance at me. Then, having given me the once over, he muttered a casual greeting, put a record on, sat himself in what was clearly ***his*** armchair and lit a cigarette.

"Been to the pub then?" His wife enquired coldly.

"Well, it's my turn, in' it?"

Hence, having in a succinct manner assessed his whereabouts for the past few hours, the woman uttered a quick 'goodnight' and promptly disappeared upstairs. I rose up to follow suit but the man suggested otherwise.

"You don't have to go simply because she's going… You like Gordon Lightfoot?"

I stared at him blankly. Gordon Lightfoot? I had never heard of him. I came from Paris, how could I possibly know of anyone from the estate called *Gordon Lightfoot*? Eventually, guessing my poor understanding of the language, the man showed me the record sleeve of an LP and said:

"That's him. He's a singer. Great songs… you'll like his music."

Boy, didn't I feel stupid. Anyway, we listened to the track: *If you could read my mind, love…* Then he looked at me all mellow and smiled.

"That's my favourite track… very romantic. Don't you think?"

I nodded with a smile.

"What kind of music do you like?"

I hardly knew any music at all but with Johan never far from my mind, I did remember one group.

"*Ze Bittels.*" I replied in my best French accent.

"*The Bittels?*" He quizzed, ogling me oddly. "Oh, you mean the Beatles, yeah?"

"Yes, *Ze Beatels*," I parroted, trying to get my tongue around the diphthongs…

By now, I was too tired to attempt to speak any more English. So I stood up.

"I go to bed now."

"Oh, I'm sorry. I do apologise for keeping you up so late. You must be very tired after your long journey. Good night, then."

"Good night."

"And tomorrow morning, you can stay in bed as long as you want."

Thank God for that, I thought, and promptly disappeared up the stairs.

On that first night, once I was tucked away in bed, the family cat came into the bedroom, jumped on the bed and curled himself up for the night. I stared at it briefly to assess his wild instincts. Satisfied that the little creature was more domesticated than wild, I quickly fell asleep.

A few days later, the organiser came to visit. The hostess had phoned her with some concern. Sitting in the lounge leafing through some magazine, I overheard my hostess say:

"But she never talks… she never says anything!"

The organiser mumbled a few words, not knowing exactly how to respond to this rather unusual problem.

"She's probably shy and her English is very limited." I heard her say in my defence. "There's also the fact that she lives in a boarding-school, so she's probably not used to talking to adults."

"I can't get her to eat either. She'll only eat cereals or beans on toast."

"Well, you've got to understand that this is her first visit to England and she probably isn't used to eating different food. But I'll have a word with her and see what I can do."

At that moment, both women walked into the lounge. I got up to greet them. The organiser greeted me in French.

"*Bonjour*, Martha. You're fine? Are you happy here?"

"Yes, I'm fine."

"Mrs L. is worried about you because you don't seem to communicate very much. Do you understand when she speaks to you?"

"Er… yes… sometimes."

"So you're fine, then?"

I paused, wondering how much she was prepared to hear; then I suddenly blurted out:

"I'm bored. There's nothing to do and no one to talk to."

"Ah!" The organiser replied. "I might be able to help you here. There's another girl who's staying near Maidenhead, not too far from here. Denise... Do you know her?"

"No."

"I'll give you her address and the name of her family, and perhaps you could go and visit her. In the meantime, I'll ring her family to let them know to expect you some time. *D'accord?*"

Wasting no time and holding the piece of paper in my hand, I walked to Denise's house. There, we introduced each other, talked about school, about the other girls we knew and listened to music.

"The little boy of the family is five and he loves to dance to the music of: *Sugar, sugar.* He knows all the words. Do you want to see? I'll call him. Andrew! Andrew!"

Soon after, a little boy appeared.

"Do you want to listen to some music, Andrew?" Denise asked. "What do you want to listen to?"

"*Sugar, sugar,*" the little boy replied, all coy, with his head sinking deep into his shoulders.

"All right," Denise said, "I'll put the record on and we'll dance, ok?"

As soon as the music started, little Andrew, spurred on by Denise, put his hands on his hips and started dancing while belting out the lyrics. I watched the two of them dancing and singing together, surprised at how at ease Denise seemed to be with her family and how friendly they were towards her. And for the first time in my life, I wished I could be like someone else. I wished I could be like Denise, be able to move and mix freely and join in without feeling inadequate and being overwhelmed by feelings of awkwardness and embarrassment. I wished I could be normal, but without a mentor or a guide, I did not know how to.

When it was time for me to go home, Denise and I plotted our next visit.

"I'll come and see you tomorrow if you like." Denis volunteered.

"Yes, do come. I'm so bored but how are you going to get there? Is your family going to drive you?"

"No, I'll just borrow their daughter's bike."

"They don't mind?"

"Of course not. Has your family got a bike?"

"The little girl has."

"Oh well, if you ask to borrow it, I'm sure they won't mind."

And so followed several days when Denise and I cycled to and fro on the mostly deserted roads between Bracknell and Maidenhead.

After a few days of this, however, the little girl began to complain. As I was about to leave, already astride on her bike, her mother appeared abruptly at the door.

"You must understand, this is not your bike, it's my daughter's bike and she wants it. So, I don't want you to borrow it again, do you hear?"

Without a word, I dismounted the bike, left it on the drive and walked off to Denise's house.

Towards the end of the holiday, I began to have some inkling about the state of affair between my hosts. Each seemed to live independently from the other and took it in turn to go out to the pub. The woman seemed to resent more and more the dishevelled look of her husband and as soon as he would leave the lounge, she would spray the room liberally with generous squirts of lavender scent. As for him, he did not seem to care; as long as he could have his beer, his cigarettes and listen to his favourite records, he was perfectly content. Caught in the middle of this marital turmoil, I observed how their daughter seemed to be the only one happy to babble away to her mother and father, seemingly oblivious to the tension mounting between the two adults.

Chapter 11

At the end of my first English campaign, I returned to Paris and to the staid atmosphere of the godmother's apartment. For some reason, the latter was growing suspicious of me and took to locking me in the apartment for hours on end every time she needed to go out. Her paranoia extended to locking her bedroom and the piano, especially the piano, ever since one of her friends had noted that I played the piano better than her. Left alone to idle the hours away, I was able to reflect on a summer that had changed me for ever. Still floating freely in my bubble of happiness with only Johan inside it, I spent most of my pocket money on records so that the familiar melodies would recreate the mood and atmosphere of the happiest days of my life. In my daydreams, I relived over and over again the most memorable moments that had turned my life upside down, visualising the house, the orchard and the valley, smelling the glorious scent of pine and fresh earth and smiling at the happy images constantly rolling inside my head with flashbacks of stunning clarity and luminosity like the limpid waters of a river of dreams.

While I swooned around the godmother's abode with my head permanently buried in some heavenly cloud, preferring to have her out of my hair rather than in it, she began to resent my cold indifference. Like a guard towards an amenable prisoner, she wanted to establish a rapport, some sort of connection that would bring her closer to the alien creature that invaded her world every weekend, but to no avail. She clearly resented me... or rather my looks, unable as she was to get over the fact that I was... er... terribly ugly. The very sight of my glasses used to send her in an apoplectic fit. She even threatened to break them if she saw me wear them again, especially in front of her friends. It was almost as if she regarded me like a pustular wart stuck to her side, and would sooner reach for a pair of

Marigold rather than touch me with her bare hands. Quite frankly I did not care because if the godmother found me irrevocably ugly, no one else seemed to have noticed.

Paris also seemed to be going through the upheaval of a second adolescence. The air was no longer filled with the loud fracas of revolutionary chants, of windows exploding or of police sirens whining, but with the metallic din of scaffoldings being erected, pneumatic drills digging up paved roads, electric saws cutting through sandstones and builders dropping planks of woods, hailing each other and wolf-whistling at anything in skirts. Old crumbly buildings were systematically demolished to make way for ultra modern luxury apartment blocks and glass clad shopping precincts. To the excitement and delight of many Parisians who delighted in everything English, a rather snobbish attitude back then, the very first Marks & Spencer was built and officially opened by an English gentleman dressed in a pin-striped suit with a red carnation on his lapel and coiffed with a bowler hat, and swinging along his side a tightly rolled up long thin black umbrella as a symbol of his sharp wit. He was supposed to impersonate Colonel Thompson from the best-selling book of the time 'Colonel Thompson's Notebooks', although of course, here in Paris nobody had ever heard of him, except my English teacher to whom I shall forever be grateful for introducing me to the wonderful work of George Mikes and his hilarious but extremely perspicacious social observations in his books 'My Little Cabbage' and 'How to be an Alien'.

Fortunately for all the lovers of classic architecture, the strict building regulations forbade the construction of high rise block within the capital, so these were speedily erected on the outskirt of the city, sprouting around the *boulevard péripherique* and transforming the suburb into a mini reproduction of New York.

As a result, the City was dusty, noisy and choking under a permanent cloud of concrete dust, and yet, I loved being back. I loved the sooty smell, the hot sticky atmosphere, the cacophony of ordinary citizens and awestruck tourists moving *en masse* on the crowded boulevards and posh avenues. I loved the hustle and bustle of a city that was alive and still kicking high on the stage of the *Moulin Rouge*, the *Lido* or the *Folies*

Bergères. But most of all, I loved being back in the folds of a city where history was being made, where the intellectual elite used to meet in cafés such as *Les Deux Magots*, place Saint Germain, or *La Coupole*, boulevard du Montparnasse – once the favourite haunts of Jean-Paul Sartre and Simone de Beauvoir – and where films stars and *vedettes de la chanson* paraded with chic and elegance on their way to *Fouquet's* on the Champs Elysées. This was a place, *the* place where everyone wanted to be and be seen, a status quo rivalled at the time only by one other city, just across the English Channel: London. Be chic in Paris, be brash in London, that was the rigorous order of the day.

<hr />

My new school was situated in the Fourteenth Arrondissement, a tame and unremarkable district of Paris where the only cries to be heard were those of the butcher or the fishmonger selling their fresh merchandise.

Having stepped over the threshold, I found myself in the middle of a small square building, neatly divided into two halves, with the right wing housing the école élémentaire and where I would repeat my year and with the left wing reserved for the *Lycée Technique Catherine Labourée* where students could study vocational courses in secretariat and accountancy. One tall solitary tree propped up in the middle of the small tarmac yard provided the only greenery among the grey buildings. This was mainly a day school with only a handful of boarders drafted in from the extended suburb.

The first boarder I met was a petite rounded girl called Marie-Sophie, who showed me around the building with a permanent smile beaming through her thin lips. She talked non-stop and I was quite happy to listen to her babbling away for her obvious state of happiness and contentment was a clear indication that the regime here would not be too harsh. After we had visited the dormitory on the top floor where I left my bag, she took me to the refectory on the ground floor where she offered me a glass of water. I asked about the teachers, especially about the English and German teachers as these had become my favourite subjects.

"Hum… I'm not sure about the English teacher. She's all right… a bit old fashion, looks like an old maid really, but she's all right. Now, Mme Dubernet is the German teacher and she's a dream, really lovely but my favourite teacher is the Maths teacher: Mademoiselle Deschamps…"

Deschamps? Did she say *Deschamps*? I knew that name. It wouldn't by any chance be…? No… it couldn't possibly be. It would be too much of a coincidence.

"Oh, she's fantastic, I simply adore her, she's wonderful…"

While Marie-Sophie launched herself into an ecstatic elegy of mathematical wonders, I was trying to dismiss outright any thought that I might be familiar with the name, that I might already have had a close and frightful encounter with that particular teacher although… I had my doubts…Could she really be…? Marie-Sophie continued to eulogise her charismatic presence, the strong hold she had on her pupils and her well-deserved status as the best teacher in the world. No, absolutely not, it could not be her, and yet…

"This Mademoiselle Deschamps…"

"Yes?" Marie-Sophie was looking at me with wide eyes, eager to tell me more.

"What's her first name?"

"Her first name? Why… I don't know. We only know her as Mademoiselle Deschamps."

"What does she look like?"

"Well… it's difficult to describe. She's tallish and slim… Her hair is always swept back in a *chignon*… you know, in a bun pinned at the back of her head… and she often wears bright red lipstick."

"Oh my God, Marie-Sophie! I think I know her."

"No! I don't believe you!…Do you… really?" She exclaimed incredulous.

"Yes, yes… Has she got a wart on her upper lip?"

"Well, I don't know; I've never noticed really… Actually… come to think of it, yes I think she has… or has she? Oh my God, I'm not sure now!"

"Is she strict, I mean really really strict like everyone is terrified of her?"

"Hum… I wouldn't say terrified though she can be quite scary at times."

Marie-Sophie was now ogling me with a weird look in her eyes.

"Oh my God!" I exclaimed again, bristling in my seat. "I'm pretty sure it's the same teacher, but I knew her as Mademoiselle Germaine and she used to be the headmistress of my first school here in Paris."

"Germaine… So that's her first name." Marie-Sophie repeated

dreamily. "I've often wondered what her first name was… And she used to be a headmistress? That doesn't surprise me. She's so clever, so intelligent… yeah, I can see her as a headmistress. Of course she's strict but… I adore her."

"You know, the one thing I remember about Mlle Germaine was that she was always fair, extremely fair."

At that moment, a nun came in. It was Sister Marie-Joseph, the nun in charge of the junior boarders.

"Right girls, are you all settled then?"

"Yes, Sister." We chorused.

"I showed her where her bed is and where to put her things." Marie-Sophie reported.

"Oh good." Sister Marie-Joseph noted approvingly. Then turning towards me she added: "I've put you in the bed closest to my room so that I can keep a close eye on you. From what I've heard of your past behaviour, I'm going to need to."

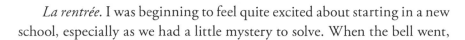

La rentrée. I was beginning to feel quite excited about starting in a new school, especially as we had a little mystery to solve. When the bell went, Marie-Sophie grabbed hold of my sleeve and pulled me towards our line.

"I can't wait to have Maths." She whispered, tucking herself behind me.

"Neither can I." I replied under my breath.

As we walked along the corridor on the first floor, I noticed progress charts posted outside each classroom door which reminded me of my school in Tourcoing. It had only been four years since I had left and yet, it seemed an eternity, a lifetime away. I now felt so completely detached from that early part of my life that it seemed as if it had never existed. It had been a dream, a bad dream, and now it was over, all over for now and for ever. I had moved on to a better world, a better place, and whether I was prepared to admit it or not, it was all thanks to the godmother.

As soon as we entered the classroom, there was a real scramble all around the desks and I made straight for one right at the back of the class.

"No, no." Sister Monique, the head teacher, hailed. "In alphabetical order, please! Mademoiselle Bertrand! Here, on the front row."

Zut alors! I cursed under my breath. Why did I have to have a surname that began with a B? I always ended up sitting on the front row. Grudgingly, I picked up my brand new satchel and dragged my feet all the way to the front of the class. With her surname beginning with a D, Marie-Sophie was sitting only a few desks away from me.

At last. First Maths lesson. Marie-Sophie and I looked at each other, then at the door. The teacher walked in, greeted the class with a bright red smile, threw a cursory glance at me as she passed my desk, and sat down at her own desk. Immediately, I turned towards Marie-Sophie and winked. She smiled back before devoting her whole attention to her beloved teacher. At the end of the lesson, the class got up to go to break. I was already out of my seat ready to grab Marie-Sophie's arm when Mademoiselle Deschamps called:

"Mademoiselle Bertrand, could you stay behind, please?"

I stood in front of my desk and waited for the other pupils to leave the room. When the last pupil closed the door, Mademoiselle Deschamps came towards me with a big smile.

"Well, well. I thought it might be you when I saw your name on the register. What are you doing here?"

Gosh, so much had happened lately that I had almost forgotten why I was back in the Fifth Form.

"I failed my exams." I mumbled sheepishly.

"What, you? I don't believe it!" She exclaimed incredulously.

Here we go again, I thought. I'm not that clever, you know, and in fact… the proof is that I was pretty stupid to fail my exams in the first place. But the teacher did not seem to be put off by my abysmal failure which, if anything, confirmed everybody's belief that I was lazy beyond measure. In fact, contrary to what I expected, she seemed positively pleased to see me.

"Well, never mind. Welcome back. I do hope that together, we can make you succeed. However, you'll need to work hard."

"Yes, Mademoiselle, I know."

Hence I settled happily in my new school where for the first time ever I felt I had an ally amongst the adults. It augured well. I made my way downstairs feeling as light as a feather and emerged into the playground. Straight away, I spotted Marie-Sophie sitting on the bench situated underneath the chestnut tree. I walked briskly towards her.

"Well?" She asked with bated breath.

I took a deep breath. Marie-Sophie cupped her hands over her mouth ready to muffle an ecstatic scream. Then I told her.

"Yes, it's her. It's Mademoiselle Germaine."

Marie-Sophie screamed.

"Oh my God, I don't believe it! Are you sure?"

"What do you mean? Of course I'm sure! If you don't believe me, call her *Mademoiselle Germaine* and see how she reacts."

"Oh, I couldn't, it'd be too rude."

"It's not rude. That's how we used to call her."

Marie-Sophie paused briefly to gather her thoughts. Then she decreed:

"I think I'm going to ask her… not because I don't believe you. I just want to see her reaction."

Suddenly, as I was watching the other girls playing around me, something or rather someone drew my attention. Over there, standing by the main entrance, I had just caught sight of a familiar silhouette. I gasped in complete surprise.

"Oh my God, Marie-Sophie! I've just spotted someone else I know."

With no further explanation, I ran off.

"Mathilde! Mathilde!" I shouted. "Hi! What are *you* doing here?"

Mathilde glared at me as if she had never seen me before.

"I'm a boarder at the *Lycée*." She declared hauntingly. "I'm studying for the *baccalaureat technique* in accountancy."

Her lofty attitude intrigued me. This was not the 'Mathilde' I knew, the giggling and mischievous adolescent girl with whom I had larked about for two whole years.

"Did you know I was coming here? Is this why you're here?"

"No, my dad decided to send me here." She replied on an indifferent tone.

"Wow!" I exclaimed, unable to make out why my old friend did not sound as excited as I was. "What a coincidence. It's incredible! Are you pleased?"

"Well, it's just another school."

Her flat remark left me totally perplexed. I could not understand why, after two years of having fun together, playing games, breaking rules and declaiming together poems and once even a whole passage from *Le Cid*, all she could manage to articulate was a cold and indifferent greeting. Then a thought occurred to me: was she actually looking down on me because I was repeating my year?

Raising her gaze, she looked away and into the distance as if searching for someone else. So I left.

At the end of break, I went back to Marie-Sophie and as we lined up in our respective classes, I tugged on her sleeve.

"Have you asked her?" I whispered.

She turned towards me and whispered from the corner of her mouth.

"I've not even seen her yet! Give me a chance."

Several days later, Marie-Sophie still had not plucked up the courage to ask the Maths teacher about her first name.

"Oh, I can't," she finally admitted, squirming with shyness. "Anyway, it's easy to see that you two know each other. I can tell by the way she speaks to you and besides... you're the only one in the class who's not scared of her."

"I used to be, though. But I know what she's like. She's a great teacher and... she's fair... she has no favourites."

Marie-Sophie may have been disappointed at hearing those words for I soon discovered that she herself was the star of the class and unlike me, she was conscientious, studious and diligent in all aspects of her work. In fact, after a few weeks at the school, the head teacher decided that perhaps we should share a desk in the hope that this unlikely pairing would instil some discipline in me and boost my academic performance. If it worked for me, it certainly did not benefit my new ally who was found to be paying less attention, showing less concentration and giggling a little too much. So the teachers held counsel and we were soon separated. Sister Monique shook her head in despair.

"I don't know what we're going to do with you, Mademoiselle Bertrand."

Well, don't you worry yourself, Sister, I said to myself. I knew exactly what I was going to do: work at my Maths for a start, because the way the marks were calculated at the exam, if you passed your Maths, it was virtually impossible to fail the whole exam. However, the question was: could I do it? In the past, having been too busy concentrating on playing my next hand at poker, I had not paid the blind bit of attention to the workings of mathematical equations that the teacher had painstakingly scribbled on the blackboard. Back then, due to my lack of attention, I considered the task as impossible as deciphering Egyptian hieroglyphs, and no wonder. However, with Mademoiselle Germaine as my teacher, it was the same game with the same rules but with a new coach who knew how to make the players win.

Another unforeseen event happened which helped me put my plans into action, and once again, it was all to do with my natural ebullience, my youthful effervescence, my overflowing gaiety which adults systematically branded as 'unruly behaviour'.

While adults scratched their heads, had words with me and examined closely my *fréquentations* within my peer group to try and get to the root of the problem, I knew exactly what the matter was: I was in love… and not just with Johan. I was in love with Paris, with the murky waters of the river Seine and the magnificent trees lining its banks; I was in love with the stifling weather, the sooty smell of the underground, the constant drilling noise of road works and of the metallic saws cutting through the sandstone of crumbling buildings; and every time I saw something old or new, my eyes threw sparkles of wonder and delight on every sight and every sound around me because everything looked so beautiful, so wild, untamed and untameable by the rigidity and inflexible minds of human beings who had not understood that life, like love, cannot be contained within the gilded cage of a free spirit. And there, dear adults, lay my problem.

Constantly at pains to try and stem the unstoppable flow of surging emotions, I had become even more exuberant, more effervescent and totally indomitable.

One day, as I made my way to the reception to ask permission to go out, lo and behold, who should be there but Sister Odile from the orphanage in Tourcoing.

"Well, well," she exclaimed eyeing me up and down. "If it isn't Mademoiselle Bertrand!" Then, turning towards Sister Monique, she enquired: "How is she these days? And her behaviour… much improved?"

Sister Monique shook her head in despair, produced a loud sigh and confessed:

"I'm afraid she's quite a handful. Totally ill disciplined."

"No change there then." Sister Odile surmised before adding: "Yet, God knows we tried… yes, God knows we tried."

One consequence of this was that my peers were irresistibly drawn towards my joyful self and cheerful moods and before I knew it, I had become one of the most popular girls in the whole school.

"Why? Why?" I asked the girls.

"Because you're not afraid to stand up to them…"

"Yeah… and you answer back!" Another declared.

What? I exclaimed to myself. Was this really how they saw me?

If I was left baffled by my sudden popularity, Sister Marie-Joseph was very clear about the devastating effect my undesirable influence had on the younger girls. The day she really panicked was one morning when, from the chapel's window, she saw a line of girls forming a spontaneous line in front of me as I was making my way to breakfast, so that each could receive their good morning kiss. Immediately, her voluminous robes and veil flew down the stairs and seconds later, her flustered silhouette burst into the playground. This circus, as she put it, had to stop here and now. Consequently, I was segregated from the rest of the girls, given my own bedroom and my own individual study.

What kind of punishment was that? I snorted to myself. Pupils' parents would normally have to pay a fortune for such privileges. Secluded in my very own haven of peace, I was enjoying a lifestyle usually accorded to university students and, it could not have come at a better time. Away from all distractions, I was able to practise solving Maths problems, lengthy equations and geometrical puzzles. At night, with no one to shout 'lights out', I was able to read at leisure and indulge in an overflow of emotions which I then poured into a profusion of effusive letters and romantic poems. Life, back in the heart of Paris, had never been better.

What happened next, however, came as a complete shock. The changes happened imperceptibly at first. One day, out of the blue, Sister Marie-Joseph brought a record player in the dormitory and put a record on. Some girls started dancing.

"Teach me how to dance." She asked.

So we showed her some basic steps and soon, she was twisting away with the rest of us. I had never seen her look so relaxed and, dare I say, happy. Following this, she took the habit of bringing the little portable record player and asked us to bring some records so she could learn more dance steps and hear the kind of music we liked. Gradually, she became more friendly and less and less starchy though the one barrier that remained immovable was… her nun's habit.

What I could not fail to notice was the fact that Sister Marie-Joseph was beginning to show a desire for 'rapprochement'. A lot less abrupt in her manner, she sought to engage in more mature and friendly exchanges. Her own room at the end of the dormitory had always been regarded as a secret realm locked away from our prying eyes. Now, I was enjoying the exclusive privilege of being invited in as a most honourable guest for short impromptu meetings during which we discussed books and music while she sought my opinion on various other matters. Once even, she took the bold step of totally ignoring the strict social code that prevented any kind of interactions between adults and their charges, to talk freely about her past, her family and herself. I was staggered and baffled at the same time by this sudden familiarity, and while she slowly drafted me into her own world, sitting in her comfortable armchair and looking at the single family portrait propped up on her bedside table, all I could think was: I shouldn't be here, not in **her** bedroom. Admittedly, I was the oldest girl in the junior section but having so far been ignored by the majority of the adult population, I did not know what to make of this sudden attention. So I remained aloof, distant and indifferent. And since I was wholly involved at the time with me, myself and I, subsisting in my own private world inside my own invisible happy bubble, I never once noticed how Sister Marie-Joseph appeared to be increasingly bothered by my cold and detached attitude towards her, how she was inexplicably fussing over me, checking that I had all my books and homework and that I was making good progress in Maths.

Frustratingly, I found myself at the centre of her attention when all I desired was to be left alone. Then one day, the matter came to a head. It was one Friday evening when all the boarders had gone home and I was left behind, yet again, because my guardian was otherwise engaged. Sister Marie-Joseph appeared in the refectory where I was dining alone. Again, she tried to establish some kind of rapport and extend a friendly hand which I stubbornly refused to take. She huffed and puffed her frustration and anger, and assailed me with all sorts of questions, all beginning with 'why?'. She banged and banged on that brick wall until her fists bled but all she got in return was a cold stare. Then, as I was about to leave the refectory, she suddenly squared up to me, grabbed me by the throat and pinned me against the wall. Glaring at me straight in the eyes, she cursed:

"You're evil! You're pure evil… You've got Satan in your soul!"

Her face all flushed with a redness approaching apoplectic dimension, she kept a firm grasp and laboured to breathe while her piercing eyes, enlarged with rage and passion, continued to bore deep into my soul. She was determined to punch through that brick wall, reach out and tear a piece of me. I could feel her hot breath blowing in my face but I remained cool, detached and unaffected. I felt neither aggression nor fear, only bewilderment. Finally, she let go off me and swiftly left the room. Still startled, I stayed against the wall for a few seconds more, totally mystified and wondering what had come over the nun, then, having collected my thoughts, I made my way upstairs and tucked myself into bed with a good book.

At school, things were moving apace with an array of teachers that rated sometime high and sometime low in my personal esteem.

In small private schools, it was quite common for teachers to teach more than one subject and our bad luck was to have the most boring of the lot teaching us several of them. Thank goodness, there were others, more amenable, more inspiring and more intellectually challenging; and then, there was the odd one, the mother hen, the one who wanted to teach from her bosom, gathering her brood around her and clucking away at her subject with cheerfulness and good humour.

In the old days, Mademoiselle Germaine – whom I now had to call Deschamps - terrified us into learning something, and yet I had been wholly inspired by her impressive knowledge of Literature, Maths and the Classics. When we claimed that French and Maths were two subjects totally apposite, i.e. if you were literary minded, you could not possibly be scientifically minded as well, therefore one could only excel in one **or** the other, never in both. Not quite so, she would counter-argue and declare quite logically that the two worked on very similar principles, both being governed by rules invariably broken by a disorderly bunch of exceptions in French grammar or an unruly cohort of variables in Algebra which had to be controlled and manipulated in order to proceed with the workings of the French language or the evolutionary theorems of Algebra and Geometry. She therefore insisted that if one were good at French, then without question, one had to be good at Maths too.

For once, I had a teacher who had the ability to make us think rather than expect us to regurgitate in parrot fashion complex notions on noble topics that we were not required to understand. With her at the helm of my destiny, I knew I could not fail.

Madame Bonnard, on the other hand, our French and History teacher, and sometimes Physics, Chemistry and Biology, was the kind of teacher who would have sent to sleep a pupil suffering from a serious case of attention deficit-hyperactivity disorder. In History, for example, she would arrive in class with the textbook tucked under her arm and climb solemnly the two small steps that led to the summit of her desk. Then, she would sit down, make herself comfortable, open the book at the right page and proceed to reel out, page after page, important facts, key dates and illustrious names on such a monotonous tone that I invariably found myself drifting off to sleep. At the end of the lesson, she would set the homework by commanding: "And for next time, I want you to learn from paragraph such… to paragraph such… on page such and such." When the next lesson came, she would open her register, pick a name at random and the designated pupil would have to stand up and recite word for word a specific passage from the book. With absent eyes, the teacher would then listen to the girl stutter, wince and muddle through historical facts and figures that were often recited in the wrong order or with bits missing that invariably turned a very important historical milestone into a comical farce with the main characters and dates all jumbled up or running after each other. There was only one way to survive her lessons: bring a good book, which I frequently did. To top it all, she had one particularly bad habit: while we scribbled away answers from the book, she would busy herself by picking her nose - both nostrils at the same time, if you please – using her auricular fingers, obviously trying to be more discreet about it. Then, having neatly rolled the proceeds between the fine tips of her fingers, would surreptitiously drop the pickings over the sides of her desk. Hence with my attention sustained by this ceremonious ritual, I spent many a lesson sniggering in my sleeve or in the soft cover of whichever fiction book I happened to be reading. Once the small ritual over and with no hopes of being intellectually stretched, I would slouch back in my chair and settle into a soporific daydream that lulled me back to a small corner of Germany where I blissfully whiled away the dullest moments of my academic career.

And I had help, for another of my favourite teachers was, coincidently or not, Madame Dubernet, our German teacher, who used to wear her long frizzy hair rolled up in a bun and propped up on top rather than on the back of her head, in the same style as Victorian ladies. What's more, in the days ruled by mini-skirts, hot pants and knee-high boots, her style of clothing favoured long skirts, frilly blouses and lace with high altar necks. Mary Quant had no hold on this young woman for this particular teacher was a highly sophisticated lady who would not be swayed by a fashion trend dominated by flower power.

Alas, women have to do what women have to do. The change was imperceptible at first. Then her tight-fitting skirts began to loosen up slightly before finally giving way to flowing dresses which grew steadily in size as the months went by.

"I tell you she's pregnant!" Elizabeth whispered.

"Is she?" I asked, dreading the thought that she might be leaving us.

"Of course she is!" Odile quipped. "Can't you see how big she's got?"

From then on, each lesson was dominated by one and one topic only: is she or isn't she?

Winter was upon us and while Mme Dubernet concentrated on teaching us the Christmas carol 'O Tannen Baum', we concentrated on her ever expanding girth. But sing we would sing and these musical interludes invariably ended in fits of laughter for, by attempting to teach us a little bit of traditional German music, Mme Dubernet had revealed that she was completely tone-deaf. It reached the point where our dear teacher could not strike the first 'O' without the whole class dissolving in laughter. She got a little annoyed with us and we confounded ourselves in profuse apologies, vouching to try harder next time. So her voice, once more, rose and quivered below the 'O', and once again we tried to hit the right note above the 'O' until our voices melted into a cacophony of irrepressible laughter.

"All right!" Madame Dubernet shouted, trying to re-establish some sort of order in the classroom. "If you don't stop laughing, you'll all be in detention."

"Madame!" Odile pleaded. "We're not doing it on purpose. We're doing our best."

"Yes, Madame! We're trying ever so hard." Several voices chorused.

"Stop laughing then."

"But we can't help it!" I pleaded.

Then, Françoise who was sitting on the front row turned towards the rest of us with her arms aloft as if to appease the atmosphere and declared:

"Right everyone. We're going to try really hard this time, aren't we?"

"Yes, yes! And we promise we won't laugh!" We all vouched.

Reassured by our angelic vows, Mme Dubernet pulled her chair closer to the desk, threw her shoulders back, raised her chin as far as it would go towards the ceiling and having thus readied herself proceeded to sing. Instantly, a howling sound escaped from her rounded lips that threw the revered 'O' of '*O Tannen Baum*' into the musical wilderness and off the musical scale. We all sat rigidly in our seats, biting our lips and crunching our hands until, unable to hold on any longer, we all transcended into a rising wave of hysterical laughter.

"All right, I give up!" Madame Dubernet decreed, throwing her arms in the air. "Next time, I'll make sure I bring my portable record player."

Then, just before the end of term, she finally broke the news.

"I can see that you've all been speculating for a while whether I'm expecting or not." She said with a warm smile.

A sudden silence fell upon the classroom, each one of us paralysed in some kind of suspense as we waited final confirmation of our suspicions.

"Yes, as some of you may have guessed, I am expecting a baby…"

"Oh great news, Madame, when for?"

"Sometime in May which means that I shall be with you all next term until the Easter Holidays. After that…"

"But, Madame," I interrupted, "that means you won't be there when we take our exam!"

"Unfortunately not. However, if any of you would like extra tuition during the summer term, I shall be available at home."

Well, that was just typical. I was having a wonderful time learning my favourite language with a teacher whom we simply adored and there she was, about to leave us at the most crucial time in our academic career, to do whatever women have to do. I was totally distraught.

The final term arrived. Mme Dubernet had by now given birth to a baby girl, and I, being the only candidate opting to retain German as a second language, was sent traipsing to her small apartment in the suburb of Paris where she conducted the lessons while breastfeeding her gorgeous baby girl. There, I met Mme Dubernet's mother, a very stylish German lady who always seemed pleased to see me. The two women always conversed in German which was ideal to develop my listening skills. Eventually, when the time came, thanks to her patience, kindness and dedication, I sailed through my German exam. The examiner even nodded pleasingly at the end of the oral exam and I even think I saw him write 18/20, a mark which I speedily reported to Mme Dubernet over the telephone.

But my staunchest ally by far was Mademoiselle Deschamps. Thanks to her unwavering support and strong encouragement, I could now solve any Maths problem with perfect ease and even discuss with her the intricacies of particular equations which I liked to manipulate in different ways to see if I could arrive at the same solution. Mademoiselle Deschamps was not so taken by this freelance exercise. It was a waste of time, she explained, especially as the results were not always consistent and could not be mathematically proven. I often caught myself staring at her, more specifically at her high forehead which, I had been told, was a sign of high intelligence and to me, she was the proof personified for, whatever subject she taught, she always knew more than any other teacher I had ever encountered.

I now felt more than ready to tackle the ultimate challenge that would determine my future. In fact, this time I could not wait to sit my exams and show off how much I had progressed in the space of just one year. On the propitious day, because of the German option I had chosen, I had to go to a different school from everyone else. It was not the prospect of finding myself confronted with a problem I could not solve which worried me most but the fact that my allocated school was situated at the other end of *Boulevard Arago*, a long straight avenue, one side of which was entirely taken up by one of the most notorious buildings in the whole of

France: *Prison de la Santé*. I walked nervously along its tall grey wall at a brisk pace, constantly looking around me in case I should encounter an escaped prisoner. This was the longest and most solitary walk I had ever taken and it was with huge relief that I finally emerged at the other end of the sinister boulevard. Fortunately, I quickly located the school without getting lost and having checked my name on the list in the entrance hall, I made my way to Room B32.

In the exam room, I completed the papers with such ease that I could not help kicking myself with frustration for having so stupidly wasted a whole year of my young life. I even had time on my hands to memorise some of my answers in the Maths papers so that I would be able to check them with our Maths teacher. Once the exam completed, I rushed back to school where, just as she had said, Mademoiselle Deschamps was waiting in the classroom for our return. When I entered, she was already surrounded by girls all pressing her to reveal the answers.

"Have you seen the paper, Mademoiselle?" One of the girls asked.

"Yes, I have it right here." She said, lifting a slim bundle of papers.

"Have you got the answers yet?" Another girl asked impatiently.

"Give me a chance! I've only just got it. However, if you're prepared to wait, I'll go over the paper now."

"Yes, Mademoiselle, please!" Several of us chorused.

Instantly, there was a disorderly melee as girls grabbed the nearest desk available. Then, with bated breath, we watched our revered teacher write on the blackboard all the answers and every time she completed a question, a low murmur of delighted voices rose up and sighed with relief: "yep, I've got that… and that…".

Once all the answers had been revealed, we thanked the teacher profusely and left.

Marie-Sophie and I walked to the dormitory together.

"Did you get all the answers?"

"I think so but I'd rather not speak too soon just in case. What about you, did you get them?"

"I recognised some of them but I could not remember all of them so I don't know. Have you finished packing?" I then asked.

"Nearly."

"Are you leaving straight away?"

"Might as well. I've finished all my exams."

"What are you going to do now?"

"I'm not sure. I'd like to do my baccalaureat first then go to university but I don't think my parents can afford it."

"That would be a shame. You're so clever. Are you going to miss Mademoiselle Deschamps?"

At that point, Marie-Sophie sat on her bed, and raised her gaze towards the ceiling in a state of beatitude, then said with a heavy sigh:

"Yes… She was the best, wasn't she?"

"Yeah," I echoed. "I've always liked her, even when I was terrified of her."

We both paused and sighed at the same time. After a long pensive pause, I broke the silence.

"Are you going back to your home in the Auvergne?"

"Probably. I can't wait to get home and see my mum and dad and my big brother. I'll miss Paris, though. What about you, what are you going to do?"

"I don't know." I let out a big sigh and repeated: "I really don't know. It all depends on whether I've passed my exams or not."

"Of course you've passed. You're clever too, you know. In fact I wish I was more like you. With me, I've got to work really hard to achieve anything whereas you seem to be able to work things out just like that, without lifting a finger… or hardly."

Her remark astounded me. I had always looked up to her and admired her courage, dedication and blind determination to always produce the best possible homework and learn all her lessons by heart. She was the star of the class, brighter and shinier than anyone else, and now she was telling me she would rather be like me. I was mightily flattered.

"I did work hard, you know, but having my own study, nobody could see how hard I revised for these exams…" Then after a lengthy pause, I began to fret about the future.

"Who knows where we'll be this time next year…"

As I pondered out loud, Marie-Sophie suddenly asked:

"Do you know what's happened to Sister Marie-Joseph?"

"No. Has something happened to her?" I asked intrigued.

"She's left the Order."

"What?!!!" I was aghast. "What do you mean she's left the Order? You mean… she's not a nun anymore?"

"Yep!"

"Oh my God!" I could not help exclaim. "But why? Why did she do that? At her age, what is she going to do?"

"I don't know…"

"How do you know this?"

"We've seen her… in the street… in civilian clothes."

"In civilian clothes?... Oh my God, I don't think I'd be able to recognise her in civilian clothes. What is she doing out there in the street? Did you say hello?"

"Oh yes, we said hello. I was with Nicole. And she asked that next time you pass her, you say hello too."

"Why? Has she seen me?"

"Yes… and she was quite upset because you completely ignored her."

"But I wouldn't know what she looks like. How am I supposed to recognise her? What colour hair has she got?"

"Darkish." Marie-Sophie replied. "Anyway, I'd better get on with my packing."

"Don't go without saying goodbye, will you?"

"Of course, I won't. I'll give you a shout."

I started walking back to my room still numbed by the news. I really did not know what to make of it. Having so fiercely rejected her attention all through the year, I was now feeling sorry for her, imagining her forlorn silhouette retracing the steps of a life that had all but floundered around her. I tried to picture her in civilian clothes going about her daily chores in the anonymous outfit of an ordinary citizen but all I could visualise was a ghostly figure haunting the street in the hope of catching a glimpse of a past life that had awakened a passion she could not live with or tolerate. Left to face alone an impossible dilemma, her staunch loyalty and integrity had made her renounce her religious vows, the ultimate sacrifice she had been compelled to make for having chosen to remain true to herself and true to God.

In the middle of this inner turmoil, I heard Marie-Sophie call.

"Martha! I'm going now."

"Wait! I'm coming!" I hailed.

I quickly rushed to the other end of the dormitory and stopped dead in front of my friend, overwhelmed with emotion.

"So, that's you ready to leave then." I mumbled, not knowing how to initiate the goodbye.

"Yes... Goodbye then."

I approached Marie-Sophie and kissed her twice on the cheeks.

"It's four times in the Auvergne." She chuckled.

"All right, then." I said, obliging her with two extra kisses. Together, we mumbled a few more goodbyes and then she was gone.

I stood for a while in the middle of the corridor, still facing the door as Marie-Sophie's silhouette disappeared from my life for ever. I took a deep breath, then slowly made a few more steps all the while throwing glances around the place that would soon belong to the past... my past.

There is nothing more haunting and heart-wrenching than walking through a deserted dormitory at the end of term. As I walked across the vast empty space, I turned my head and looked at the clear blue sky through the bare windows, and I felt this pang, like a fist pressing on my stomach, the same gripping sensation I had felt when I left Sangatte for the very last time, except that this time it was stronger...much stronger.

Around the building, everything stood still. The only noises I could hear were the distant echoes of girls chatting and giggling, hailing each other and laughing. I peered outside looking for the happy sounds, just like I had done when I was a little child running away from my nightmares... but there was no one there... all the noises were in my head.

Chapter 12

The summer holidays had finally arrived. I sauntered leisurely to *la fédé* to find out what Mme Chauvineau had in store for me.

"No," she began straight away. "You're not going back to Germany. There's no point. You've done your German exam so you don't need to go back there anymore. It would be a complete waste of time and money."

"Not for me." I asserted.

"Don't answer back… and don't look at me with that insolent look!"

"But I need to go back because I want to carry on with German!" I protested.

"Well you can't anyway because at your new school they don't do German. Actually, it's not really a new school because you're going to the technical *Lycée* there. Now, do you want to choose secretarial studies or accountancy?"

I looked at her aghast, shocked even. Were these the only options opened to me? How on earth did she ever get the notion that I might be interested in either of these careers?

The problem was that I really did not have a clear idea of what I wanted to do. I had began to give it some thoughts though, ever since it had dawned on me that one day I would have to do something useful with my life.

At first, I had wanted to be a doctor because the thought of devoting myself to others without being a martyr rather appealed to me. However, when one of my classmates pointed out that only rich families could afford to pay for medical studies, I was forced to give up on the idea. Thinking further afield, I toiled with the idea of a career as a 'stewardess' to satisfy my thirst for adventure. My guardian was not keen on the idea. As far as she was concerned, being a stewardess amounted to nothing more than being a glamorised waitress and the idea of spending her working life waiting on others simply appalled her. However, I shall never forget her reaction when I came up with my third option.

"I want to be an actress." I declared, my eyes twinkling with excitement.

When she heard this, my guardian nearly choked on her croissant, spilled her coffee and stared at me horrified:

"Don't be silly, you're too ugly!"

Years later, a university friend provided me with the perfect repartee.

"You should have said you wanted to specialise in ugly parts!" Tom suggested.

I laughed at his brilliant reply, just like I had laughed at my guardian's brutal frankness.

Having run out of pragmatic options however, I settled for an occupation which would above all please me. I wanted to study Literature and write long poems and endless essays. I wanted to nurture my romantic muse and wallow in romantic novels like '*Sparkenbroke*' by Charles Morgan or plunge into Jalna, the elaborate family saga that Mazo de la Roche had created. I wanted to live in a surreal world suspended above reality and carry on dreaming about love, life and my own supreme beings. And after I had ran out of ideas, I would seek to do justice to my reputation as a human sloth by reclining nonchalantly on the sofa with my head thrown back in loose abandon. In this perfectly staged pose, I would dictate out loud my literary fantasies, just like Barbara Cartland used to do, to a hapless ghost writer who would then have to burn the midnight oil trying to make sense of my surreal dreams while I attended glitzy ceremonies and collected all the prizes, the honours and the money for pieces of writing he had painstakingly transcribed for me. Poor sod.

With my head full of ethereal and impossible dreams, how could I possibly be expected to study something as useful, pragmatic and down-to-earth as secretarial studies or accountancy?

I scowled at Mme Chauvineau.

"But I don't want to do either of them. I want to study for a French baccalaureat and go to university."

"Well, you should have thought about that when you were wasting your time playing cards all the time!"

I wanted to scream, but what was the use. She would not hear me even if I did.

"Anyway, you don't have to choose right away, you can think about it over the summer. Now, in July, I'm going to send you to an international school in Spain…"

"Spain! Why?!" I interrupted. "What for? I've never learned Spanish! I don't want to learn Spanish… it's not even one of my subjects…"

"Don't worry, you won't have to do any school work. It's a summer camp which happens to be in a school." The social worker quipped. "However, it will be educational all the same. It will do you good to go somewhere different. So, come back here on the first of July with your suitcase ready. And don't forget your identity card."

I turned my heels and left abruptly without saying goodbye. I knew it was rude and I knew that at my next visit, I would have to endure an endless lecture about the importance of good manners but how was I supposed to react when I had been told that my future had been mapped out for me, a world away from my own wishes and aspirations?

I arrived at the godmother's apartment in a foul temper.

"So, you've finished all your exams, then." She said on a jolly tone.

"Yep." I quipped.

"Good. Now you can forget about them and enjoy the holidays. When are you off again?"

"1st of July. I'm going to some place near Alicante. I don't know where it is and I don't care."

"You're in a bad mood again." She observed, as calm as a geisha.

"Yes! Because Chauvinette…"

"Madame Chauvineau, please!" The godmother corrected.

"I don't care! Chauvinette's just told me I've got to choose between secretarial studies or accountancy and I don't want to do either of them."

"They're useful careers, you know. At least, you'll get a professional qualification and you'll be able to get a job straight away when you leave school."

"I don't want to go to work. I want to go to university. I'm not choosing and that's that!" I stubbornly decreed.

The godmother knew better than to respond. Instead, she had some other news for me.

"We're going to be moving soon."

"Are we? Why? I like it here."

"Yes, but I'm wasting a lot of money renting this place. I'd rather buy my own apartment. You see, I've got to think about my old age. It'll be a good investment. It's a brand new building on the other side of *Pont de la Défense*, near Neuilly. If you like, we'll go and have a look at the show flat. That'll take your mind off things."

"Oh, I'd like that. Can we go and see it tomorrow?"

"Well, I'd rather go on Sunday. There'll be less traffic."

So, on Sunday, we piled into her brand new maroon Renault 10 which reeked of hot plastic, and drove down the *Avenue de la Grande Armée*, crossed the *Pont de la Défense*, followed the river Seine to the right and turned left at the BP offices. Soon, we arrived in Courbevoie, one of those suburban towns hurriedly being transformed into a mini New York. A few minutes later, we reached a gigantic modern apartment block with hundreds of concrete pigeon-holes for sale. Inside the immense reception area, we made our way towards one set of lifts and the godmother pressed the button number eight.

By comparison to our present abode, the apartment looked tiny. It had one bedroom, one living-room and a bathroom that was bigger than the kitchen, but, the godmother was quick to point out, it had one essential and invaluable commodity: a walk-in cupboard. I was far from impressed.

"It's rather small." I remarked.

"Well, it's the perfect size for me." She declared. "And look, that cupboard could be your bedroom. What do you think?"

"I don't like it. You'll never be able to fit a bed in there."

"Perhaps not but look, I can build a shelf here along the wall and put a mattress on top."

"It's too small." I decreed.

"No, no," she said, determined not to give up on the idea. "Lie down against the wall, I can tell you'll fit in there, I've got good eyes, I have."

So I did, and my lithe body managed to fit in perfectly within the restricted space.

"See, didn't I tell you?" She trumpeted.

"Yes, but my head and my feet are practically touching the walls. What if I grow a few centimetres?"

"Don't worry, you'll still fit in. Trust me, I'm a painter and I've got a good eye. So, as I was saying, your bed will be on that side and on this wall here, I'll get a joiner to build some shelves and a little bureau for your books and things. And see, above your bed, I'm going to have more shelves for suitcases and in the space under your bed, I'll be able to store the vacuum cleaner and brooms and mops and other bric-a-brac. There'll even be enough room to store some of your things, if you want."

Charming. My new abode was going to be a stuffy poky windowless cubby-hole. Understandably, I was not exploding with enthusiasm at the thought. My trail of thoughts was suddenly interrupted by the godmother hailing:

"Come and see the balcony!"

I reluctantly proceeded to the balcony.

"What do you think, hey? Isn't the view magnificent? We can see all of Paris from here. Look over there, that's the *Eiffel Tower*, and there, to the left, *le Sacré Cœur*. I can just make out the top of the *Arc de Triomphe*, can you see it?"

"No." I decreed petulantly.

"I'm not surprised; you're as blind as a bat. I've got good eyes, I have. Unfortunately, we're going to lose most of the view eventually because they're going to build another block right there in front of us." She said, pointing at the huge gaping hole in the ground. "Anyway, when you come back from Spain, I'll have moved in."

"Great." I sighed on a flat tone.

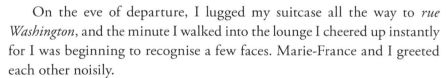

On the eve of departure, I lugged my suitcase all the way to *rue Washington*, and the minute I walked into the lounge I cheered up instantly for I was beginning to recognise a few faces. Marie-France and I greeted each other noisily.

Alerted by the rising level of noise, one of the social workers popped her head round and pleaded:

"Not so noisy, girls."

We immediately sat down on the plush sofa and armchairs and remained quiet until she left. However, as soon as she closed the door, the lively conversations resumed.

"So, where are you going?" I asked excitedly.

"England." Marie-France replied.

"Oh, no," I said, mightily disappointed. "We're not going to be together. I'm going to Spain."

"What about August? Where are you going?"

"England." I sighed.

"And I'm going to Spain then! *Quel dommage*! Never mind, maybe we'll be together again at the next skiing holiday."

Suddenly, one of the other girls chipped in:

"***I'm*** going to Spain!"

Both Marie-France and I looked at the girl who had just spoken. From my friend's reaction, I could tell that she did not know her. And neither did I.

"What's you're name?" Marie-France enquired.

"Magali."

"I'm Marie-France and... this is *Merdouille*," my friend declared pointing at me in total hysterics.

We both collapsed in a heap of laughter while jostling for the most comfortable place on the sofa. Not yet able to join in, Magali watched the pair of us larking about until Mademoiselle Cany walked in.

"Now, who's making all this noise? If I have to come in one more time, I'll throw the whole lot of you out! Martha Bertrand! Your turn to see Mme Chauvineau."

Before getting up, I whispered to Marie-France:

"Wait for me here!"

Mme Chauvineau was busy shifting bits of paper around her desk. She threw a cold stare at me and ordered:

"Right, Martha Bertrand, come and stand here. Here are the papers you need, time of the train, Gare de Lyon. You can collect your luncheon vouchers from the concierge downstairs; the self-service is not far from here, just round the corner..."

"I know... I've been before."

"Very well. Tonight, you'll spend the night at the *Hôtel Jeanne d'Arc*, near the Panthéon, easy to find, just follow the others if you're not sure. You'll need to get off at the metro station 'Odéon'... or is it 'Place Monge'?

Anyway, the others will know. Here are some metro tickets to get there. Now, most importantly, have you got your identity card?"

"Yes, it's in my bag."

"Good, that's you all sorted, then. Off you go now… and you'd better behave!"

I took the envelop with all the bits and pieces safely tucked inside it and promptly left. Back into the lounge, I waved at my friend.

"Marie-France, have you seen Mlle Cany yet?"

"Yes. Come on, let's go, I'm so bored hanging around this place."

"Can I come with you?" Magali asked.

"Yeah, of course." Marie-France said.

"What are we going to do, then?" I asked.

"First, we're going to collect our dinner tickets."

On our way down the stairs, I asked:

"Do you know the concierge?"

Marie-France looked at Magali and I with a wry smile.

"Don't we all?" She replied with a wink.

"What do you mean?" I scowled, not having the faintest idea how to interpret her remark. Ignorant of all things in the capital, and not exactly *au fait* with all the goings-on here at *la fédé*, I felt even more provincial and naïve than ever before. The godmother had a choice word to describe people like me: peasant.

"*Mon Dieu*, Martha! Where have you been? You must be the only one who doesn't know…"

"Doesn't know what?" I asked baffled.

"Well, if you're nice to Monsieur Bechamel, you get extra tickets."

"Nice? In what way?" I asked, tempted by the prospect of getting an extra portion of food.

"Come on, Martha, you're having me on…"

"No, I'm not, I really don't know what you mean."

Marie-France chuckled, winked, raised her eyebrows and made all sorts of facial expressions to try and illuminate me further. Still faced with my blank look, she finally blurted out:

"You know… special favours…"

"Special favours?… like… oh no!"

"And of course, you can always bluff! Just watch me."

Downstairs, on the ground floor, we aimed for a side door whose clear window panes were covered with a pair of grotty net curtains. Marie-France rang the bell. Seconds later, a large stout man with a shiny face came to open the door.

"Hi, Monsieur Bechamel," both Marie-France and Magali greeted cheerfully. "We've come to collect our luncheon vouchers."

"How many do you need?" The man asked on a burly tone.

"Six." Marie-France requested.

"Me too." Magali said.

"Six!" The concierge exclaimed. "Isn't your train leaving tomorrow morning? Let me check my list…"

"Well, just after lunch." Marie-France bluffed. "I'm not going with them, I'm going to England."

I watched the concierge give out the luncheon vouchers, repelled by his unshaven face, his sweaty and malodorous armpits, his grubby hands imagining them roaming all over my friends' delicate skin. The sight was too much. I took a step back to distance myself from him.

"How many do you need?" He asked abruptly.

I looked straight into his predatory eyes all sizzling with desire at the prospect of a new conquest, and replied:

"Same as them."

I grabbed the tickets and, without thinking, wiped them against my jeans before stowing them away in the zip pocket of my bag. As soon as we were out of earshot, I exclaimed:

"Oh, yuk! How can they do it?" Then, turning to my friend, I asked:

"Have you ever done it?"

"No, never! I'm not that desperate!" Marie-France decreed, clearly disgusted. "But I bet Magali has." She added teasingly.

"You must be joking! I wouldn't touch him if he was covered in banknotes."

Later that evening, a group of us took the metro and made our way to the *Hôtel Jeanne d'Arc*. The blue plaque on the wall outside boasted two red stars… Two stars? For what? We soon wondered as we traipsed on the threadbare carpet towards the dark corner of the reception desk.

There, a large matronly figure was waiting for us, counting the heads and anticipating trouble.

"Eight!" She finally exclaimed. "Well, I've only got two rooms available, so some of you will have to sleep on the floor. I'll fetch some mattresses."

She stretched her hand towards a wood panel covered in hooks behind the desk, rattled a bunch of keys and ordered us to follow her upstairs, onto the first floor. When she opened the door of the first bedroom, four girls rushed inside, giggling noisily.

"Martha!" Marie-France hailed. "I'm going with my friends!"

Across the corridor, the scary 'matron' had already opened the door of another bedroom.

"In here!" She shouted, and before taking her leave, she threw one last warning.

"No noise at night, I've got customers to think about. And no smoking in the bedrooms!"

Nicole, Claudette, Magali and I dragged our suitcases inside the bedroom. The state of the room was far worse than I expected. The faded curtains, torn in places, hung miserably against the damp patches on the wall; the carpet, or what was left of it, had crests of loose threads peaking around the edges; and the bed… dare I mention the bed. Underneath the grotty moth-eaten cover, Magali uncovered sheets that had not been washed since the last occupant had vacated the room. And we knew exactly what he had been up to for there, next to some dark pubic hair, Magali had spotted something quite revolting.

"Oh my God! It's disgusting. You know what that is," she said pointing at a yellowy stain. "It's a sperm stain!"

"Oh yuk!" The girls cried out at once.

"A what?" I queried naively. "You mean like… Oh yuk!"

Claudette peered at the bed and declared:

"I'd rather sleep on the floor!"

"Me too!" Said Nicole.

Magali and I looked at each other. I was in a quandary: I would have to either sleep on the hard filthy floor or the soft filthy bed. I did not know which to choose.

"Well," Magali finally decided. "I'd rather sleep on the bed. There's bound to be fleas on the floor."

Putting comfort before cleanliness, I too decided to plump for the soft option.

"It's always like that." Claudette stated philosophically. "Filthy… but who cares, we usually spend the night chatting anyway. Who wants a fag?" She then asked passing an unopened packet of cigarettes. Magali took one, Nicole took one but I declined.

"No thank you, I don't smoke."

"How old are you, then?"

"Sixteen."

"Ha! Still a baby!" Claudette chortled.

"I thought we were not allowed to smoke anyway." I reminded her, vexed by her remark.

"Why? What are they going to do if we do? Throw us out? Think of the money they're making out of us. They're probably charging *la fédé* for four bedrooms when we're actually sleeping on the floor. No, I bet you they won't say anything if they catch us. Go on, have one."

"No thank you."

"Gosh! You're such a baby!"

Chapter 13

Early the next morning, we scrambled out of bed, got dressed and lugged our suitcases down the metro's endless staircases and arrived at *Gare de Lyon* talking loudly and giggling with excitement.

At the end of the interminable train journey that took us through France and Northern Spain, a coach took us to the school situated ten kilometres outside Alicante. The building was a three storey concrete block divided into large light and breezy rooms with the classrooms on the ground floor, girls' bedrooms on the first floor and boys' bedrooms on the top floor. Magali and I quickly settled in our bedroom with two other girls Daphné and Muriel. Up until now, I had never paid much attention to my general appearance. Indifferent to the rigorous code of the early 70s' fashion scene flaunting outrageous hot pants, I wore whatever I liked which basically meant jeans. My hair was long, not through any aesthetic desire but simply because, after my early experiences at the orphanage where our hair was cut with a blunt razor blade, I categorically refused to let anyone touch it. As for make-up, I never wore any; I was not grown up in that way. Besides, I simply did not like that sticky substance that I had seen my friends apply on their skin or eyelids. However, sharing a room with Magali and Daphné would open my eyes to the sophisticated world of personal grooming and fashion… so as to attract boys.

"But there are no boys." I immediately remarked.

"No, not yet," Daphné replied. "They're coming next week. Apparently, they're from Belgium."

"Hmm… I can't wait." Magali purred.

Having studied closely the two girls in predatory mode, I came to the conclusion that the only things I had in common with them were my pubescent spots. However, these elaborate grooming sessions became lessons of life that held me spellbound as I tried a dash of eye shadow, a touch of mascara and a light dabbing of lipstick. The transformation over, Daphné thrust her mirror into my hand.

"Look!" She hailed, proud of her own input. "What do you think? Looks good, doesn't it?"

I hardly recognised myself. I went to the window to light up the result, turned my face sideways a few times, lifted my chin and lowered my eyelids to try and take in the full effect of this temporary transformation. However, after a few minutes of this close minutia, I decided that I preferred myself *au naturel*, without any of the artifices that made me look like someone I did not recognise. And all that for a bunch of boys I had not even met yet. I was not interested anyway… my heart was already taken.

"Go on," Magali urged. "You've got to have a boyfriend otherwise, who's going to pay for your drinks?"

"Pay for my drinks? But I don't drink."

"Gosh! You're such a baby!" She sighed as if I was a lost cause.

Hence began my Spanish holiday. In the summer camp, there were only two rules: girls must not stray onto the boys' floor and vice versa; and smoking is banned inside the building. To try and impose these rules on a group of over-confident adolescents who have just discovered their power of attraction was like asking a wild lion to… 'sit!'.

The days were mostly spent labouring hard on the beach or around the pool. After numerous make-up sessions, Magali pursued my social education by giving me my first cigarette.

"Are you sure? It's not going to make me ill?"

"Of course not. Go on, you try it… make sure you inhale."

"Inhale? How do you do that?"

"Breathe in the smoke and then, blow it out."

After several attempts, I finally succeeded, though I wished I had not for my head began to spin out of control and I struggled to walk in a straight line.

"Am I supposed to feel like that?" I asked, weaving around the place.

"You're doing it on purpose." She laughed.

"No, I'm not. I'm really feeling dizzy… I need to sit down."

"Don't worry, you'll soon get used to it but you need to practise though."

In the evening, with the school being situated in the middle of nowhere, it became imperative that we should find some form of entertainment, provided by the local disco where my friends would be able to practise their pulling powers and where I would improve my dancing skills. Feeling rather inhibited, I shuffled awkwardly to the rhythm of Stevie Wonder, Barry White, to the hit of that summer 'Pop Corn' and many more.

The disco covered a huge area with spotlights everywhere and the compulsory large mirror ball twinkling just above our heads. Upstairs on the balcony, I spotted several silhouettes dancing behind a big white screen.

"Hey, Magali!" I called. "How do you get up there?"

"Don't know. I'll ask my boyfriend."

Boyfriend? She already had a boyfriend?

"Pedro," she shouted in the ear of this tall, slim, highly manicured and mature Spaniard, "how do you get up there?"

The said Pedro waved his arm towards the right-hand side of the wall.

"Over there!" He indicated.

"Shall we go?" I urged Magali, convinced that hidden behind a large screen, I would not look a complete idiot as I tried to master my first disco steps.

She hesitated, looked at her new conquest and mouthed a few loud words before following me up the stairs.

"How old is he?" I quizzed her.

"Don't know but he's got a car."

"Wow!"

"With reclining seats!"

I stopped dead on the stairs, looked at her and gasped:

"You wouldn't!"

"Yes, I would! Come on, let's dance!" She chortled.

As I was busy concentrating hard wriggling my hips and shuffling my feet with my eyes firmly fixed on the rhythmic movements of my platform shoes, I was suddenly accosted by this young Spaniard.

"Hi! What's your name?"

I confess I panicked.

"Er… er…"

"You're Spanish, aren't you?"

"No, I'm not." I declared slightly relieved, for the young stud was clearly after a *seniorita* rather than a *demoiselle*.

"Yes, you are." He insisted. "Only Spanish girls have beautiful long hair, deep brown eyes and a dark skin."

Before I knew it, he had put his arms round my waist and was now pulling me towards his smouldering body. Roaring like a lion on heat, he dug his chin deep into his throat and purred manfully:

"You're beautiful!"

I nearly laughed. I mean, after having been told repeatedly how I lacked all the charm and beauty attributed to every other girl except me, I was not going to be taken in by the smooth talking of this little upstart who only had one thing in mind. Definitely not. So I laughed.

"Why are you laughing?" He asked, somewhat upset by my lack of appreciation for his smooth words. "You are beautiful," he insisted. "I'm Spanish and I know what beautiful girls look like."

"Well, I'm not Spanish." I decreed on a firm tone.

"OK, then, what's your name?"

"Martha."

"Maria? You see, I knew you were Spanish."

"No, not 'Maria', Martha!" I shouted.

"No, no. Your name is Maria; I can tell."

"If you don't believe me… the proof is I can't speak Spanish."

"Yes you can, you're just faking. You're clever; I can tell you're clever, you speak languages."

In the meantime, Magali had gone back downstairs to rejoin her new conquest. I was cursing her under my breath for abandoning me at the hands of a determined young Spaniard who had decided that *when you've got to have it, you've got to have it*. In the end, there was only one thing I could do.

"I have to go now. My friend's waiting for me downstairs."

He grabbed my arm very firmly.

"When can I see you again?"

"Tomorrow… I'll come back here tomorrow," I vouched, hoping for a quick release.

Only after my repeated assurances did he let go of my arm.

Needless to say, I made sure I did not return to the disco for several days afterwards.

When Magali returned to the room, very late at night, she could not wait to talk about Pedro.

"I'm in love." She declared in a state of pure ecstasy.

"You can't be," I stated categorically, "you've only just met him."

"Oh, but I love him… I know I love him… He's so gorgeous… and you know what he did?"

I was not ready for that kind of detail.

"Tell me tomorrow," I yawned. "I'm really tired right now; I just want to go to sleep."

"OK, I'll tell you all about it at breakfast."

Oh God, does she have to? I tossed and turned under the bed sheet and soon fell asleep.

———————◆◇◆———————

The weekend arrived disgorging a coach load of young Belgians, all in their late teens. Suddenly, the building seemed crowded. Everywhere we went, the cool plenitude that had reigned in the deserted corridors around the school was filled with manful voices hailing each other, laughing and bantering, peering cheekily into the girls' corridor to throw a cheerful "Hi gals!" while we ran away screaming in shock, horror… and laughter.

Our first opportunity to scrutinise the new intake came that evening at dinner time. The tables having being set in a U-shape, we were able to study discreetly but at leisure the looks, the dress sense and the potential of each candidate without making it appear too much like an identity parade. With her expert eye, Magali had already singled out her favourites.

"Martha!" She whispered. "Don't look now but there's a pair of twins over there. They're really cute."

Inevitably, I looked.

"Don't look now, I said!"

"Oh my God!" I exclaimed. "They're absolutely identical!"

"OK," Magali continued. "Which one do you want?"

"What?! I don't want one… I don't want to choose."

"For goodness sake, Martha! You've got to have a boyfriend, otherwise you're going to find yourself all alone while everybody else will be out having fun. Go on, choose one."

"All right," I sighed, looking at the identical pair with a cold and indifferent eye. "I don't know which one to go for, they're so identical."

"OK, then" Magali decreed, "I'll take the one on the right and you take the one on the left."

"How are we going to know which is which?"

"Ask their name, idiot!... Hang on! They're getting up! Come on, let's go!"

Making sure we appeared to be, by sheer coincidence, leaving the refectory at the very same time, we followed them in hot pursuit.

"Hi!" Magali greeted keenly. "I'm Magali and this is my friend Martha."

"Hi!" Both twins echoed at once, looking rather overwhelmed by our premature assault.

Emboldened by my friend's direct approach, I then asked:

"What's your name?"

"I'm Christophe."

"And I'm Christian."

"Do you want to go outside? Magali suggested. "We're going for a smoke."

"Well, we've got to get changed first. We're planning to go to town later."

"So are we!" Magali declared with a big grin.

"Are we?" I asked, failing to remember making any plans beyond having an after-dinner fag in the gardens. She answered by giving me a sharp dig in the ribs.

"Come on, Martha! Let's go and get ready. The coach leaves in an hour." Then turning back towards the twins, she hailed: "See you later!" to which both twins replied: "*D'accord!*".

Back in the room, we found Daphné sitting on her bed with her hair rolled up in a towel, peering at her hand-mirror while holding a small metal instrument close to her face.

"What's that?" I had to ask.

"It's a comedo extractor." She declared scientifically.

"A what?"

"You know, it's a thing to remove comedos."

"What are *comedos*?"

"Blackheads! You've never heard of blackheads before?"

"Oh yeah, I've heard of blackheads. I just didn't know they were called *comedos*."

"Come on, Martha! Get going or we're going to miss the coach."

While Magali rummaged frantically through her vanity case, I sat on my bed pondering over the events.

"I'm never going to be able to tell them apart…"

"It's easy," Magali interrupted. "Christophe is the one with the stripy trousers and Christian with the plain trousers."

"Oh well that's great!" I retorted cynically. "What if they change their trousers, which they'll probably do…"

"Don't worry about it. Find some kind of mark or beauty spot on their faces. Look at their watches, they're bound to wear different watches. Anyway, you still haven't said, which one do you want to pick?"

"I think I'll go for Christophe."

"OK, I'll have Christian, then."

"No, on second thoughts I think I'll go for Christian."

"Come on, make up your mind!"

"But I can't! As soon as I pick one, the other one looks more attractive."

"For Christ sake, Martha! What does it matter! They're identical!"

"All right! All right! I'll stick withChristophe, then."

"At long last! OK then, do you want to borrow some make-up?"

"Like what?"

"Some eyeliner, eye shadow, lipstick?"

"I don't mind. Will you put it on for me though, because I don't want to make a mess of it… but I don't want any lipstick."

"You've got to have lipstick otherwise how is Christophe going to see you in the dark?"

"In the dark?..."

"Yes, if we go to a disco, it's going to be dark, isn't it"?

Magali shook her head in dismay at my complete ineptitude of worldly things and came towards my bed with eyeliner and eye shadow in hands.

"I don't know… Living in Paris, you're supposed to be more sophisticated than me. I come from peasant country, I do. You can't get more provincial than Toulouse."

"Yes you can; and you've had boyfriends before…"

"Well, you're a baby, aren't you? I can see I'm going to have to sort you out… OK, how's that?"

"Have you got a mirror? Which colour have you put on?"

"Green."

"Green? I don't like green."

"It suits you. Now which lipstick do you want?"

"Lipstick?" I asked, panicking a little. "I told you, I don't want any lipstick."

"Come on, you've got to have a bit of lipstick."

"Maybe next time. I don't want to put too much on, you know, I might scare myself."

We were the last to board the coach where from the very back seats, both Christophe and Christian were staring at us.

"Come on," Magali said, taking the lead, "let's go and sit with them."

Still bemused by our unsolicited attention, the twins watched us take our seats right next to them. As the coach tumbled along the bumpy road, Christian eventually put his arm round Magali's shoulders. Following his brother's lead, Christophe put his arm around mine and while the coach rattled gently along the scorched landscape, the rocky hills and the parched trees, I smiled inanely. Oh my God, I've got a boyfriend!

In town, the boys and their Belgian cohort took us to a bar on the esplanade. The place was bustling with tourists and revellers of all ages. We sat outside the café on the terrace from where I watched, totally fascinated, the cosmopolitan crowd strolling by at a leisurely pace. All around us, the atmosphere was hot and balmy, but at our table, the ambience was smoky and sizzling with the spirit of youth… and whisky and coke.

As the days passed, the rules began to blend with the hazy sunshine, and guidelines to blur in our sultry minds. Monsieur A., the director of the camp, began to fret. He did not wish to upset anyone but there had to be some kind of limit for our own sake, clear boundaries within which to contain our youthful effervescence and natural propensity to pair off. Several times, he panicked as well-established couples kept appearing and disappearing without him having the faintest idea of where they were or worse… where they had been. He did not really want to lecture us, but felt obliged to have a word with us at dinner time, during which he begged us not to cross a 'particular line'. Naïvely, I thought he meant that we should not stray in each other's corridors.

Strategically, Monsieur A. had located his room on the girls' floor right next to the stairwell door so that he would be able to detect illicit footsteps creeping up or down the stairs in the dead of night. And he had heard some. Yes, he had heard some, and he wanted to let it be known that, should these illicit activities occur again, the culprits would be in real trouble. We all knew what he was referring to because only a few nights ago, the boys had raided our floor under the cover of darkness and we, girls, were plotting a return attack… but it would not be tonight. No, best wait until Monsieur A. had calmed down and reverted to his usual unflustered and nonchalant mood.

Several days later, the word was being passed around: Tonight, be ready tonight.

"What time?" I whispered.

"Don't worry, we'll come for you." Jacqueline conspired.

It was pitch black outside. The moon had disappeared beyond the shadowy lanes of the Milky Way, refusing to grant us the feeblest beam of light that would help us guide our steps towards the stairwell. I heard someone gently push the bedroom door open.

"Who's there?" Magali whispered.

"It's me, Jacqueline. Are you coming?"

"Yeah, yeah, I'm coming. Martha, are you awake?" Magali whispered.

"Yes, I'm awake. What about Muriel?"

A voice groaned from underneath a sheet.

"I'm not coming."

"What about Daphné"? I asked.

"I'm already up." She whispered.

"Where are you?"

"I'm standing by the door."

"I can't see a thing, how am I going to see where I'm going?"

"All right, everybody." Jacqueline quipped. "Walk in a line and grab the nightie of the girl in front… and keep to the wall. Ready?"

I fumbled my way towards the door, grabbed someone's nightie and shuffled along, making sure I kept close to the wall. At the head of the mutinous crocodile file, Jacqueline, sure-footed, was leading us towards the stairwell while the rest of us, anticipating the fun ahead, tried to muffle our giggles.

"Stop giggling!" Jacqueline said in a loud whisper.

Moments later, we heard the hinges of a door opening. Keeping in a straight line like a tame flock of blind sheep, we all followed her in. The door hinges creaked more loudly. In the stairwell, Jacqueline fumbled around to find the light switch when suddenly a deep voice boomed and barked in the thick of darkness:

"What's this? Who's there?"

"Oh my God!"

Someone screamed.

Instantly, a mad scramble followed as we all scurried back to our rooms giggling and laughing. Monsieur A. jumped out of bed and ran after us. I will never know how we managed to run back to our beds without bumping into the walls, doors or furniture but within seconds, we were all tucked in our beds pretending to be asleep. Some of the girls simply fell into the first bed they came across. From under the bed sheet, I heard Monsieur A.'s footsteps thundering from room to room wanting to know what we could possibly be doing in his room.

"You were going to play a joke on me, weren't you? Well, I'd better warn you, I'm not one for practical jokes!" His voice boomed. "What are you doing in here? That's not your bed! Go back to your own bed!"

Seconds later, he squared himself in the doorway of our room and switched the light on. As I peered discreetly from under the bed sheet, I caught sight of him standing erect in his skimpy pants, and with his chest all swelled up, ready to shout more warnings.

"It's no good pretending you're asleep! I know who did this!" He carried on, "and I shall not hesitate to have a word with the culprits tomorrow morning."

As befitted Monsieur A.'s easy-going temperament, the director could not bring himself to take 'punitive actions'. Flanked by the other two meek supervisors in the middle of the refectory, he wrung his hands repeatedly, jerked his head nervously and pleaded with us once more to behave and act within the agreed guidelines.

The rest of the day was spent reliving the event of the previous night and quizzing Jacqueline on her faux-pas, though we all agreed, she had a strong defence.

"It was pitch-dark." She pleaded. "I couldn't see anything. It's not my fault if I opened the wrong door."

Chapter 14

At the end of the holiday, Magali waved goodbye to Pedro, vouching her undying love for him and pledging to learn to speak Spanish fluently. Then, back in the school building, she went to seek solace in Christian's arms.

On the train journey back to Paris, we cuddled up to Christophe and Christian, kissed, exchanged addresses, and promised to write.

With so many hours to kill on a train journey from Barcelona to Paris, Magali and I managed to catch up with each other. In this way, I discovered that my friend enjoyed an enviable freedom during the school year. Unlike the rest of us, she was staying not in a boarding school, but with Mme Garrier, a charming widow who lived on her own in a suburban house, a short train ride away from where the godmother stayed.

"Please, you will come and visit." She begged.

Absolutely, I promised. I would have gone to Timbuktu if she had asked, just to get away from the godmother.

Magali became a close friend with whom I ended up spending most of my weekends. What I admired most about her was not her long frizzy hair which bounced freely around her face like a lion's mane but her perfect teeth, her spot-free skin and her long slim legs. Also, when it came to homework, she was extremely diligent and superbly disciplined. She was also incredibly tidy which led me to think: what on earth is she doing with me?

There was no doubt that Magali was more sophisticated than me. She knew about fashion, had impeccable taste in clothes, make-up and accessories. However when it came to music, thanks to my travels, I was streaks ahead of her. She liked Cliff Richard and adored Claude François on whom she kept a thick scrap book. She also had a big poster of Mike Brant on her bedroom door, the pop singer who at the height of his fame committed suicide by jumping out of a window. By contrast, I liked the Beatles, the Bee Gees, Simon & Garfunkel and Nina Simone. But we were united in our musical taste by one singer whom we discovered together while listening to the hit parade: Mark Boland. Yes, we loved T Rex, especially the song 'Metal Guru' because the way he screams at the beginning of the record always made me feel like a bit of a rebel. A rebel? ***Moi?***

Over the following months, Magali would mould me into a sophisticated young woman and provide me with a safe haven whenever I wanted to get away from the godmother. What she got from me in return, I was not entirely sure.

Her first priority was to do something about the way I dressed.

"What's that you're wearing?" She would say on a tone that really meant '*God Almighty, Martha, what do you look like?*'

"Why? Do I look that bad?"

"Yes. It's dated and it doesn't suit you."

"But that's all I've got." I whined, "The godmother gives me my clothes, mostly passed down from her friends."

"Don't you know that you are entitled to an allowance for your clothes?"

"No."

"You don't know!" Magali exclaimed. "Martha! Where have you been?"

"Nobody told me." I retorted.

"We're all allowed 300 francs for the winter trousseau and 300 francs for the summer trousseau." She explained. "Didn't you get anything for this summer?"

"No." I replied, flabbergasted.

"Well, next time you see Mme Chauvineau, ask her."

"What if she says 'no'?"

"She can't. You're entitled to it. Go on, you ask her."

"All right, I will." I pledged, feeling rather uncomfortable at the idea of asking for money. I was already torturing myself with the thought that I would have to grovel and beg for something I was entitled to… and to Chauvineau of all people. I was beginning to think I would never be able to do such a thing, but Magali was right, I had to do something about my overall appearance.

In the meantime, we had to get ready for our next trip. England beckoned again. To my delight, I discovered that Magali was coming too. We had both been assigned to a new town that was blossoming on the outer edge of Reading, the same place and the same estate where I had ended up after the disastrous expedition of the previous year.

Before our next adventure, though, we would have to endure an overnight stay at the ghastly *Hôtel Jeanne d'Arc*. However, ignoring the filthy state of the bedrooms, we lay on the bed and talked all night, only stopping to light up a cigarette.

"Do you think our Belgian friends will write?" I wondered aloud.

"'Course they will. Though I don't really care if they don't... Christian was a bit boring, if you ask me, not my type really, too *bourgeois* for me."

"I'm not sure I like the idea of staying with a family *au demi-pair*," I declared, changing the topic. "What does it mean exactly?"

"It means that the family gets half of the money they would normally get and in return we have to do a bit of housework." Magali explained.

"Like what?" I asked, horrified at the thought of having to lift a finger at any time, let alone when I was on holiday.

"Don't worry, it won't be much, a bit of hoovering and washing up... and baby-sitting..."

"Oh God, I hope they don't ask me to do the ironing, I can't stand ironing!"

"Well, if they ask, just say you don't know how to iron. Basically, if they ask anything you don't want to do, just say you don't know how to. That's what I did last year and I ended up doing hardly anything at all!" Magali scoffed.

Hence reassured that my holiday would not be spoiled by an overload of housework and baby care, I turned over and went to sleep. Outside, it was already daybreak. In a matter of hours, we would have to trudge all the way to *la Gare du Nord*, bleary eyed and with our arms aching from pulling our heavy suitcases which, in those days, did not have wheels. Before boarding the train en route to Calais, Magali rummaged through her handbag and offered me a cigarette.

"Oh God, no thanks." I said. "I really couldn't, not first thing in the morning. I really need to eat something though."

So we stopped at the station kiosk and bought some croissants and pains au chocolat.

It was during the ferry crossing to Dover that I first witnessed my new friend in full action. Passing remarks on unsuspecting passengers and crew, she tested the field, studied their reactions and reviewed their situation with a flirty eye.

After a while, her eyes arrested on the young steward who was coming towards us balancing a tray on his hand.

"Yes, ladies, what can I get you?"

"You for a start…" Magali giggled, flicking her hair back and fluttering her eyelashes. "… and after that, I'll have a coke."

Visibly flustered, the steward then turned to me.

"Me, I'll 'ave orange juice."

As he was about to fetch our order, Magali grabbed his leg.

"Oooo… you have strong legs… What's your name?"

"Dave." He replied, beginning to look interested.

"Do you have a cabin on board… where you sleep?"

"Well, it's not exactly a cabin, it's…"

"Can I see it?"

The steward hesitated.

"Er… I'll get your drinks first."

We watched him walk towards the bar where he whispered a few words to one of his colleagues, without seeming in a hurry to return to our table.

Magali bristled in her seat.

"He's taking a long time. What's he doing? Look, Martha, he's serving other people! I bet he's forgotten all about us"

"Hardly! Maybe they were before us…" After a short pause, I asked: "You're not going to go with him, are you?"

"Why not? He's got a cute little bottom… I love men with cute little bottoms."

Finally, after ten long minutes, Dave returned with the drinks.

"You took a long time." Magali scowled.

"I'm sorry, I had to serve these other people first. I finish my shift in ten minutes… maybe, if you're still interested… you know…"

Magali smiled.

"I'll be waiting… right here."

Dave then turned to me.

"If you're also interested, you know, my mate Mark…"

"*No sank you, I'll just have ze orange juice.*" I replied giggling.

As soon as the steward left, Magali leant towards me and said:

"Remember, Martha, the best way to get a free drink is to get a boyfriend."

A few minutes later, Dave returned.

"I'm free now," he told Magali. "If you're still interested…"

Magali jumped out of her seat.

"See you in a mo., Martha, and behave yourself while I'm gone."

A good half hour passed before Magali was back with me.

"Guess what?"

"What?" I parroted keenly, expecting a blow by blow account of her little escapade.

"He's going to bring us some drinks."

"What? For free?"

"Yeah! For free!"

"Here you are, young ladies, one coke and one orange juice." he said, devouring my friend with his hungry eyes.

Emboldened by her first conquest while still at sea, Magali ran her hand up and down his leg and said with a cheeky smile:

"Thank you very much. It's been a pleasure meeting you."

To which, the steward retorted with a broad smile:

"The pleasure was all mine," before retreating speedily back to the bar.

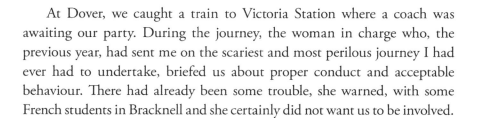

At Dover, we caught a train to Victoria Station where a coach was awaiting our party. During the journey, the woman in charge who, the previous year, had sent me on the scariest and most perilous journey I had ever had to undertake, briefed us about proper conduct and acceptable behaviour. There had already been some trouble, she warned, with some French students in Bracknell and she certainly did not want us to be involved.

"Another important thing, everyone" she said, "no one should ask for the key to their family's house, understood? You should not come and go as you please. The families are responsible for you, so do not make their job more difficult by asking for a key to their house. They need to know where you are at all times. And finally… quiet please, I've nearly finished… May I remind you of the English lessons that have been organised for you? The attendance last year was very poor. These lessons are not optional, they are compulsory and they are there to help you learn or improve your English. So, can I please repeat my plea that you all attend these lessons? It's only two hours every morning at the Youth Club in Bracknell, so it's not asking much of your time. Right, any questions anyone?"

Mrs Miller scanned the coach.

"No? Very well. I shall be coming round in a minute to give you the names and addresses of your families. If you think of a question in the meantime, you can ask me then."

"Can we have the radio on, please?" A girl shouted.

"Yes, Radio One please, driver!"

Mrs Miller proceeded to give us the names and addresses of our respective families to the sound of *Superstition* by Stevie Wonder.

I nudged Magali.

"Did you ask for a key last time you were here?"

"'Course I did."

"And the family didn't mind?"

"No… but then, they don't seem to know they're not supposed to give us a key."

"Are you going to ask for a key this time?"

"Too right I am. I've no intention of going to bed at the same time as the local peasants. Besides, the disco doesn't finish before eleven o'clock."

"Oh… there's a disco?"

"Yeah. Nothing like the Palladium in Paris though, but you know, the choice is either staying in with the old folks and drinking '*another cup of tea, my dear?*' or fraternising with the locals on the dance floor."

"So the family you stayed with were old?"

"Old?" Magali exclaimed. "Ancient you mean, so ancient I thought they'd just come back from the Napoleonic wars!"

We both burst out laughing just as Mrs Miller levelled up with us.

"What are you up to, you two?" She chided.

"Nothing, Mrs Turner, just joking." Magali giggled.

"Right, well, there's the names and addressed of your families. As you can see, you won't be staying far from each other but I strongly recommend that you keep away from each other, otherwise your English is never going to improve."

Glancing at my piece of paper, I immediately recognised the name of the road. Noticing my reaction, the leader chipped in:

"Yes… it's just across the road from where you were staying last year, and there's quite a few others staying in the same area, so you shouldn't be bored this time."

"She won't be if she stays with me." Magali quipped.

I glanced at my friend and we both burst out laughing again.

"Yes, just as I thought… You still have a lot of growing up to do, you two." Mrs Miller noted, shaking her head in disbelief.

Roughly two hours later, the coach stopped near the small town square. Eager families were gathered in a large crowd on the pavement, craning their necks to catch a glimpse of faces through the coach windows.

"There's my family!" Jacqueline shouted from the seat directly behind me. "Hi! Mrs Martin!" She waved, pressing her large breast against my face.

Some families cheered at the sight of familiar faces. Young children squealed with excitement and rushed to the coach door.

"Mind yourself, young lad!" The coach driver warned.

"Could you please keep the exit free?" Mrs Miller pleaded.

Armed with her clip-board, she began to pair off parents with students, waving her ball-pen and ticking boxes each time a family was united or reunited with one of us.

"Martha Bertrand!"

"Here, Madame."

Before alighting from the coach, I quickly turned to Magali.

"You've got my address, haven't you? You will come, won't you? Will you be able to find it?"

"Don't worry, I'll find it."

"When will you come?"

"Soon."

"How soon?"

"Martha Bertrand!" The leader's voice shouted again.

"All right, Magali. Got to go! See you soon!"

I grabbed my bag and rushed down the steps.

"Ah, there you are." The leader sighed before herding me towards a young couple with two cute little girls clamped on their legs.

"Here you are. This is Mr and Mrs D." She said, introducing my hosts. Then, turning to my hosts, she said: "And this is Martha Bertrand."

"How are you?" Mr D. greeted, extending a friendly hand.

I understood his greeting but I did not know what to say in return so I just smiled. As I looked at Mr D.'s smiling face, I was immediately struck by his extraordinary appearance. The man had huge side-burns and short black hair with an elaborate quiff that looked as if it had been starched on top of his head. Compared to the fulsome figure of his wife, he stood tall and thin in his tight-fitting jeans. As I exerted myself to lift my suitcase, he immediately jumped to my aid.

"Let me take your suitcase," he offered kindly. "By the way, I'm David and this is my wife Linda and our two little nippers: Sophie and Lucy. We're going on foot. The house's just round the corner." Then, pointing at the square concrete building that was the Youth Club, he added helpfully: "You might like to know they have discos in there… Is it every Friday they have them, Linda?"

"Yes, I think so, dear." His wife confirmed.

As they spoke, one of the little girls squeezed past us.

"Daddy! Daddy! I want to hold your hand!"

"Just a minute, sweetheart, I'm carrying Martha's case. Why don't you hold Martha's hand instead?"

The little girl looked at me, all coy and shy.

"I don't want to, Daddy." She finally said, wringing her hands.

"Go on! She's not going to bite you!"

Five minutes later, we came to a row of small terraced houses. Mr D. carried my suitcase upstairs and deposited it in the small box room at the front of the house.

As soon as I was settled, Mrs D. set about to organise my daily chores.

"Can you iron?"

"*No.*" I replied firmly.

"Hoover?"

"*Yes.*"

"Wash up?"

I nodded again.

"Good. I'm glad you can do something. Now, I'm making beans on toast for tea. You like beans on toast?"

"*Yes, sank you.*"

Relieved, she made her way to the kitchen where she grabbed a basket full of clean laundry. As she opened the back door, a tiny black puppy bounded in. The little dog jumped and barked and greeted everybody, including me. I could not resist grabbing it.

I settled in the family routine, hoovering every morning, helping with the washing-up, the laundry and other little chores to absolve myself from the fact that I refused point blank to do any ironing.

I did not know what Mr D. did for a living. I could only guess that he must be some kind of freelance trader because some evenings, unmarked boxes would arrive at the frond door containing whole stacks of various merchandise like shirts and ties, and whole suits still wrapped in their cellophane bags. There was also the odd consignment of watches that shone like the best quality fake gold and which tinkled like brand new coins. Furtive customers would then tiptoe to the front door and whisper their orders.

When it came to clothes, Mr D.'s pride and joy was undoubtedly his Teddy Boy outfit which he used to wear in the old days.

"But not anymore," he admitted with a tinge of regret in his voice. The craze had passed.

I had to explain that I had no idea what a Teddy Boy was. Knowing that words would have very little effect on me, he immediately ran upstairs, donned on his magnificent suit and re-appeared a few minutes later, carefully patting his starched quiff. Going straight for the record player, he put on a record and executed dancing steps in his brothel creepers, twisting his knees and hips to the sound of rock 'n roll.

"That's Elvis!" He beamed, all excited. "He's the king of Rock 'n Roll... but *here* in this house, I'm the king!"

He then grabbed his wife and performed an energetic jive while the little girls giggled on the sofa, clutching their dolls.

All his wife could do was to roll her eyes and chuckle as she tried to keep up with the brisk pace.

Fortunately for her, the next track was '*The Wonder of You*', and they all sat down again. Sophie and Lucy stood up from the sofa to make room for their parents and settled themselves on their parents' laps while Mr D. looked adoringly into his wife's eyes and declared warmly: "You know, that's my favourite track of the whole record."

Mrs D. returned his adoring look, kissed her husband and rested her head on his shoulder.

A few days later, Magali called.

"Ah, *salut!*" I effused. "Did you find the place easily?"

"Yeah. I just asked."

"*Mrs D., zis is my friend Magali.*"

"Hello." She greeted from behind the ironing board.

"Hello, Mrs D..."

"*We are going to town now.*" I carefully enunciated. "*Where is town, please?*"

"You go to the end of the street here, turn right, go under the bridge and then turn left. The town centre is there, just beyond the Weather Centre."

"*Sank you, Mrs D...*"

Just as we were about to leave, Mrs D. shouted:

"Remember, tea's at five!"

"*Yes, Mrs D.*"

On our way back from town, Magali decided to call on Jacqueline.

"You know where she lives?" I asked.

"Yes, she lives in the next street over there. We need to find out about the disco. She's been here before so she'll know all about it."

"Great, I can't wait to go to the disco."

A few minutes later, we stopped outside a white front door and rang the bell. Jacqueline bounded to the door and greeted us with several sets of noisy kisses.

The lady of the house invited us in and immediately offered us a cup of tea and biscuits, then proceeded to quiz us about our plans.

"What are you going to do this weekend? You know, there's a disco on Friday night."

"Oh, please, Mrs Martin," Jacqueline begged, "can I go?"

"Of course you can. You need to go out with your friends and enjoy yourself."

"Will you stay up for me?"

"Yes, of course. It doesn't finish too late, I don't think, about eleven o'clock."

"Yes," Jacqueline agreed. "If it's the same as last year, it starts at eight and finishes at eleven."

"We'll all go together, then." Magali suggested.

"We should ask Françoise and Sophie, they might want to come as well." Jacqueline added.

"OK, then, we'll come for you at seven thirty." Magali said.

"Great. I'll ask the others to come here, so that we can all walk together. See you Friday, then, Bye!"

As we walked back to my hosts' house, I mentioned *en passant*:

"You know, eleven o'clock is late for Mrs D. She usually goes to bed at ten."

"Ask for a key to the house, then."

"But we've been told not to."

"Don't take any notice of that." Magali replied dismissively. "We know that, but your family probably doesn't."

"I don't think I should."

"Well, I have." Magali trumpeted, flaunting a latch-key.

"Oh my God!... All right, then. I'll ask."

We fixed the time and place for our next meeting on Friday and after the normal ritual of kissing each other twice on the cheeks, we parted.

Leaning nonchalantly against the wall in the doorway, Mr D. watched us with a bemused smile and remarked:

"Do French girls always kiss each other like that all the time?"

Chapter 15

After a lot of hesitation, I finally plucked up the courage to ask Mrs D.

"*Please*," I began, feeling as awkward as if I was about to confess a naughty deed, "*can I 'ave a key of ze 'ouse?*"

Mrs D. looked perplexed. I could not tell whether her lack of an instant response was due to her trying to decipher my appalling English accent or whether it was because she had clearly understood my request and was deliberating the outcome.

"You want a spare key?" She asked.

"*Yes, please. I'm going to ze disco and ze disco finishes at eleven o'clock.*"

"Hmm… I do have one somewhere… I'll look for it later." Then she added: "Make sure you don't lose it though, and when you come back at night, make sure you don't make too much noise so you don't wake up the girls."

"*Yes, Mrs D. Sank you Mrs D.*"

At about seven o'clock on Friday night, Magali called. After greeting Mr and Mrs D., we stole upstairs to put some make-up on.

"What colour do you want?" Magali started.

"Blue, but can you put on the eye-liner first and I'll apply the eye-shadow after."

"Do you want lipstick as well?"

"Hmm… I'm not sure…"

"Try a little. What you do, you put it on and then use a cotton bud to remove the excess; that way, you'll only have a touch of lipstick."

"Okay, I'll try that."

Having dabbed on a shade of blue eye-shadow and a touch of lipstick, we were ready to leave. The last thing we heard as we made a point of closing the front door gently was someone shouting:

"Don't forget your key!"

Further down the road, we met up with Jacqueline, Sophie and Françoise. Wearing her favourite dress that swept the ground with its flowery pattern, Jacqueline stood taller and larger than the rest of us. Sophie sported her favourite brown slacks and Françoise a pretty chiffon dress. Both Magali and I had opted for miniskirts paired with plain blouses. Earlier that evening, I had studied the length of my skirt in the mirror, calculating with an expert eye the exact surface covered between the hips and the knees to check whether, in the words of Sister Monique, the skirt was barely longer than a finger nail or wider than a belt.

The five of us arrived outside the disco just after eight o'clock. The whole place seemed strangely quiet and… totally deserted.

"Maybe we've got the wrong time," Françoise speculated.

"Or the wrong day." Jacqueline quipped.

After a few minutes, a man appeared at the door, looking as if he was in charge of the place.

"Why don't we ask him?" I suggested.

"Who's going to ask?" Jacqueline wondered looking at the rest of us. "Martha, you go and ask."

"Why me?" I protested. "Magali, your English is better than mine, you go and ask him."

So, Magali walked up to the man to enquire about the disco and we all crowded around her to hear the answer.

"No," the man replied, adamant. "No more discos for August. Too much trouble with French students."

What do you mean no more discos? How were we supposed to survive in this alien neighbourhood without the only form of entertainment that we knew… for a whole month? We stood on the pavement speechless in our best disco gear and with nowhere to go.

"What are we going to do?" I eventually asked.

We glowered at the concrete shell of the Youth Club, then at the deserted pavement and empty road.

"Where else can we go? Jacqueline, you've been here before, you must know of another disco."

"No, I don't."

"Perhaps we should ask where there's another disco." I ventured.

Some unsuspecting passers-by, startled by our sudden approach, gave us a short, sharp reply before shuffling away at speed, probably in fear of being caught loitering.

Suddenly, Jacqueline had a eureka moment.

"Why don't we stop cars and ask them?"

"Yeah, yeah!" came the unanimous reply. "Let's do that!"

Without further ado, we lined our platform shoes against the edge of the pavement and began to wave frantically at passing cars. All ignored us.

"It's not working." Jacqueline sighed. "We'll just have to jump on the road."

So, when the next car came along, we tried to stop it by jumping in front of it. The car swerved widely and I just caught sight of the driver shaking his head, clearly shocked.

The next car that happened along turned out to be a little mini with three young men inside. Again, we jumped in the middle of the road waving frantically. The car stopped. The window wound down and a bewildered young man stuck his head out.

"*Disco?*" We immediately shouted in unison. "*Where's ze disco?*"

The three occupants exchanged a few words, chortled in anticipation and replied:

"Disco? Yeah, yeah, we know a disco!"

"Come on," said the driver. "Jump in!"

"What!" I said to Magali. "All five of us? There's already three of them in the car. We'll never manage to get all in."

Jacqueline had no such worries. She was already sliding her large frame into the front seat of the cramped mini, squashing the young man who was already sitting there. Screams and laughter followed as the rest of us tried to fit in the back of the car.

By now, the packed mini looked more like a Vietnamese pot-belly pig than a car. Nevertheless, it limped off, its exhaust scraping the tarmac every time it hit a bump on the road.

Suddenly, the three young men squeaked together:

"Nick nick! Nick nick!"

"What's that?" We asked, baffled by their strange sense of humour.

"There's a police car coming. Get your heads down!" The driver shouted.

Immediately, we squashed ourselves as low as we could below the car windows.

"Oh my God, Martha!" Magali exclaimed. "I've got my head between his knees!"

Immediately, screams of laughter welcomed her remark.

"Don't mind me!" The young man joked. "Pleased to meet you! My name's Frank."

He then shook a hand.

"Who's hand is that?" He asked highly amused.

"Mine!" Sophie yelped.

Once the danger had passed, we proceeded to make the introductions and discovered that both the driver and his passenger friend were called 'John'. To avoid any confusion, John the passenger would from then on be referred to as 'Jack'.

"Is it not confusing?" Jacqueline asked.

At the back of the car, Magali was busy plotting her next conquest.

"The driver isn't bad looking," she surmised. "I like men with dark hair and blue eyes. I think I'll have him."

"Oh, I was going to go for him." I said, disappointed.

"You can have the other one." She directed.

"I don't like him… too skinny… looks a bit of a wimp… and he's got a moustache, yuk!"

"Don't worry. It's only for the holiday, after that you can forget about him…" She tried to convince me. But far from being convinced, I squinted at the young man, unable to detect a single redeeming feature.

"No, I don't like him." I decreed.

"Where are we going?" Jacqueline enquired, on the off-chance that someone was paying attention.

"To a disco." John replied.

A while later, the mini turned into the car park of a large red-brick house which had a picture sign hanging above the main door.

"We're going to stop here for a drink first," John declared.

"*Is zis a disco?*" I asked, distinctly unsettled by the quietness of the place.

"No, it's a pub. We'll go to the disco later." Frank replied.

Jacqueline was feeling uneasy.

"Are we allowed in? None of us are 18."

"Don't worry," Frank reassured us. "Just keep your backs towards the bar and nobody'll notice".

Not notice? Only the other day when I trotted off to the corner shop to buy a packet of cigarettes, the woman had peered over the counter to look me up and down and had breathed through the sharp end of her nostril: "are you sixteen?" So, God knows how I was going to pass for an eighteen-year old.

Inside, we stood at a fair distance from the counter in a homogenous mass hoping to look eighteen or more. From there, we watched in awe the barman pull some dark, almost black liquid topped up with whitish foam into enormous glasses, and we stared in amazement at the young men drinking it.

"*What is zat?*" I asked.

Frank lifted his glass and explained:

"That's Guinness, that is. Very nice. You want to try it?"

"*No sank you.*"

John had started to buy the first round.

"Orange juice? Coke? Lemonade? Bloody hell Frank, I think we've just picked up a nursery class!"

Then turning to me he said:

"You can't come to a pub and order orange juice and lemonade!"

"*Okay, zen, I'll 'ave a peenapple juice.*"

John chuckled discreetly.

"You mean pine-apple."

As I waited for my drink, I diverted my eyes away from the counter in order to observe the unfamiliar scene. Needless to say, I did not understand much of what was being said because in spoken English, somehow half of the syllables seem to disappear. And then, in between the missing syllables, something mysterious, surreptitious and unobtrusive slips in: the vernacular. Ah… where would we be without the vernacular? How could any of us experience the kind of intimate *rapprochement* that exists between friends, neighbours and every country folk without the vernacular? Not that it worried me though. I was still at the primitive stage where I did not even know what to reply if someone asked me quite innocuously: "How are you today?"

Suddenly, my attention was irresistibly drawn towards our little group. Over there, standing between Magali and John, I spotted Jack, the one that I had instantly rejected and written off, forthrightly discarded and categorically refused to befriend, engrossed in a flirty conversation with Françoise. In one instant, I saw my free drinks and taxi disappear. ***Excuse me, but…***

I elbowed every man and woman out of the way and made a bee-line for my intended… *Phew*, talk about a near miss! Having thus supplanted any potential rival, I proceeded to use all the charm I could muster. Of what I said, I have no idea how much my intended understood, but - and make no bones about it - the message was crystal clear, unambiguous and unequivocal, and, judging by his reaction, clearly received.

Having successfully paired off, Magali was by now well ensconced with John, and I with Jack. Whether he intended to or not, Frank was the only one to remain on neutral ground. Perhaps he already had a girlfriend. Anyhow, whatever the state of his domestic affairs was, he was clearly not interested and was happily chatting about anything to anybody.

"So," Françoise asked again. "*Where's ze disco?*"

"Ah!" Frank finally admitted. "We don't know, but we're going to a party and if you'd like to come with us, I'm sure it'll be all right."

Jacqueline and Françoise shook their heads.

"No, I don't want to go." Françoise decreed. "I don't like being surrounded by total strangers."

"I'm bored" Jacqueline confided with a heavy sigh. "I want to go home."

"I'll give you a lift back home, if you like, my car's in the car park behind the pub."

"Yes, please!" The girls chorused.

"What about your friend? Does she want to go home too?" Frank asked, referring to Sophie. Having overheard, Sophie prompted:

"Yes, I think I will."

Compared to the rest of us, Sophie was reserved, quiet and uncommunicative in the extreme. Her style of dress was always conservative and the colours rather subdued, ranging between bottle-green, navy blue and dark brown.

A few minutes later, Frank disappeared with Jacqueline, Sophie and Françoise. John intimated to Jack that now might be the time to make a move.

"You want to go to a party?" He asked Magali.

"Yes!" She replied enthusiastically.

"*What's a party? Is it ze same as a disco?*" I enquired.

"Well, not quite. We go to someone's house" John explained, "and we drink lots and lots of beer…"

"*Can we dance zere?*"

"Yes, if you want. There's always music, loud music, so you can dance all you like."

"*Okay, zen, we'll come.*"

After a short drive in the dark, we arrived at a house that was packed with people. A solid block of amorphous silhouettes was crowding the front door so we entered through the back door and as we passed through, I espied several large tins stacked up on the kitchen table surrounded by many bottles in various state of emptiness.

"*What's in zere?*" I asked, intrigued.

"Beer. There's a gallon of beer in each tin."

"*Wow!*" I exclaimed, before turning my nose up.

"Is that all you drink? Orange or pineapple juice?" John asked as if it was quite abnormal.

"*Yes. Me, I don't like alco'ol.*"

"But you can't have a good time without a proper drink!" He remarked.

"*Well, me, I can.*" I insisted.

What was really stopping me from enjoying myself right now was the fact that there was not a square inch free on which to dance, so I decided to consult Magali.

"I'm getting bored."

"So am I." She replied.

We both relayed our feelings to the men.

"You want to go home now? But we've only just arrived."

Regardless of how he felt, a few minutes later, we were back in the car. Magali sat at the front and I settled on the back seat with Jack.

By the time I got back home, it was nearly one o'clock in the morning. Jack got out of the car and accompanied me to the door.

"When can I see you again?" He asked, almost whispering.

"*Why are you whispering?*"

"I don't want the others to hear."

"*Well, I don't know,*" I replied, hesitating.

"Shall I call on Sunday?" He finally breathed with a hint of impatience.

I was somewhat shocked that anyone should be interested in me. I was not used to this. What's more, his insistence of wanting to see me again made me feel trapped but I was on holiday, so it would eventually come to an end and I would be free again. Very reluctantly, I ushered a very timid 'yes'. Then, as the true gentleman that he really was, he came closer to me and asked:

"Can I kiss you goodnight?"

I squirmed with shyness. Oh, God, did he really have to do this?

Suddenly, a voice hailed from the car.

"Come on, Jack, it's getting late and I've got to go to work tomorrow. We've still got to drop Magali off."

"All right, I'm coming!" Then Jack turned to me and added quickly: "Okay for Sunday, then?" Then he rushed back to the car and waved, his face beaming with a big bright smile.

Chapter 16

With our foursome firmly set into two unlikely couples, the days shortened dramatically and the nights lengthened beyond the scale of time. If, in the middle of all this, my hosts feared losing track of my time, my daily routine was, reassuringly for them, clearly determined, albeit organised around my somewhat hectic social life. I usually got up and, bleary eyed, shuffled downstairs to have breakfast, regardless of the time of day, do a bit of hoovering and washing up, then disappear for the rest of the day… and night, which prompted Mr D. to declare once, with a rather mystified expression on his face:

"I don't know what you get up to at night, but you're never up before midday."

Whether he expected an answer in return, I could not tell for my reading of minds in a foreign language was not as perspicacious as it normally was. Instead of a reply, I simply shrugged my shoulders and thought of Gordon Lightfoot and his beautiful romantic ballad: *"If you could read my mind, love…"*

For one thing was certain. If Johan had opened my heart to a sublime and supreme love that only existed on a spiritual plane, John was slowly introducing me to a more earthly, palpable love that communicated itself through romantic gestures, and through desires and wishes whispered in words. This was too new for me and I did not know how to respond.

Our free time was spent mostly wandering aimlessly around the small town and talking about our conquests. Sometimes, we would catch the bus to go to Broad Street in Reading. Once even, we thought we would surprise John by calling at his little shop. Getting his business card out of her handbag, Magali read the address.

"How are we going to find it?" I said.

"We'll just ask." Magali replied.

When we got there, we stopped on the pavement opposite the shop to see if we could catch sight of him.

"John was right, it is a small shop." I noted.

"There he is; he's just come out of the storeroom. Come on, let's go and surprise him!"

And surprised him, we certainly did for as soon as John saw us, he panicked.

"What are you doing here? I'm not supposed to socialise during working hours!"

"We thought it would be a nice surprise." Magali explained, going towards him to give him a kiss. To her surprise, John pushed her firmly away.

"No, no! Don't kiss me here! I'm working! You're gonna have to leave!"

"But I wanted to see you." Magali said, rather disappointed by his brusque rebuff.

"Sorry, I can't see you right now, I'm busy."

"Can't we just pretend we're customers?"

"Ok, if you want, as long as you don't come anywhere near me, I'm working. Look out, there's my assistant; she could report me, you know."

After a few minutes, I nudged my friend.

"Magali, I think we should go. He's clearly not happy with us being here."

But Magali did not respond. She was too busy eying the assistant, a young girl with long blond hair and a fresh and friendly face.

"Have you seen his assistant?" Magali whispered from the twisted corner of her mouth. "I don't know why he doesn't go out with her. She's rather attractive... too attractive for my liking."

"Maybe *she* doesn't fancy him."

"I don't see why not. I'd go out with him if he was my boss... given the chance."

At long last, we made for the door.

"Bye!" We chorused.

"See you later, bye!" John waved hugely relieved.

In the evening, we often grabbed a burger or fish and chips and cruised along the streets while listening to the latest hits on Radio 1 in John's mini before going to a pub. In this way and under the bemused stare of our respective boyfriends, Magali and I crooned along with Rod Steward, Carol King, T-Rex and the hottest teenage idol of the day Donny Osmond; and every time Maggie May, It's Too Late, Hot Love/Get It On or Puppy Love came on the radio, we bounced on the car seat and shouted: "louder! Louder!"

One evening, John, turned up all excited.

"Hey," he announced, "there's a new disco that's just opened by the river. It's called 'Riverdance', d'you fancy going?"

"Yeah! Yeah!" we shouted simultaneously.

"Calm down, girls, calm down." John pleaded. "We're going!"

Soon, John was steering the car through deserted streets, rectilinear estates until we finally reached the silvery coil of the Thames River. In the distance, we spotted a white wooden building festooned with multicolour lights running all around the roof.

"That's got to be it." John noted.

Magali wounded her window down.

"Yes, I can hear ze music."

A few minutes later, we entered the packed disco hall with the biggest dance floor I had ever seen. Familiar hits pounded the giant speakers and the loquacious DJ, perched high up in his little glass cubicle, gesticulated energetically while encouraging the static crowd to 'come on dancing'. Quickly we settled at a table which we had to share with strangers all hyped up and excited, just like us. We ordered drinks, lit a cigarette and sat back to observe the scene. And what a staggering sight it was. While up there, in his box close to the gods, the DJ exhorted himself to get people to dance to a wide range of music, nobody, absolutely nobody was prepared to make the first move. Puzzled by this complete social inertia, Magali and I looked at each other.

"That's strange, nobody's dancing. Why is nobody dancing?" We asked the boys.

"Don't know" came the reply, "perhaps they're too shy."

"Well, I'm not going to sit here all night doing nothing. We came here to dance and dance we shall." Magali decreed.

"Me too," I seconded.

"Come on, Martha, let's start the action. Let's show these peasants how it's done."

Upon which, Magali grabbed my arm and together, we made straight for the middle of the enormous dance floor. Free to hog the limelight, the two of us twisted, twirled and danced under the startled gaze of hundreds of onlookers. We giggled and mocked the young crowd too insecure to make a move. We sneered at their poor fashion sense that had boys and girls wearing trousers right up to their armpits with yards of superfluous material flapping around their skinny and sometimes not so skinny frames. As the DJ put on the next record, he hailed into the microphone: "Come on, everyone, join these two lovely ladies on the dance floor and show us what you can do. Here he comes, it's T-Rex!"

Several people moved closer to the edge of the wide open wooden floor. We could see them jiggling on the spot, still too shy to venture any further.

The DJ rattled his microphone again.

"Come on, everyone! This one's for you! I want to see everybody on the dance floor! Now!"

His words finally took effect. All of a sudden, we were swamped by a surge of flared jeans, frilly blouses and flowery dresses with their tight bustier almost squashing our noses. Suddenly, before we had time to react, the dancers fell into spontaneous lines and started to perform synchronised moves in synchronised steps, advancing, retreating and turning all together like a massive tidal wave which forced us to the edge of the dance floor. We froze on the spot, neither of us having ever witnessed anything like it. Stunned by this strange spectacle, Magali and I looked at each other. The only thing we could do now was to take some time out.

Back at our table, I could not help but ask:

"*Do people always dance like zat?*"

"Well, yeah… it's the latest, in' it?"

Curious, Magali and I continued to stare, totally mesmerised by the line formations that went against our own idea of independence of movement and expression.

Late that night, John drove us home.

"What are you doing on Thursday?" Jack asked, always eager to plan our next sortie.

"We can't see you on Sursday." I declared. *"We 'ave to go to London to visit St Paul's Cazedral."*

"Why? You want to go and visit a church!"

"No, we don't want to but we have to, it's obligatory." Magali explained.

"Come on, surely you don't have to. You're on holiday."

Of course we were on holiday which was why the prospect of visiting a cathedral appealed to us as much as counting the number of 'Smiths' in the telephone directory, but there was no avoiding it.

"We 'ave to because we've missed all ze ozer excursions, and we're going to be in real trouble if we miss zis one too."

"Oh, what a pity." John remarked. "It's my day off and I was going to take you to see the Victory in Portsmouth."

"Ze Victory? What's zat?"

"That was Nelson's flagship." John replied, somewhat surprised that we had never heard of it.

"Nelson? Who's zat?"

Now, he looked shocked.

"Surely, you must have heard of Trafalgar?"

At this point, all the historical pointers clicked together, but feeling in a rather mischievous mood, we decided to remain obtuse.

"Oh yes, of course, we know Trafalgar Square!" We guffawed.

"'ave you been to Trafalgar Square?" I asked Magali in a chuckle before John quipped:

"No, I don't mean Trafalgar Square; I mean the battle of Trafalgar, between Napoleon and Nelson."

"Oh yeah, we won zat one, didn't we?" Magali teased, laughing.

"Yeah, of course we did!" I seconded before collapsing in laughter.

The men shook their heads and stared at us in complete disbelief.

"You're having us on, aren't you?"

"Oh no, me, I know nocing about 'istory. It's too boring but I've 'eard of Trafalgar and zat king zat invaded England, yeah 'im… you know… Norman ze Conqueror!" I giggled, purposely making my English accent sound worse than ever.

"It's not Norman! It's William the Conqueror!" John corrected.

"Ah yeah, but 'e was Norman, wasn't 'e?"

Loud laughter greeted my cheeky reply.

"Right, well I can't hang about all night." John reminded us. "It's all right for you lot. You're on holiday and you can sleep all day if you want, but I've got to go to work tomorrow to earn more pennies so that we can see each other again and have a good time."

"Okay, then. See you Friday. I'll ring you." Jack whispered, giving me a light kiss on the lips.

"Ok, bye!" I hailed in return.

The following morning, I opened one eye to glance at my watch. Through my myopic gaze, I thought I read 'ten o'clock'. Good, the coach was not due to leave before eleven o'clock. I tossed over to go back to sleep when loud bangs resounded on the door.

"Martha! Martha! Your coach is leaving in fifteen minutes!" Mrs D. shouted through the door.

"What!" I screamed, springing out of bed like a mad hare.

I grabbed my clothes, my bag and stormed out of the house. From there, I ran all the way to the Youth Club where we had been told to wait for the coach. Out of breath, I greeted the others who were already gathered there, all looking remarkably refreshed, polished and highly manicured. I scoured the familiar faces, looking anxiously for my friend. I did not see her but I spotted an old acquaintance. With her long blond hair among heads of long black hair, she could be spotted a mile away. Yes, there she was, Nadine, the very same from *Saint Vincent*.

"Hi," I said timidly.

"Hi," she replied with a quirky smile.

"You're staying in Bracknell too?"

"No, Ringwood. My family dropped me off here this morning."

"Are they nice?"

"Yes, they're great!" She replied emphatically.

Then, spotting Jacqueline, I shuffled towards her.

"Where's Magali?" I asked.

"She's just coming."

Seconds later, I heard someone running and as I turned around, I caught sight of Magali's black mane being blown about in the wind.

"Phew!" She said out of breath, "I've just made it!"

"I nearly didn't!" I told her.

When the signal came to board the coach, Magali and I rushed up the steps.

"Go for the back seats!" Magali ordered. "We'll get a better view."

Once we were comfortably seated in our favourite seats, we were finally able to relax. Magali ogled me with a queer eye.

"You look as if you've fallen out of bed."

"I have. I don't have an alarm clock so I didn't know when to get up."

"Do you want to borrow my hairbrush?"

"Oh, thanks. I didn't have time to do anything. I just ran out of the house."

"I've got a small mirror too if you want to borrow some make-up."

"I can't be bothered. We're only going to St Paul's Cathedral."

"We might meet someone, though."

"Please, Magali, spare me. I'm not interested."

"Ah! There you are, you two." The leader exclaimed as if she had made a sudden discovery, before ticking our names on her clip-board.

"*Bonjour, Madame Miller.*" We greeted politely.

"You didn't come on the last excursion to Beaulieu…"

"*Beaulieu?*"

"Yes, Beaulieu." She repeated. "It's one of the largest English estates with the biggest private collection of classic cars…"

"Oh yeah," Magali interrupted. "We didn't go because we're not interested in cars."

"That may be so, but excursions are not optional, they are compulsory."

"We didn't know that." We pleaded in each other's defence.

"I also see from the register that you haven't been to any of the English classes either."

"Classes?!!!" We both exclaimed at once.

"Yes, English classes, especially organised to improve your English."

"Gosh, I'd forgotten about them," I admitted.

"We're all right, Madame." Magali prompted. "Our English has improved a lot, hasn't it, Martha?"

"Yes, Madame, we've had a lot of help. Our families are ever so helpful, aren't they, Magali?"

"Well, make sure you don't miss any other excursion, all right?"

"Where's the next one?" I enquired, just out of interest.

"Oxford Street and Trafalgar Square."

At the sound of the familiar name, we both collapsed in a heap of laughter.

The leader glowered at us, rolled her eyes to the ceiling, turned her heels followed closely by her clip-board, and exhaled exasperated:

"You two are so immature!"

Moments later, the coach huffed and puffed before coming to a stop outside the steps of St Paul's Cathedral. The leader grabbed the microphone and announced:

"Here we are everybody: St Paul's Cathedral. We're going to visit the cathedral and its famous Whispering Gallery. Afterwards, you will have some free time to have a look around the shops. However, I want everyone back here at three o'clock. Is that clear? Three o'clock and don't be late; we don't want to be stuck in traffic jams for hours."

Unbeknown to her, and to me for that matter, Magali had made quite different plans. As the group began to climb the ceremonious steps, she snagged my arm and whispered:

"Stay right back."

I looked at her, puzzled.

"Stuff her 'whispering gallery'!" Magali whispered. "Wait until the group goes inside and then, we'll just go."

"Go where?"

"To the shops of course."

"But we don't know where they are."

"It doesn't matter, we'll just ask."

"What if Madame Miller ask us questions about the cathedral?"

"Don't worry, just say you didn't understand."

We climbed two or three steps just to pretend we were following, then, when the coast was clear, we scarpered.

Back on the pavement, we stopped the first passer-by that happened along.

"*'Scuse me, Mister, where's ze shops?*"

The old man looked startled, even fearful I thought. However, soon reassured that we were not about to mug him, he raised his hand, lifted his cloth cap and scratched his forehead before pointing his finger southwards.

"The shops? Over there."

"Thank you, Mister."

We ran following the invisible line of his pointed finger and soon came upon a street which had a big banner suspended across the street. We ambled slowly, transported along by the festive ambiance, the colourful window displays and the music blaring out of every shop. We stared, mouth gaping, at the array of young people sauntering down the street in loud shirts, tight jeans or flowing skirts, at men and women all with long hair and festooned with flowery headbands and colourful beads beating on their exposed chests. Some marched down the street in brown leather sandals or flip-flops with a big white daisy covering their toes. Shop assistants, who stood idly on their doorsteps, hailed us to come inside to have a look at their display. With nothing else to do and no rush to go anywhere, we stopped frequently to browse at leisure through stacks of multicolour T-shirts with wide funnel-shaped sleeves and small round mirrors sewn at the front. We rummaged through hundreds of silk tunics and silk scarves, all genuine articles from India. We scoured trays upon trays of beaded jewellery, multicoloured bangles and other 'hippiesque' apparels, but all we really wanted was something that would remind us of our first trip to London. Eventually, among the thousands of items we scrutinised, picked and examined only to discard, we found exactly what we were looking for: a white T-shirt with printed on the front a large union jack shaped like a heart pierced by Cupid's arrow.

For fear of getting lost, we chose to return early back to the steps of St Paul's rather than venture any further. There, we met up with Nadine and Sophie. Together, we sat on the steps and lit up a cigarette.

"So," I began, addressing Nadine, "you've bought anything?"

"Not much, a T-shirt, some earrings and things."

"We've bought a T-shirt too." I said, whisking it out of the plastic bag. Then, I enquired about her family.

"Your house is not far from mine, if you wanted to, we could meet up one day."

"Yes, I'd like that."

"You see, I'm a bit bored with my family... Actually it's not really a family, I'm staying with this old man who lives on his own... very nice he is and very funny... but you know, not exactly my kind of company."

"Oh? He has no wife?"

"No, he's never been married. He likes cooking, though... but he's still an old man. I could do with some company... Do you fancy going to Reading with me one day?"

"I don't mind. When do you want to go?"

While I chatted to Nadine, Magali was busy catching up with Sophie. Suddenly, she hailed me all excited.

"Martha, guess what!" Magali shouted.

"What?"

"Sophie is going out with Frank!"

"With Frank? You mean, Frank from the party? Oh my! Well done Sophie! Go on, tell us more. What's he like?"

For all reply, Sophie darted a killer stare at Magali. Whatever she had told her was in complete confidence and now she regretted having breathed a word of it. All she could do now was to retreat inside 'Fort Knox'. So we backed off. Fancy her having a boyfriend, though!

Back at my hosts' house, I walked straight into the lounge.

"Hi!" Mrs D. greeted from behind the ironing board. "Nice to see you back so early for once. Did you have a good time? What did you think of St Paul's, then? Did you buy anything?"

For all reply, I lifted the plastic bag and said:

"*I bought a T-shirt.*"

At the sight of the plastic bag, Mrs D. squealed:

"You've been to Carnaby Street?!"

"*Carnaby Street?*"

"Yes, there, that's the name on your bag."

I looked at the bag, then at her, totally puzzled.

"You've never heard of Carnaby Street?"

"*No.*" I said, thinking 'should I have?'

"Everybody's heard of Carnaby Street, here in England. It's *the* place to shop. All the stars and famous people go to shop in Carnaby Street."

"*Oh, really?*" I lilted, remaining firmly unimpressed.

"By the way," she continued. "We're going to Southend on Sunday. Would you like to come with us?"

Noting my perplex expression, she added:

"It's a seaside resort… you know… by the sea. There's a pier and a fair. The kiddies love it."

"*Yes, I'll come.*" I accepted. Then, after a moment of reflection, I asked: "*Can my friend come too?*"

"Which one?"

"Magali."

"Oh, Magali; yes of course she can. It's going to be a bit of a squash in the car, but I'm sure we'll manage."

On Sunday, Magali arrived wearing her new T-shirt from Carnaby Street. We clambered into the car with the two little girls squashed between us on the backseat. We strolled along the promenade, on the pier, and had our photograph taken with tiny monkeys all dressed up in frilly gear. Just as the photographer pressed the button, the little blighter nibbled my finger which made me grimace just as the shutter clicked.

Strolling along the promenade, it soon became clear that Mr D. was more interested in our hectic social life than what was going on around him in Southend. Leaving his wife to walk at a leisurely pace holding her little girls' hands, he squared himself between the two of us and began to prod, pry and gesticulate. Unable – or unwilling – to articulate a proper reply, we giggled instead and the more Mr D. probed and pried, all in good humour of course, the more we giggled. Having gained little or confused bits of information, he suddenly pointed at Magali's neck and asked:

"What's that you've got there?"

We burst out laughing.

"So you've got a boyfriend then. That was quick."

More laughter. When we eventually calmed down, Magali pointed at me and trumpeted:

"She's got one too!"

"Magali!" I shouted angrily, whilst I fumbled self-consciously with the scarf I had strategically tied around my neck. Mr D. looked at each of us in turn with a knowing smile and finally said:

"Well, girls, I don't care what you get up to… but just be careful."

Chapter 17

On a bright sunny day, Nadine and I eventually met up. She was the only reminder that we had once lived in a ghastly godforsaken place, but here in another country, a foreign land, those memories had long disappeared, buried in their murky past, a past that neither of us wanted to revisit, permanently relegated with a steely resolve behind the fortress of our minds. 'Neither a saint nor a martyr be', let it be our motto for life.

That afternoon, we took the bus on our way to Broad Street in Reading. With both of us in the full throes of a carefree adolescence, we could not do or say anything without giggling or laughing. Some people got annoyed, exasperated even, others happily joined in.

Once we boarded the bus, we chatted and giggled until a thought occurred to me.

"By the way, do you know where we're supposed to get off?"

Neither of us knew so we turned around to ask advice to the passenger sitting behind us. Whether it was the fact that we both turned around at the same time or the unexpected sight of a large lady with blue-rinsed hair smiling back at us, I do not know but we both burst into an irrepressible laughter, and try as we might, we simply could not stop. We made several attempts to pose our question but never managed to articulate a single word beyond the first syllable. Fortunately for us, the extremely good-natured lady did not take offence and simply continued to stare at us nodding her head magnanimously, her face beaming with a friendly smile.

When the bus eventually turned into the main street, the blue-rinsed lady tapped Nadine on her shoulder, pointed at the window and helpfully indicated:

"The shops. There's the shops."

As we waited for the bus to come to a full stop, we deciphered the small adverts plastered all around the ceiling and to amuse ourselves, we proceeded to read them out loud, with every single word pronounced as if it were a French word. Our linguistic antics succeeded in cheering up the whole bus and as we got off, I noticed that every single passenger was smiling.

Moments later, we hopped onto the crowded pavement with no other intention than to while away the afternoon strolling along, observing, scouring and passing comments on the passers-by, the window displays and the odd flash of eccentric fashion parading down the street. At about four o'clock, we rested our feet in the nearest Wimpy bar, shared a banana split and plotted our return home.

It was now approaching five o'clock and the queues at the bus stops were beginning to form long orderly lines all along the pavement. From the Wimpy bar window, we stared at them in horror. Nadine spoke out first.

"Well, stuff them! I'm not queuing!"

I looked at the queues, then at Nadine.

"What are we going to do then?" I asked.

"We'll just go to the front of the queue!"

"Really?"

"Come on, let's go!" She said, rising abruptly from her seat.

Once outside, she set out her plan.

"What we'll do, we'll just go to the front of the queue and just pretend that we're checking the number of the bus… and then, we'll just stay there until the bus arrives. If people start complaining, just pretend you don't understand. I've done it before, it's really easy!"

Just as planned, we marched to the front of the queue, craned our necks to read the various numbers out loud and in French in order to use the language barrier as an excuse to justify our blatant lack of courtesy and manners. Having executed our plan with youthful aplomb, we giggled in our sleeves and felt quite pleased with ourselves for this small victory was nothing less than our rebellious streak turning into an act of bravado, except that this time, nobody was laughing with us.

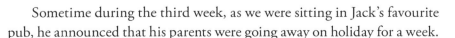

Sometime during the third week, as we were sitting in Jack's favourite pub, he announced that his parents were going away on holiday for a week.

"Great!" Magali exclaimed. "We can go to your house!"

"No, you bloody well can't!" He blurted out.

So, the pub rounds resumed, often followed by another impromptu party at someone else's house where we sipped our fruit juices to the general dismay of the gathering who had never encountered anyone who did not drink alcohol. In pairs, we slouched on sofas, armchairs or on the floor listening to music; and it was in the smoky atmosphere of some stranger's lounge that I cultured a more sophisticated taste in music, that I discovered new sounds like Deep Purple, Led Zeppelin, Pink Floyd, the Moody Blues, the Who, Neil Young, James Taylor and others. In this world of mods and rockers, totally alien to the rigid set up I was accustomed to, where the mere mention of a boyfriend would have branded me loose, amoral and profligate, I was evolving, blossoming and maturing while learning the lessons of life and the rules of love. Here, I was free to communicate and interact like any normal teenager, even if the language barrier often forced me to act out the words I wanted to express. And it was during one of those late nights that I saw, through the nebulous filaments of our lit cigarettes a new life emerging, and at that moment, the beginning of a plot began to weave inside my head, that perhaps if I wanted any semblance of a normal life without being nagged to death, I would have to move to England, but you know… only if you want to… you don't have to make up your mind now… you're still young… there's plenty of time… but perhaps… one day… maybe… think about it.

In the dark and sultry night, I was beginning to lose sight of the demarcation line.

Quite beside me, myself and I, I had also noticed a gradual change in Sophie. She was showing herself to be more communicative, more willing to share and participate but still within the confines of her very strict boundaries. As for Frank, always the perfect gentleman, he was taking things easy and very slowly, the main reason being that Sophie was only fifteen.

Later during the week, the little mini broke down, so the men decided to hire a car. We continued to pester Jack to let us go to his house but this turned out to be quite a touchy subject. The idea of having his mates sprawled all over the immaculate furniture of his parents' pristine house, guzzling beer from giant cans, trampling all over the mite-free carpet and stinking the place out with cigarette smoke and late night curries did not appeal to him in the least. However, he hinted, he was not against the idea of a tête-à-tête on the sofa, holding me firmly in his arms whilst listening to Deep Purple, Carol King or the Pink Floyd. In actual fact, he quite nurtured the idea of the two of us being alone together in his own little world without his posse of friends constantly heckling, jeering and bantering; and all the while I was taking notes, observing his arms forming a protective cordon around me, listening to his sweet nothings whispered in my ears which I did not always understand. It did not matter anyway for the language of love is best expressed without words.

Then one day, we met up, just the two of us. We sauntered along the university campus which happened to be a short stroll away from the house. With his hand clasped in mine, we watched the squirrels scurrying away, the wild birds singing and the swans gliding on the lake. We listened to songbirds, to their wings fluttering excitedly, to the summer breeze rustling the branches and leaves, and to tender words whispered in the wind. We lost ourselves in a pensive silence, full of romantic thoughts and unspoken words which we both understood should be left undisturbed. Those delicious moments spent together taught me not to be scared, that I would not lose my independence by being involved in a one-to-one relationship. Slowly, I was coming round to the idea that it was all right to matter to one person, and one person alone.

Chapter 18

When Magali and I met up again, we resumed our mundane chatter... and her adventure. Like an obliging listener acknowledging with indifference the eclectic melange of fact and fiction, I giggled and laughed and shrieked in pretend shock and mock horror. Then, we would light up a cigarette.

That evening, in the pub, John reiterated his offer to take us to Portsmouth to see the Victory. Not that we were all that interested in Nelson's exploits or keen to study from up close the roll-call of his spectacular victories. All we wanted, really, was to abscond from a tedious programme of boring English lessons and even more boring excursions.

When the day came, exhibiting a closer allegiance to England rather than France, we sported our new Union Jack T-shirts. However, above our giggles and cheeky repartees, clouds gathered and started extending their multifarious arms. It was a dull and manky day but fully absorbed with our companions while listening to Tony Blackburn chiming our favourite tunes on Radio 1, neither of us noticed the rain patting on the car windows, nor the wipers squeaking loudly on the windscreen. At the back of the car, I listened to the music in a dreamy state, snuggled in Jack's arms.

In Portsmouth, the wind and rain had cleared the quayside from any living souls. As we got out of the car, we were instantly whipped up by a strong gale. Posing for a brief photo or two in front of the imposing bow of the fully restored Victory, we shivered in our skimpy T-shirts and urged the men to get a move on.

"Don't you want to go around the ship?" John asked.

"No!" Magali and I vetoed.

I glowered at the slippery gangway and declared:

"It's too cold! I want to go back in ze car."

"Come on," John pleaded. "We've come all this way... and you don't even want to have a look around the ship. Go on, just for a little bit, so that you can say that you've been on Nelson's flagship."

"We've seen it and we're on it!" Magali quipped.

John shook his head, half bemused but disappointed all the same. After Jack had finished capturing the moment with his Leica camera, we all piled back inside the car.

"*We can go to ze shops.*" Magali suggested.

"Bloody hell! I don't want to go to the shop, it's boring." John interjected.

"Not only that," Jack remarked. "Parking in Portsmouth is a nightmare. No, we'll just go back and explore a pub or two on the way."

"*Yeah, yeah, good idea.*" I firmly agreed.

Before long, the car windows steamed up and I had nothing to look at except the view of my conquest sitting right beside me, ruffling his moustache and with him staring back at me as if I were a peculiar '*object d'art*'.

Chapter 19

The following days flew by, filled with rounds of pubs, the occasional stroll in the local park or the regular outings to the shops.

By now, Mr and Mrs D. had become well acquainted with John and Jack, so well in fact that when I first introduced the young men to my host family, it felt as if I were a daughter introducing her boyfriend to her parents. Mr and Mrs D. chatted with them and besieged them with questions, mostly to find out about the young men's background, just as caring parents would do. John seemed rather reticent to talk about his family, so Jack took over and boasted about the five uncles he had on his father's side. The verdict was that Mr and Mrs D. found them to be perfectly respectable young men whose company they could trust. So when they asked if I would not mind babysitting one evening, and I replied by asking: "Can I invite my friends?", they readily agreed.

As to be expected, the inevitable questions about our parents rose. I mumbled and fumbled awkwardly with words because quite frankly I was not willing to reveal the truth. There was no need. I wanted people to see me the way I was, i.e. ebullient, effervescent and vivacious, and not as a poor little orphan who had been rescued from Vietnam.

The final week drew to a close. Soon, we would be boarding the coach en route to Victoria Station. We made plans how to spend the last evening together and after a short sortie to the local pub, the four of us met up at John's house. We chatted about all sorts of things, the birds and the bees… but not the future. We talked about friends, school, college and life in general… except the future. And it made sense, for in the present, where Magali and I were firmly rooted, the future was too far, too distant, standing out like a surreal leap in time that we adamantly refused to take.

"I've got something important to tell you." Jack suddenly declared, "But I'll tell you tomorrow… at the station… just before you leave."

"Why? Why not now? Come on, tell me now." I insisted.

"No, tomorrow. I'll tell you tomorrow."

At eleven o'clock at night, rather unusually early for us, we asked the men to drive us home.

On the way back to Bracknell, the men decided to stop for fish and chips. We watched them stand in the queue, waving at us and mouthing words through the steamed-up shop window. Unable to decipher their muffled words, we decided to join them inside the shop.

"Better lock the doors!" Magali advised, pressing all the little knobs down. We entered the shop and joined the men in the queue. As we came out, John tried to open the driver's door and finding some unexpected resistance, looked quizzically at us.

"I've locked the doors!" Magali trumpeted.

"But the keys are still in the ignition!" John exclaimed.

"Oh no!" We screamed and giggled.

"Never mind," John sighed. "We'll eat the food and deal with the car later. It can't be that difficult to break into a car; there's one stolen every minute."

Reassured by his on-the-spot statistic, we ate our fish and chips in complete peace of mind, joked and bantered about Magali's bright ideas and listened to John declare in his usual cool:

"Don't worry, girls, we'll have you home in a jiffy. If all else fails, I'll just ring the AA."

"You're a member?" Jack enquired.

"No, but I'll soon be."

I turned towards Jack.

"What's ze AA?"

"It's a motoring organisation. If you break down, they come and rescue you."

"While we're waiting, perhaps you could tell me now what you wanted to tell me tomorrow…"

"No, I'd rather not. Just be patient; I'll tell you tomorrow."

Intrigued by all this secrecy, I scratched my head, racked my brain, went over the last twenty-four hours to see if I could pick up any clues that would give me a hint as to what important secret he was about to reveal.

Soon after, we watched the men walk around the car, tap the windows and search for a gap somewhere… anywhere.

"Break a window." Magali suggested.

"I don't want to do that. I've only just had the car back from the garage… and it's going to cost me more money to repair it. No, I'll go and make a phone call and see if I can find someone to come and help."

Upon which, he disappeared back inside the shop but they would not let him use the phone. Cursing under his breath, he set about to look for a phone box. A few minutes later, he returned with his head hanging low.

"I can't get hold of anyone, they're all out."

While the men pondered what to do next, we decided to have another look at the car, tried all the doors again and stepped back, feeling helpless and defeated.

It was now well past midnight. The shop assistants had long left and a few minutes later, the shop owner turned the lights out, locked the door and rolled down the metal shutters.

"Right," said John on a firm tone. "I'm going to phone the AA."

"But you're not a member," my companion pointed out.

"I know, but I've got to do something. We can't spend all night here."

"I'll never be able to get up tomorrow morning," I whinged.

"Don't worry," Jack riled. "You won't have to because at this rate, you probably won't have a chance to go to bed anyway."

"I'm tired." I whined again.

Jack drew me closer to him and insisted:

"Don't worry. We'll get you home before dawn."

"And anyway," Magali added in French, "we'll be able to sleep on the coach and on the train, so don't worry about it."

I knew that, and I was trying not to worry about it but I wanted to go home, to my bed and sleep so that I would be all refreshed to enjoy the journey. More than anything, I loved travelling. It was an urge to satisfy this insatiable thirst I had to explore a world that stood way beyond the hermetic perimeters of a boarding school stuck in the heart of the city with no greenery and no view. This is why I needed to be wide awake in order to absorb the Englishness of the scenery and the landscape. Otherwise, how else would I be able to relish the sights, the smells, the places that would add to the rich canvas on which I was busy weaving the tapestry of my life? That's why I wanted to go to bed. That's why I needed my sleep.

Finally, the AA man, our rescuer, our saviour, arrived. By now, it was three o'clock in the morning. Using a metal hanger in the shape of a hook, he prised it through the top of the window, caught the handle to wind down the window and created a gap wide enough to reach the key. Manoeuvring the hook carefully, he slowly prised the key out of the ignition and pulled it ever so gently through the window. As soon as the key was safely out, John grabbed it.

"Yeah! Yeah!" We screamed, followed by resounding "Hurray! Hurray!"

The AA man turned to John.

"Sir, may I suggest that you always carry one of these?" He said, showing him the twisted metal hanger.

"I might very well do that." John acquiesced. "Come on, everyone, in the car!"

During the short trip back home, Jack asked me at what time the coach was leaving.

"At eight o'clock," I replied. "From the Youth Club."

"Well, don't worry, we'll come and pick you up, so you won't miss your coach."

"Will you?"

"Yes, we will; in fact, we'll get as much sleep as you, because we've decided to sleep in the car, outside your house."

"Oh really?" I exclaimed, not knowing whether to believe him or not.

"Only joking! But we'll come and pick you up if you want to."

"Yes, I'd like zat."

Why did I ever doubt him? The following morning, the car pulled outside the front door. From my bedroom window, I could hear its little engine clicking away in the silent street. Mrs D. came and knocked on my door. She was in her dressing gown. I quickly got up and dressed, threw all my belongings inside the suitcase, sat on it to close it, lugged it down the stairs into the entrance hall and went into the kitchen.

"Would you like something to eat before you go? You've got time to grab a bowl of cereals."

"No sank you. I'll just 'ave an apple. 'ere's your key and sank you very

much for letting me come and stay 'ere…" Then, after a short pause I asked: *"Would I be able to come back?"*

"Yes, of course, but if you do come back next summer, we hope to see a little more of you."

I smiled at her remark. At that moment, the bouncy steps of Mr D. creaked down the stairs.

"You came back rather late last night. That was silly, with a long journey ahead of you. I don't know how you manage it."

"It's not my fault. We couldn't open ze car door. It was locked and ze key was inside ze car."

"Right, well, I'll get dressed and take you to the Youth Club."

A noisy crowd was already gathered outside the Youth Club. The first friend I spotted was Nadine.

"How's your old man?" I chuckled.

"Oh, he's not taking it well. He's drowning his sorrow in a glass of milk!" Nadine chortled back. At that moment, I spotted Sophie as she was getting out of a car.

"Hi, Sophie!"

"Hi!"

"Frank didn't come with you, then?"

"No, he's working."

"*Quel dommage*! Have you seen Magali?"

"Not yet."

"God, I hope she makes it. We had a rather unexpected late night, last night."

"Why, what happened?"

"I'll tell you on the train." I replied, craning my neck and searching for my friend.

Eventually, a Ford Anglia pulled up. I rushed to the car.

"Gosh! I really thought you were not going to make it."

"Come on, Martha, you know me, I don't need that much sleep. Is John there yet?"

"No, not yet. Do you think they meant it when they said they would follow the coach?"

"I don't know. They'll probably stay in bed and sleep all day."

"Yeah, that's what I thought."

Just as we had given up on them, a little blue Mini screeched to a stop.

"Magali! They're here!"

The two men got out of the car. We rushed to greet them and stayed with them until it was time to go.

When the time came to board the coach, Magali and I rushed in to secure the back row so that, from the high seats, we would be able to wave, send kisses and sweet messages to our men cramped all the way down in their little mini. On the journey, we lost them a few times at junctions, traffic lights and roundabouts but every time, they managed to rejoin us with a big smile on their faces as we continued to wave at them and kiss them through the back window.

Victoria Station. How exciting. The hustle and bustle of airports and train stations always made me dream.

Inside the coach, the leader grabbed the microphone.

"All right, everybody. Here we are at Victoria Station. I hope you've all had an excellent holiday. I know that some of you have been extremely busy getting to know the locals **rather** too well, but I hope that somehow, you've found the time to improve your English. Make sure you do not leave any of your belongings on the coach and I hope to see you again next summer. Now, can I remind everyone to have your tickets ready with your passports or identity cards… And please, stay together because from now on, you're on your own and I don't want anybody to miss the train."

After which, the leader quickly disappeared inside the station to find out which platform we should aim for while we stayed behind, on the pavement, labouring on with our heavy suitcases.

"Can you see them?" Magali asked.

"No. Do you think they've got lost?"

"Surely not."

"But… did they actually say that they would meet us at the station?"

"They said they might."

All the while, our heads kept jerking around the four corners of the station, hoping to catch sight of the men. An uncontrollable shiver ran through my entire body, and I did not know whether this was due to the sudden drop in temperature inside the station or some other feeling I could not identify. Suddenly, Magali shouted:

"Here they are! I knew they'd come!"

We stopped dead in our tracks and waited for the men to catch up with us.

"Where have you been?" I immediately chided.

"We had to find somewhere to park the car." Jack explained, visibly anxious to reassure me.

We fell into a warm embrace, but did not kiss – not in public! Jack kept saying – and stayed locked together for a few minutes, until Magali urged:

"Come on, Martha, we've got to go."

So, Magali and I picked up our suitcases and it is at that precise moment that Jack grabbed my arm. I immediately called out to Magali who was already marching ahead.

"No!" Jack pleaded. "I want to speak to you on your own."

I looked at him, more intrigued than ever.

"You know the other day… I said that I had something important to tell you… Well, you know … if the two of us get on well… perhaps we could continue to see each other and perhaps… stay together."

I was stunned. Was my fragmented English conveying the correct message? Had I heard all the words and captured their proper meaning? Was he really asking me to…?"

Noticing my intrigued look, he added almost in a whisper:

"What I mean is… perhaps we could get engaged and…."

"What?!!!"

I was shocked, so shocked that I burst out laughing and called out to my friend.

"Magali! Guess what!"

But Jack immediately pulled me closer to him and pleaded:

"No, please, don't tell her. Don't tell anyone. Let it be a secret… our secret."

I looked back at him, still in shock. His face had a tender look that begged me to remain silent.

"All right," I agreed. "It will be our secret."

"Come on, Martha, we've got to go!" Magali shouted.

At last, we parted and as I made my way towards the train, trudging my heavy suitcase, I kept turning back to look at his forlorn face, at his arm waving sadly in the distance and I waved back, smiling at him and sending millions of kisses.

Inside the compartment, Magali and I settled around a table by the window. I wanted to tell her the news but I had given my promise.

"Come on, Martha, you can tell me. What did he say?"

"I promised not to tell." I replied, trying to look as detached and indifferent as I could.

But inside I was panicking. In my inexperience and naivety, I had never considered the fact that a relationship may have a beginning... which could very well lead to... eternity.

Bloody hell! I thought. All I wanted was a free drink!

Chapter 20

I returned to Paris and to the godmother's empty apartment. On the other side of Paris loomed the staid atmosphere and dull colours of an institution where music and laughter were banned, where posters representing anything other than a religious icon were torn off the walls, where the stifling silence was only interrupted by the monotonous drone of nuns at prayers filtering through the cold stone walls.

Thankfully, the godmother was often out and school had not yet started so I put some music on and let myself float through delectable sensations and emotions stirred up by the big hits of that summer: '*I'm still waiting*' by Diana Ross or '*Maggie May*' by Rod Stewart.

As I reflected upon love, life and destiny, I began to discern the making of a path, though as yet undetermined and still too blurred for me to be able to see what the future held for me. Not that it worried me too much. As far as I was concerned, the present was the most wonderful era purely dedicated to the insouciance and effervescence of youth. What's more, totally free from the tight reins of parental or adult authority, my friends and I enjoyed an independence and freedom rarely bestowed on adolescents growing up in the heart of Paris. Footloose and fancy free, we stumbled into the riotous 70s' determined to enjoy every bit of it; and with a dedicated hedonist like Magali, I was in good company.

Back in our respective abodes - Magali with Madame Garrier and I with the godmother - we kept in touch by telephone and met up almost every weekend.

Sophie began to join in.

At school, I had now joined the senior section though, before being allowed in, the head teacher, the acerbic Sister Marie-Cécile, made me sign a contract in which I vouched to behave myself (*what do you mean?*),

162

obey the rules (*what rules?*) and do as I was told (*like learning stupid pages by heart?*). Having been forced to choose a career path that conflicted with my own wishes and aspirations – Accountancy is for people who live in the real world, not for dreamers – I had to resign myself to sit through classes where on the blackboard teachers drew T-shaped transactions, commercial graphs and diagrams, and wrestled with complicated equations invented to analyse company curves meandering through a vast grid of carefully calculated percentages. We handled counterfeit money, dealt with faked documents and faked cheques, and created faked bank accounts with outrageous overdrafts. We happily settled fictitious bills and gladly accepted dubious remittances. All these varied and tedious tasks were performed with alacrity and with a certain degree of resilience mixed with our typical brand of juvenile humour, but inside, my head was sizzling with anger and frustration. These were dangerous times when the whims and caprices of youth roared with confidence, leapt with both feet into conflicts and clashed head-on with any figure of authority. Often, parents or guardians, weighed down by their heavy baggage of experience and wisdom, flailed their arms in despair wondering how to tame the wild spirit, how to approach and cajole the rebellious mind in order to reach a subdued compromise.

Ever since discovering that, because of my destitute state, I was 'unpunishable' – since I had nothing, nothing could ever be taken away from me – I had developed the mind of a warrior: I was untouchable, better still I was invincible. That may be so but I was in no mood to misbehave. My head was swooning with too many happy memories. As such, I spent most of my time floating in my dream bubble well above the real world while adults were pulling the strings to bring me back to earth. How dare they?! From then on, I adopted the countenance of an impenetrable brick wall with my eyes firing deadly sparks, should anyone say as much as 'hello' to me without asking permission first. I was so incensed by the way adults had decided on my future that any attempt to communicate became a confrontation that soon escalated into an irresolvable conflict. These were difficult times, especially for my teachers who often had to consult with Madame Chauvineau to try and work out how to deal with me. They did not want me in their school, I did not want to be there, but Madame

Chauvineau was still holding on to the reins tightly, doing an expert job at keeping all the key players staying together.

Fortunately, I was often able to escape to the smooth waters of friendship for I had reconnected with Martine. How different she seemed since our 'casino' days, as she appeared more serious, more reflective and far more mature than me. She had even lost that mischievous spark that had first drawn us together. We never played poker again and instead, indulged freely in literary and philosophical discussions brought on by the books she had to study for the French *Baccalaureat*.

"Have you read *'Candide'*?" She once asked.

"No." I replied, getting ready to deliberate the author's worthiness as one of the greatest philosophers ever to have graced the soil of France. Voltaire, my man, my cynical friend who had decreed that *'it is better to be hated than ignored'*, and who had teased my good humour more than once with his perspicacious quotes and sharp words. I readily embraced his quirky philosophy with the eye of a shrewd opportunist who would rather use his wisdom as a weapon than a dull form of erudition, for I had always suspected that our great Man of Letters was having us on. Once I had read his tale of eternal optimism, my suspicions were confirmed. While Molière wrote farces to mock the *Bourgeoisie*, Voltaire wrote comical dramas disguised as 'œuvres philosophiques'. What a let on! And I loved him for it, for his sheer intellectual audacity, for his staggering pedantic pomposity, for his amazing ability to make us laugh while laying bare the tragedies of life… and also for the fact that he did not like Shakespeare, calling him a 'charlatan!'. *'All is well in the best of all worlds'*, he kept declaiming in his usual lofty manner after having tortured and butchered everyone in *'Candide'*. What a tease! What a man!

At weekends, Magali and I had a very set routine. Saturday night was usually spent at *The Palladium*, a disco in the Latin Quarters where my friend had managed to wrangle up free entries by flirting outrageously with the doorman, and free drinks by using the same ruthless ploy with a love struck barman. Many a time, the two of us turned up to her romantic rendezvous with various barmen, waiters and even the odd American tourist she had collected along the way.

Very reluctantly, Sophie would sometimes join in, mainly because we refused to hear which part of NO she meant. Her surly and complex temperament did not quite fit in with our exuberant nature but, determined as we were to cheer her up with the brash sound and crazy beat of 70s'pop music, we dragged her along by the arms and by her feet suspended high on platform shoes.

Her parents had the good fortune to own a country residence on the outskirt of Paris, and on the few occasions we were not in the mood to jiggle at *The Palladium*, we would descend on her, laden with the latest pop records and cigarettes.

Arriving at her house, our first priority was to raid the fridge where Sophie's step-mother had left some palatable treats knowing that we would be visiting. Later on, orange tea leaves were vigorously stirred and served in dainty porcelain cups.

While all three of us lay in front of the ornate fireplace in the lounge, the soulful sound of records like '*Papa was a Rolling Stone*' by the Temptations brought back memories of our trip to England which had seen us transformed from young girls into young women.

Sophie looked forlorn.

"Sophie, why don't you get yourself a boyfriend who lives here? Come on. Next time we go to *The Palladium*, you'll have to come with us!"

"Oh, I don't know that I want to…" Sophie sighed.

"We're not asking you, we're telling you even if it means we have to drag you there!" Magali insisted.

"But I might not be in the mood…"

"Trust me, with us for company, you'll soon be, won't she, Martha?"

"Of course, you will. You don't have to do anything you don't want to but you know… just listen to the music; it's great music, that'll cheer you up."

And so we did. The first time we went as a trio, we ended up with some young dudes who claimed to be a pop band on the line of Pink Floyd. Chat-up lines were becoming more and more sophisticated. Of course we did not believe them. However, keen to prove their musical status, they took us back to their house after the disco, somewhere in the suburb. If I did not know what 'minimalism' was, I soon discovered it here in their lounge which was sparsely furnished with white furniture arranged around a black-lacquered grand piano standing supreme in the middle of the vast room. Two electric guitars were propped up against the white wall right next to the large French windows.

"Do you want us to play one of our songs?" Magali's suitor asked.

"No," we all cried out at once. "We're too tired. We want to go to bed."

It was four o'clock in the morning and dawn was breaking.

The following morning, having quite forgotten the previous night's antics, I woke up not knowing where I was, in a strange bed with a young man smiling at me.

"How did you sleep?" He asked softly.

"Like a log." I replied, smiling back at him.

"You look amazingly beautiful first thing in the morning." He said.

I peered at him incredulously through my myopic gaze, put his remark down to another chat-up line and smiled.

Noises from the kitchen made me want to get up. I was about to call my new friend when I suddenly realised that I could not remember his name.

"Er..." I began.

"Yes?"

I started to giggle with embarrassment.

"I'm sorry... I can't remember your name."

"My name? George."

"Right, George. Let's go for breakfast, I'm starving."

"Breakfast? You don't want breakfast now, it's gone midday."

"Is it? Well, whatever, I'll eat anything, I'm starving."

When I finally made it downstairs, Sophie was already there, bright eye and bushy-tail.

"Gosh, Sophie, how do you do it?" I exclaimed before asking: "Is there anything to eat?"

"Not much. Typical bachelor's pad. There's some cereals."

"Yuk, I don't like milk. By the way, whose house is this?"

"Don't know."

At this moment, Magali appeared in the doorframe wearing a man's shirt.

"Hi!" She greeted, trying to flatten her hirsute mop of hair. "Is there any coffee?"

"I'm boiling some water." Sophie replied, looking terribly organised.

"Good morning, girls!" A cheerful voice hailed. "Or should I say 'good afternoon'!"

It was Magali's companion.

"Patrick, have you got any food?"

"Well, let's see." He replied, going straight for the fridge. "We've got eggs, bacon; you like that kind of stuff? Very English…"

"We know," Magali giggled. "We've been there… several times."

"Ah! What's cooking?" George asked as he entered the kitchen.

"Bacon and eggs. Have you got anything else?" Patrick enquired.

"Let me have a look in the cupboard."

"Where's the other one?" Magali asked.

Patrick looked puzzled.

"You mean Jean-Claude? Where are you, Jean-Claude?" He shouted.

"In the lounge! I'm going through the music sheets."

Patrick turned towards Magali and relayed:

"He's in the lounge, already working… and on a Sunday!"

"So, you really are a band?" She questioned again.

"Of course we are. We're not well-known yet because we've only just started, but one day, we'll be the biggest band in France."

"Wow!" We exclaimed altogether, rather incredulously.

George stood behind me stroking my long hair.

"What's the plan for this afternoon?"

"Well, we have to go home soon." I said.

"Would you like to hear one of our songs?"

Simultaneously, Magali cried out "No!" as I shouted "Yes!"

The men laughed.

"Come on, Magali, we've got to hear at least one song." I said.

"After breakfast, then. I've got a sore head" She decreed.

So, after breakfast, Jean-Claude sat at the piano while Patrick and George grabbed a guitar each.

"Who's the singer?" I asked.

"It varies, but for this song, it's me." George replied.

We settled ourselves on the leather sofa, lit up a cigarette and sat back to listen to the music. It was modern and pleasant to the ear, more of a romantic ballad than a pop song. At the end of the song, we nodded appreciatively but Magali could not wait to move on. Cutting short any discussion about the musical merits, she asked, quite abruptly I thought, if any of them could drive us to the nearest metro station. George volunteered but before we left, they made sure that we had their names and telephone number. However, the spirit of youth is fickle and we parted, not entirely convinced that we wanted to see them again.

As often happened, we ended up strolling along the Champs Elysées, shared a banana split at the Wimpy - the only place where we could afford to eat - and finally went home.

The godmother came to greet me at the door.

"Did you have a nice time at Sophie's?"

"Yes, although we spent most of our time trying to cheer her up."

"What a shame… Anyway, have you done your homework?"

Chapter 21

My new boarding school was slowly growing on me. With only twenty four of us, the atmosphere in the boarding house itself was somewhat relaxed. Mademoiselle Marie-Chantal, the supervisor, was a brainy student who studied some brainy subject. She was tall and lanky, skinny even, rather gentle in her manner and very softly spoken. To wake us up in the morning, she would put a record on. Classical music was not exactly to our taste so we asked if we could choose something else. When it was my turn to choose, I would pick 'Puppy Love' by Donny Osmond or 'Mamy Blue' by the Pop Tops.

For a long time I believed that any kind of friendship should remain exclusive. Now I was making friends with girls who, in my awakening mind, had a higher intellectual level than me, which allowed us to bond over a book or discuss philosophical essays – Philosophy was a compulsory subject in the Baccalaureate stream – while dissecting with avid interest the exact nature of the relationship between Mlle Marie-Chantal and Sister Marie-Cécile.

I did not know what was going on and quite frankly I was not interested, though one day I had to sneak back into the dormitory as I had forgotten my PE kit. Just as I entered the main corridor, Sister Marie-Cecile came out of Mlle Marie-Chantal's bedroom. Oh God, I thought, I'm in trouble again. I stood at the door waiting for the usual volley of reprimands. However, to my complete surprise, it was **her** who started reeling out reasons why she should be coming out of Mlle Marie-Chantal's bedroom in the middle of the afternoon. Without saying a word, I scurried off to my room keeping my head down, grabbed my bag and quickly left before it dawned on her that *I* was also in the wrong place at the wrong time.

In this new boarding-house, two friends stood out, Francine and

Yvette, for, like me, they were passionate about books. Literature opened our minds to the different levels of friendships and, inevitably, to those of love. Through it, we discovered that men, quite unlike the primitive and uncouth specimen portrayed in Natural History Museums, were perfectly capable of beautiful, refine and noble sentiments. Hence, with the purity and innocence of mind that still existed in our teenage years, we studied in awe the close bond between Alexandre and George in "*Les Amitiés Particulières*", the passion of Jean-Christophe for Oliver in the trilogy "*Jean-Christophe*", the love between brother and sister in "*Les Enfants Terribles*", and the tormented idyll of Verlaine for the fickle and insouciant Rimbaud, all of whom suffered the same agony and pain caused by the unrequited love we encountered in "*Le Rouge et le Noir*", "*El Cid*", "*La Chartreuse de Parme*", or "*Les souffrances du jeune Werter*".

Through Literature, I was beginning to understand what happened to me in that beautiful corner of Bavaria… but not how. In the past, a sense of complete control over my emotions had earned me a reputation for being aloof, distant, indifferent and even cold as a stone. Now, my heart was in complete disarray. For the first time in my life, I was no longer in control and just like an alchemist frantically searches for the magic recipe to make gold, I wanted to seize, dissect and take control of each wonderful vibe that reverberated through my entire body, unaware that I was trying to connect to the physical plane an ethereal realm which did not exist beyond the basic level of human consciousness. I was completely lost, totally confused… but deliciously so.

And so it was that Martine, Francine, Yvette and I spent many happy hours discussing love and lovers. Johan was still the exclusive love allowed inside my invisible bubble but as I discovered more and more divine beings, my precious bubble expanded and got more crowded by the day. Writers, composers and pop icons were happily and merrily mixing together. Beside Johan, Voltaire, Rousseau, Hugo, Dickens, Balzac and Emile Zola, I now had for company the Beatles, Pink Floyd, Simon & Garfunkel, the Bee Gees, James Taylor, Carol King and later Carly Simon. I also had to include Dusty Springfield, not simply because I adored her soft and husky voice, especially when she sang 'Some of Your Loving', but also because she had a schoolgirl crush on Carly Simon.

Incidentally, in the matters of love, my dear friends showed a particular interest in my own affairs. And so it was that one day, I found Francine and Yvette milling at the back of the classroom. They looked as if they were plotting something, and sure enough, as soon as I entered the classroom, they hit me with the question:

"Bertrand! Are you a virgin?"

What?!!!

I stared back at them, shocked by the directness of their question. In that awkward moment, I think I would have preferred to discuss the metaphysical relativity between consciousness and the conscious mind.

Anyhow, quite apart from our literary, musical and metaphysical discussions, we were developing an keen curiosity in the occult, despite the fact that none of us believed in ghosts. As for the perennial question whether there was life after death, this particular conundrum was far too advanced for me. If there existed a metaphysical link between life and death, I had not as yet grasped it as I perceived my own existence as an existential entity moving inexorably along a very palpable timeline called 'the present'. No newspaper reports could convince us of the existence of nebulous or vaporous spectres floating in mid-air, intent on scaring the hell out of unsuspecting onlookers, without providing us with some kind of tangible proof. We wanted to 'see' before we could believe.

It is in this frame of mind that one winter night, Francine, Yvette, Martine, Marigard and myself ordered all the boarders to vacate the study room so as to allow us to perform a 'séance'. All the girls filed out obediently and quietly … except one.

"I'm not going." Marlene protested. "I haven't finished my homework."

"We won't be long." We assured her.

"I've got an essay to write. I'm in mid-sentence. I can't go right now."

We all looked at each other.

"We've got to do it tonight." Martine whispered. "There's a full moon."

Suddenly, Marigard came up with an idea. She turned towards Marlene.

"I've got a pair of special glasses you could borrow. There's no lens but they have lights on either side of the frame which means you'll be able to carry on with your homework in the dark if you like. Would you like to borrow them?"

Marlene looked incredulous. After a short pause she sighed.

"All right."

Swift as the wind, Marigard returned with the special frame, gave them to Marlene and went to switch the main lights off.

"Have you got them on?" She asked, her deep voice resounding in the depth of darkness. "The little switch is on the right hand side."

Almost instantly, two globular eyes pierced through the darkness and directed its blinding rays straight at us.

Satisfied with its brightness, Marlene resumed her homework while we, the amateur spiritualists, settled around a table, joined fingers, closed our eyes and began calling out the spirit of Sister Marguerite, the nun in charge of the laundry who had departed the previous year.

The silence prevailed. Holding our breath, we listened out for the faintest sign of the invisible soul breathing out some message from beyond the grave. But none came. After numerous attempts, Marigard opened her eyes and instantly froze in her chair. There, right in front of her, two bright eyes were staring straight back at her. A loud piercing shriek tore through the air. She pushed the table and ran out of the room. Panic-stricken, we all stood up and scrambled as fast as we could out of the door, screaming. None of us had any idea what terrified Marigard but no one had any intention to peer in the dark to find out.

At that very moment, Sister Marie-Cecile appeared down the corridor. She stared at us, aghast, trying to understand the cause of our fits of laughter. Swiftly, she rushed towards the study room, switched the lights on, and gasped, horrified, as she surveyed a scene of complete devastation with chairs upturned and the table on its side.

"What on earth were you doing... in the DARK?!"

Only one girl was in a fit enough state to answer that question. Alas, Marlene remained steadfastly glued to her chair, totally rigid and looking rather shell-shocked as she slowly pointed the searing light beams... straight at the nun!

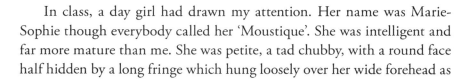

In class, a day girl had drawn my attention. Her name was Marie-Sophie though everybody called her 'Moustique'. She was intelligent and far more mature than me. She was petite, a tad chubby, with a round face half hidden by a long fringe which hung loosely over her wide forehead as if she were trying to hide her sharp intellect. At first, I kept my distance, feeling unable to compete with her. I was quite content simply to admire her from my seat and observe in total admiration the way she put teachers on the spot if she detected the slightest weakness or flaw in any of their theories or thoughts. Although I wanted to, I could not bring myself to approach her. I was in such awe. Then one day, in the playground…

"Hi Martha!"

I turned around. It was Moustique.

"Hi!" I replied, desperately trying to look as cool and detached as I could, while inside feeling mightily flattered that she had at last acknowledged me.

She wanted my opinion on some topic we had discussed in class. As we talked, we felt an instant connection which made us both wonder why we had waited so long to become friends.

Then, totally out of the blue, she declared:

"You know, I hated you at first."

"Really? Why?!" I was dumbfounded.

"Because you're better than me in French."

"What!" I exclaimed, somewhat shocked. "**You're** better than me! Your essays are far more intellectual and mature than mine."

"I don't know about that… but you have a really nice style… yes, I like your style."

If the path of our new friendship began to run smoothly, it soon rang alarm bells with the authorities. Sister Marie-Cécile, who could not conciliate the sight of a good student mixing with the most notorious rebel she had ever known, was determined to avert an imminent disaster. She contacted Moustique's parents.

"What did your parents say?" I enquired eagerly, feeling more anxious than I cared to admit.

"They just laughed! I mean… they know me and they trust me so if I tell them that you're not like that, they're more likely to believe **me** than a bloody interfering nun. In fact, they want you to come and visit."

"Oh really? I'd like that."

In the eyes of some, or the deranged mind of a sexually obsessed nun, our friendship had reached the intensity of inseparable lovers. When both Moustique and I happened to miss school on the same day – I do not know where my friend was but I, for one, was at a Modern Art Exhibition at the *"Grand Palais"* – Sister Marie-Cecile put two and two together and came up with… two.

The following day, we were summoned by Mme Garband, the school secretary who was also in charge of detention.

"Mademoiselle Bertrand, you're in trouble again! Where were you, you two, yesterday?"

Moustique and I looked at each other and burst out laughing. Finally, having composed herself first, my friend began to protest vehemently.

"Why does everybody automatically assume that, because we happen to be missing class on the same day, we're bound to be together?"

Mme Garband shrugged her shoulders and gave us a resigned look as if to say: 'sorry, I'm only doing my job', before writing our names on the detention list. There was nothing remotely mean, nasty or vindictive about this lady *"d'un certain age"*. She was the most docile of creatures who had the great misfortune to work for a big bad wolf disguised as a nun and we respected her hugely for it.

Needless to say, the reviled nun never had a hold on us and together we solidly remained. Occasionally, I would spend the weekend with Moustique. Despite having sworn that I would never ever go for a walk again in my entire life, we went for extended strolls in the woods of Fontainebleau. There, we organised picnics, fed the ducks and lay on the grass discussing the conceptual symbiosis of love and friendship; and as I listened to the fresh green leaves shimmering above our heads and gazed at the white clouds rushing through the clear blue sky, I suddenly realised that for the first time ever, I had found someone with whom I could connect, someone who had a great sense of fun but who could challenge me intellectually like no one else had ever done before. Relying on an unadulterated wisdom mostly acquired outside school, we discussed anything, from the meaning of life to the astounding music of Pink Floyd. We pondered about love, unaware that through our deep friendship we had already sown the seeds of love. Yet, despite our deep soul-searching conversations, we did not take ourselves too seriously. What's more, we knew that we were living the best years of our lives and were determined to make the most of them. Viewing the adult world with Voltaire's cynical eyes, we readily adopted his outlandish sophism: *all is well in the best of all worlds*, because, as far as we were concerned, it was the truth, the only truth.

Our conversations revealed that Moustique had a bohemian soul, open-minded and open-hearted. She had the courage to speak out in the face of injustice, even if it meant clashing head on with Sister Marie-Cécile – often to defend me.

And so it was that one day, the whole class returned late from the lunch break. Intent on lighting up the sombre atmosphere of a cold establishment, we hummed the Pink Panther tune as we wounded our way up to the top floor. As we sat at our desks in hysterics with the teacher frantically trying to restore some order in the class, Sister Marie-Cécile suddenly burst in and thundered: "Mademoiselle Bertrand, you will be punished for this!". Instantly, the classroom erupted with a loud and sustained 'boo!' that forced the nun to beat a hasty retreat. A resounding 'Hurray!' punctuated her swift departure.

Moustique was the most loyal and wonderful friend anyone could have wished to have. Unfortunately, having been a free agent for the best part of my life, I was beginning to struggle with the demands of a close friendship. Of all my childhood friends, she was the one I would have loved to keep. After an ardent friendship during which we practically behaved like twins but which I found increasingly stifling, it became almost inevitable that we should end up losing each other. It happened after we left school and despite my longing to re-connect those indelible ties that crossed and criss-crossed our hearts, they finally gave way, eroded to the core by the fickleness of time, by too many imponderables and by an insurmountable obstacle called 'adulthood'.

Chapter 22

At the end of my two years at the *lycée*, we took our vocational exams. I knew I had done well because my favourite topic came up and when we asked for the answer to our teacher, I had the very same result than she had. Nevertheless, when the time came to go and get my results, I was so nervous that Martine volunteered to come with me. When we reached the entrance hall of the school, a thick crowd of overexcited pupils were already pressing hard against the notice board frantically searching for their names. I could not get anywhere near it. Fortunately, Martine managed to wriggle herself to the front and soon shouted.

"Martha! Martha! Your name's there! You've passed!"

"Have I?" I exclaimed, unable to believe her at first. "Are you sure?"

"Yes," she replied, pointing at a dark line on the notice board, "it's right there… Can you see?"

"Yes, I see it!" I shouted back, although all I could see were short black lines going up and down several pages, but Martine was quite adamant that my name was right there where her finger pointed, so I rushed back to school to spread the news. There, I shouted to Madame Garband, the receptionist, "I've passed!", to which she replied with a wry smile: "Well, Mademoiselle Bertrand, I don't believe it! How on earth did you manage that?".

Sister Marie-Cécile, who had left the door of her office open because of the summer heat, caught sight of me, shook her head in complete disbelief and riled:

"Mademoiselle Bertrand… you don't deserve it."

I threw my head back, looked at her in sheer defiance and smirked at her pointless remark.

My next stop was *rue Washington* for I knew exactly what I wanted to do. Contrary to Madame Chauvineau's plans, I did not want to leave school, I was far too happy there. And by passing this exam, I had earned my reprieve; I had proven that I was worthy enough to join the Baccalaureat stream.

———————◆⟐◆———————

Madame Chauvineau looked at me, incredulous.

"So you've passed! Well I am surprised…"

"And you said…"

"I know what I said…" She interrupted curtly. "I suppose I have to give it to you, haven't I? So you're quite happy to continue with your studies despite the fact that, as you put it, you hate accountancy?"

"Yes, I want to study for the Baccalaureat."

"Very well. A promise is a promise. I'll put your name down for next term, but on the condition that Sister Marie-Cécile will have you back."

To my complete surprise, the head teacher did accept me back and this time, unconditionally. Joining our class was a young nun in her mid 20s' who, like us, was studying for the Baccalaureat. As to be expected, I picked a desk as far away from her as the size of the classroom would allow.

"No, Mlle Bertrand." The teacher called out. "I'd like you to sit next to Sister Veronique."

What!? I was horrified. What was the school trying to do? Turn me into a nun? Reluctantly, I dragged my feet and schoolbag toward the appointed desk. I sat down, huffing and puffing, making sure that everyone knew how I felt. However, during lessons, I would occasionally slide furtive looks at the nun, usually when she was absorbed in some accountancy exercise, to study her features, scrutinise her face and perhaps even catch a glimpse of her soul. What made her give up her life for God, I wondered? She was so pretty with clear blue eyes that looked straight at you and melted instantly any lurking rebellious streak.

The teacher who insisted that I share a desk with Sister Veronique was a man, possibly in his late thirties, called Mr Grivard. He was the very first male teacher I had ever encountered and… in my considered opinion, not a prime candidate for reproductive purposes which, in an entirely female environment, was a blessing for us all. He had none of the chic normally associated with your standard French citizen, and lacked the finesse and elegance of a man keen to make a good impression on impressionable young girls. His suits were invariably a size too small for him, exposing well-worn socks which did not always match. If he did not have time to grab last week's handkerchief, he would turn towards the wall to sneeze and splatter his germs all over the blackboard which invariably sent us in heaps of laughter.

On the odd occasion when he did turn up in a rather smart suit, we would greet him with wolf whistles and sycophantic words of admiration.

"Wow! Sir! You look grand!"

"Sir! Have you got a new girlfriend?"

"Sir! You're not going for an interview, are you? We'd hate to lose you."

"Sir! What aftershave is that? Did your girlfriend buy it for you?"

All our remarks were received with his usual good humour for Mr Grivard was the most affable teacher I had ever come across, blessed with the patience of a saint and a splendid sense of humour, always responding to our relentless teasing with a quirky smile and the occasional well measured repartee. And boy did he need them! Having to wrestle on a daily basis with the original bunch of St Trinian's girls, he often had to think fast in order to rein in gently over-excited girls who were more interested in his love life than the manufacturing cost of a loaf of bread. Unfortunately for him, the effervescence of youth is almost impossible to tame. Blythe spirits were already plotting their next mischief. And so it was that one day, Elizabeth, who could have been mistaken for Jane Birkin's sister, so naturally beautiful she was, turned up in class with pages of naked men which she waved around the classroom before surreptitiously slipping them inside Sister Veronique's folder during morning break. Acting to perfection the old adage: 'see nothing, hear nothing, say nothing', we waited with bated breath for the young nun's reaction. There was none. Absolutely none. Needless to say, we were all mightily disappointed.

"Did she actually look at them?" Virginie asked on our way to the gym.

"I don't know. I didn't dare look." I replied truthfully, feeling slightly embarrassed by the whole episode.

We never found out what Sister Veronique did with the naughty pictures. And please, don't ask me! We only shared a desk, not the confessional!

After another morning break, Mr Grivard arrived in the classroom.

As usual, we welcomed him with teasing remarks about his appearance. He smiled. As he shook his bag to retrieve his notes, he took out a pencil case and books and lay them on his desk in front of him. He looked mildly puzzled.

"Who do these belong to?" He queried on the same tone as if he had asked: "What's the name of the river that flows through Heidelberg?"

The class fell silent. Someone glanced at Elizabeth.

"How should I know?" She protested. "They're not mine."

Next to me, Sister Veronique was wringing her hands and blushing… but she remained silent. At that particular moment, I turned towards her and felt her acute embarrassment. So I got up, went to the teacher's desk, grabbed the young nun's belongings and returned them to her without uttering a word. Without further ado, the lesson began.

Mr Grivard, we subsequently discovered, was a romantic at heart. One day, he revealed, almost like a boast, that he was particularly keen on poetry. To my dismay, Francine hailed:

"Martha's keen on poetry too!"

From then on, Mr Grivard would find any excuse to keep me after class. I only had to yawn to be told I had to stay on after school. During those exclusive moments, while I performed some futile exercise on the blackboard, the teacher would scan my body with the minutiae of an MR scan machine. I could feel his gaze sear a trail from the top of my left shoulder, slowly penetrating the well-defined contours of the upper body, caressing with his eyes the smooth rounded form of my breasts, before lingering further down wherever his imagination took him. Then, in a perfectly composed manner, he would cross his legs and start a discussion on some poem he had read, eager to hear my opinion. I was quite amused by his little games, almost enjoying the ephemeral status of an exquisite "objet d'art", i.e. free to be admired… but not to be touched.

Chapter 23

For some time, there had been rumours that the government wanted to wind down the F.O.E.F.I. The treaty of Geneva was coming to an end and quite besides being cute little orphans along with the unfair special treatment we had been given over French children from poor families, our upbringing was costing them a fortune. So, someone made the decision that from now on, during school holidays, we would have to work. Having become used to a privileged lifestyle, the news horrified us.

The news was confirmed on my next trip to *rue Washington*.

"No," Madame Chauvineau started. "You're not going back to England. It will be useful for you to get a summer job. It'll give you a sense of responsibility and help you mature a bit… I hope. So, when you return from Spain, I'm sending you to a *colonie de vacances* on the coast of Normandie, you'll be a supervisor there in a nice summer camp not far from the beach…"

"But I don't want to go there!" I interrupted.

Totally ignoring my outcry, the social worker continued on a neutral tone:

"Most of the children there are from the *Assistance Publique*, so you'll be able to relate to them…"

"I don't want to go! I want to go back to England to improve my English!"

"That's so typical of you. You are such a selfish girl! You only think about yourself. Well, it'll do you good to think of someone else for a change. So, you're going and that's that!"

"OK. If I go to that *colonie de vacances* and I get a good report, can I go to England during the Easter holiday, then?"

"I don't know… We'll have to see. I'd rather deal with one thing at a time…"

"The English family wants me to go back." I interrupted again. "If they write to you, will I be allowed to go?"

"I don't know… We'll have to see. As I said, I prefer to deal with one thing at a time, so we'll see how it goes and then maybe, *if* you get a good report from the Mother Superior…"

"What!" I blurted out, horrified. "The summer camp is run by nuns!"

I let out a huge exasperated sigh, crossed my arms across my chest, tapped my foot on the floor and refused to listen anymore.

"There's no need to get all upset. I'm doing this for you, you know."

I stared back at her with a straight penetrating glare that left her in no doubt as to what I was thinking.

"After all," she bluffed. "Didn't you once say that you wanted to be a skiing instructor? You love skiing, don't you? Well, you won't be able to be a skiing instructor if you've had no pedagogical experience…"

I knew straight away that it was a ruse to bring me around, but not being entirely au fait with the exact qualifications required to be a skiing instructor, her argument began to sway me more than I expected.

"All right, then. As long as I can go to England at Easter…"

Madame Chauvineau breathed a huge sigh of relief.

"Believe me," she went on. "It's going to be an excellent experience for you."

Unconvinced, I turned my heels and left abruptly, muttering to myself that if they expected me to go to church, they had another thing coming. I ranted and cursed under my breath but at least I was going to Spain first.

Chapter 24

As always, we met up in the lounge of *la fédé*. By now I knew most of the girls. The first face I always looked out for was that of Marie-France. Sitting on the armrest of one of the armchairs, she flicked back her unruly mop of straight black hair to reveal a moon face beaming with a permanent cheeky smile. Her overflowing youthful effervescence never failed to cheer me up. Then, in amongst the others, there was Marie-Jeanne, unusually tall for a Vietnamese girl, sitting in her corner, knees together, quiet and reserved. Not far from her, on the sofa, Claudette was busy holding counsel with a small posse of younger girls sitting on the edge of their seats and listening to her every word. With her angular and masculine features, her hair cropped to the roots and her general countenance of a cowboy looking for a fight, she could easily have been mistaken for a ruthless thug. But we all knew that, underneath that John Wayne's drawl, there was an ultra sensitive soul, soft and gentle and always on the lookout for someone in need of help. Over there, in the other armchair, Claire, an acquaintance from the orphanage, was sitting like a queen in waiting. If anybody had the gall to ask her about that dreaded place, she would instantly stiffen up and clam up, as if some invisible shutters had suddenly slammed down. As the onlooker stared back in fear of having stirred troubled waters, she would declare quite flatly: "I don't remember anything!". With Claire, just like with Nadine, our relationship was strained, marred by memories that we all wanted to erase, obliterate and send to oblivion. Unfortunately, with each one of us standing as a painful reminder of those terrible days, it was hardly surprising that we should not be able to enjoy each other's company.

Apparently, Michèle was there too but she had changed beyond recognition and I did not recognise her.

After the initial greetings, we quickly got on to the more important

182

business of finding out who was going where. Marie-France and I sighed in despair as we discovered that, yet again, we would not be travelling together.

"I thought you were going to ask Chauvinette." She whined.

"You know I can't ask her anything. The witch can't stand me!"

"You just don't know how to go about it. You need to do a bit of crawling… and a bit of grovelling…"

Me? Get off my pedestal and grovel? Sorry, the jump was simply too high. Soon, the banter resumed, just like in the old days. Suddenly, someone flew the door open and shouted:

"Quiet, girls! You're being far too noisy again. Now, who's next to see me?"

It was Mademoiselle Cany. Instantly, silence fell upon the room. Céleste put a timid hand up and said:

"I think it's me, Mademoiselle."

"All right, then. In you come. Come on, girl, I haven't got all day!"

Mademoiselle Cany could not help but be brisk in her manner and in this respect, she reminded me of my teacher, Mademoiselle Germaine. Both women were about the same age, same built and, as far as we knew, without the usual appendage of a partner. However, we all knew something extraordinary about Mademoiselle Cany's past… she was an unmarried mother. With this vital piece of information, it was easier to understand why Mademoiselle Cany was so much more understanding and lenient towards her charges. Not like Madame Chauvineau who did everything by the book and smirked under a halo of righteousness, giving herself the authority and the power to throw the rule book at us every time we strayed ever so slightly away from the righteous path. With two personalities so totally apposite, it was almost inevitable that some kind of conflict would arise between the two women for it was a well-known fact that the two could not stand the sight of each other. So, despite Mademoiselle Cany's abrupt and short shrift ways, we would rather be confronted by her than by the caustic tongue of the woman sitting at the desk right next to hers.

"You're staying at the hotel *Jeanne d'Arc* tonight?" Marie-France enquired.

"Yeah. What a dump!"

"I know but it's great though because we can talk all night. Have you collected your meal tickets for supper?"

"No, not yet. Shall we go and get them now before the big rush?"

"I've got mine." Marie-France trumpeted, fanning my face with them. "So you'll have to go and get yours on your own."

"Oh no! I'm not going on my own to see Monsieur Bechamel. I don't like him... He's so repulsive!"

"Yeah. You have to watch his hands! You see the walk-in cupboard there?"

I looked at a narrow door tucked away in the far corner of the room.

"Well, he'll find any excuse to get you to go in there with him!"

"No!" I exclaimed in mock horror.

"Have you ever been in there?"

"Yeah, when I got my stuff for skiing..."

"Well," my friend interrupted. "At the far end of the cupboard, there's a small staircase that leads to what used to be the maid's quarters."

"Really?" I said, pricking up my ears.

"So, it's just like a bedroom up there, with a bed and everything..."

"Wow! So the rumours are true, then!"

"Oh yeah, there're definitely true. You know... if you want extra meal tickets... or anything else... it's really easy, all you have to do..."

"Oh yuk! Don't say anymore. It's too disgusting. Just the thought of his hands... Yuk!" I spat out, shivering in disdain.

"I know several girls who've been up there..."

"Oh yeah? Who?" I enquired keenly, my curiosity getting the better of me.

"I'm not telling!"

"Oh, go on! I promise I won't tell!" I insisted.

At that moment, Magali walked in.

"Hi!" Magali greeted somewhat shyly.

All eyes fell on her. When it came to fashion, Magali was our number one role model oozing with style and elegance in her flared jeans and white blouse. We all stared at her, checking her clothes for her dress sense, her make-up which was always kept to a minimum when she came to see Mademoiselle Cany, and her shoes because if there was anything notable about Magali, it was the way she was always impeccably dressed and immaculately turned out. As she squeezed herself into the already crowded sofa, we made quick mental notes of her designer clothes wishing we would look as smart and as trendy as she always did.

"Hi, Martha. I can't wait to get to Spain. Do you know who else is going?" Magali enquired on a casual tone.

"Well, some of them. There's Claire, Chantal… I think Céleste is going too."

"Céleste?"

"She's with Mademoiselle Cany."

"Are you going?" Magali asked Marie-France.

"No, I'm going to England."

"We don't go on holiday together anymore." I lamented. "Perhaps, we'll go skiing together?"

"I don't think so. I don't think there'll be anymore skiing holiday…"

"What?!" I exclaimed in horror. "No more skiing?"

"Well, that's the rumour. Apparently, the government is withdrawing all the funds." Claudette explained.

"Yeah, I've heard the same rumour." Marie-France seconded.

"Oh no!" I cried out in despair. "That's my favourite holiday!"

"I can see their point of view, though." Claudette continued. "After all, France withdrew from Vietnam after the fall of Diên Biên Phu. That was back in the 50s', but they're still taking on Vietnamese orphans who were born in the 60s', well after the French defeat. It's the Americans who should look after them now, not the French Government. In fact, I've even heard that The F.O.E.F.I. is going to be shut down."

"Oh God! I hope it's not true!" Magali exclaimed. "What are we going to do?"

"Well, they can't very well throw us out in the street just yet, but it's bound to happen." Claudette continued. "They'll probably let us finish our education and then… within a year or two…"

I made a quick mental calculation. I would be out of school in two years time which meant that there would be no chance whatsoever of my going to university. I sighed in despair. The *Baccalaureat* would be my final qualification. Then, I would be thrown mercilessly into the big iron jaws of modern society. I panicked. I did not even know how to shop for food or cook for that matter. Help! I cried out in my head, I'm not ready.

"Let's go to the Wimpy." Magali suggested cheerfully.

"I can't come yet, I'm still waiting to see Mademoiselle Cany." Marie-France remarked.

"I'll wait for you if you like. Boy, it's stifling in here. Can we not open the window?" I asked.

"No. In the words of Mlle Cany: only peasants hang out of windows. Come on, Martha, Marie-France will join us later, won't you? Let's go. I'm dying for a banana split."

"All right, all right. I'm coming. See you later, fatso!" I hailed to my friend.

"Don't you worry, Merdouille! I'll get my own back later!" Marie-France chuckled.

After a brief stop at Monsieur Bechamel's door to collect my meal tickets, Magali and I strolled down the Champs Elysées as far as the Wimpy. We sat as close to the glass doors as possible so we could have a good view of all the tourists and passers-by. The waitress, in her frilly apron and air-hostess hat, came to take our order and we giggled heartily as we listened to her shout: "One double wimpy, a '*salade niçoise*' and a banana split with extra cream!"

In the evening, our instructions were that we should not arrive at the Hotel *Jeanne d'Arc* later than ten o'clock. So, we strolled up the Champs Elysées, then took the metro to the Latin Quarters and wandered aimlessly until nearly ten o'clock. On the way, we met up with Claudette and Céleste and agreed that we would all share the same room.

At the hotel, the same matronly woman was waiting for us, watch in hand.

"You're late!" She barked. "It's after ten o'clock!"

None of us responded to her remark except to give her a cold and arrogant stare in a way only teenagers can. She growled again before taking us straight up the stairs. Once inside the bedroom, we inspected the floor and the bed. As usual, the sheets had not been changed but at least this time, they were not soiled.

"I'm having the bed!" I declared, throwing myself on it.

"I don't mind," Claudette said. "I'll sleep on the floor. It's just like camping. I love camping."

"Ok. I'll share the bed with you, then." Magali decided.

"Oh! I wanted to sleep in the bed." Céleste whined.

"Too late." Magali decreed. "I'm having it. You can have it next time!"

We quickly got into our nightclothes, then sat up in bed or on the floor for a long night of chats and gossips regularly interrupted by us lighting up a cigarette.

"Don't forget to open the window." Claudette warned.

This time we flew to Spain rather than take the train, and after a short coach journey, we arrived at the small seaside town called *Playa de Aro*. The house consisted of two apartments joined up together. The ground floor had been transformed into a large kitchen and dining room with, on the other side of the corridor, the sleeping quarters for the younger girls who were all French and the leader, Madame Lefèvre, a tall and formidable middle-aged woman who had the big straw hair, the square jaw and the brash manners of Melina Mercouri, the Greek actress. She was fun and she wanted us to have fun too. Her task was made easy by the fact that this was not a mixed camp. As such, she was able to impose only the minimum of rules which concerned mainly mealtimes and bedtime. However, and she was quite firm on that, no gallivanting at night, she had requested.

Our quarters were upstairs on the first floor where the main lounge had been transformed into a vast dormitory. Another smaller dormitory was situated on the other side of the kitchen and there, sandwiched between the two dormitories, lay another room, probably the dining-room, which had been transformed into a large bedroom with only two beds in it. Magali and I immediately rushed to take it but that room, we were soon told, was reserved for the supervisors. They had not arrived yet. They would be arriving later that day or maybe tomorrow. The thought of having two supervisors living right in the middle of our sleeping quarters appalled us and thinking fast, before anyone else had time to react, both Magali and I grabbed the two beds furthest away from their bedroom.

As we proceeded to unpack, I could not help looking at one of the girls in our group. She was as black as the ace of spade and we were dying to find out how she had ended up being a Vietnamese orphan, but because we did not want to offend her, we never asked. Her name was Géraldine and she loved to laugh which easily made up for poor Sophie's black moods. The holiday augured well.

On the first morning, we were woken up by the sound of hand-clapping and two cheerful male voices.

"Come on, girls! Time to get up. Breakfast is served! You've got ten minutes to get dressed!"

Shocked and bewildered, I peered over the bed sheet but could not make out who I was looking at through my myopic gaze. Seconds later, I heard the supervisors' flip-flops clack down the tiled-stairs.

"Who was that?" I asked sleepily.

"Martha! Did you see them?" Magali breathed excitedly.

Still lying down, I fumbled around the bed to find my glasses.

"No, who were they?"

"The supervisors. Can you believe it?"

"Why? What did they look like?"

"Oh my God, Martha! You won't believe this. They're both young and ever so dishy!" Magali effused.

"You're exaggerating, as usual. We've never had young and dishy supervisors. They've always been like a bunch of old witches!" I declared, finally getting out of bed.

"Come on. Let's go to breakfast and see for yourself."

In the make-shift dining-room, both supervisors were standing on either side of Madame Lefèvre. When everybody had arrived, she turned to us with a broad smile and introduced the men.

"Good morning, everyone. I trust you all slept well. I apologise if you were woken up during the night by the arrival of our new supervisors but their train didn't arrive until midnight. However, here they are: Didier on my right who is a student in physiotherapy, and on my left here, this is Gérard who has just completed his first year as a PE teacher. Now, they're going to look after you for the month. So please, be nice to them and stick to the rules; that way we can all enjoy ourselves and have fun."

Gérard was a medium height muscular fair-haired young man with large pectorals and a tight bum, but despite his rebounding compact muscles, he looked remarkably shy and reserved. Our direct stares were clearly making him feel rather uncomfortable, and he smiled quirkily while fixing his gaze on the pattern of the ceramic tiles under his nervy feet. We, girls, eyed him keenly, admiring with sheer boldness a very fine specimen of the human species.

Alas, any aspiring contender would soon be disappointed for when the owner of the apartments came to check that everything was fine and that we had settled in nicely, young Gérard became totally absorbed by the sight of this bouncy, heavily made-up, sun-kissed and mature blonde sauntering towards him. He was smitten on the spot. We rarely saw him after that although we did occasionally hear him… in the bedroom stuck between the two dormitories… or on the beach where he staggered at around midday with his back covered in scratches, which meant he could no longer swim for the sea water penetrated his skin and stung mercilessly his love wounds. The first time he went into the sea after a prolonged night of passion, he leapt out of the water as if pursued by a pool of hungry sharks and fell to his knees on the sand, wriggling in agony. From then on, the love-struck supervisor was reduced to sitting on the beach wearing a loose T-shirt or with his towel covering the whole of his back.

"Poor sod!" Didier surmised. "I don't know why he continues to hang out with that tigress. It's ruining his holiday."

With Gérard out of the running, we were left with Didier. What struck me straight away about him was the way he had stood in the dining-room with his head erect scrutinising our faces with the penetrating stare of a body-guard. He was not that much taller than Gérard and his muscles were more subtly sculptured around his solid frame but his whole body oozed with vigour, energy and confidence. Suddenly, his eyes were upon me and I flicked my hair back in a nervous tick, unsettled as I felt by the sustained gaze of his deep brown eyes.

Once the first flushes of youth had been cooled by the icy currents of the Mediterranean sea, we proceeded to organise our evening entertainment. There were two local discos, the *Maddox* and the *Memphis*, both situated within walking distance of our holiday abode. After the first night out during which the girls had befriended the staff from the *Maddox*, Géraldine rushed to me and said:

"You speak German, don't you?"

"Yeah, but only a little bit though."

"And you also speak English, yeah?"

"Not much and my accent is awful."

"Yeah, but you've been to Germany and England, so you can't be that bad…"

"Yes, but I'm not that good either."

"Well, you see, the DJ is looking for someone who can speak French, English and German to make a recording to tell the dancers when the disco is about to end…"

"What?" I quizzed.

"Yeah, you know, to say something like: 'we've come to the end of the evening, we hope you've enjoyed yourself and hope to see you back soon…' or something like that."

"I couldn't do that, I'm too shy."

"Come on, Martha," Magali butted in. "You know you can do it!"

"You've been to England," I reminded her. "And your English is definitely better than mine so why don't you do it?"

"Because I did Spanish at school, so I can't speak German."

"Come on, Martha! Do it!" Germaine insisted. "because in return you get to go in for free for the rest of the holiday and we, *your* friends, get to go in at half-price!"

I had no idea how my enterprising Vietnamese friends managed to wrangle that one but one afternoon, they dragged me very firmly towards the *Maddox* and introduced me to the DJ. We climbed the iron staircase right up to his glass dungeon overlooking the dance floor and found him twiddling hundreds of knobs on a large electronic console.

"So," he said, "which one of you is going to make the recording?"

Both Magali and Géraldine pointed at me and chorused:

"Her!"

I greeted the DJ with a shy "Hi!".

"Okay. This is what I'd like you to do. I'll do the Spanish version and you do the French, English and German. Is that okay? Don't worry, it's not difficult. I've written down in French what I want you to say, then you can translate it in English and German."

I looked at the piece of paper and read pretty much what Germaine had said.

"Well, if you don't mind, I need to write it down."

"That's okay. Here's some paper and a pen."

With the help of my acolytes, I translated the sentence and used my friends as an audience on which to practise my accent and diction.

"So, are you ready?" the DJ asked.

"Yes." I asserted with confidence, with paper in hand.

"Here we go then…"

After the recording, the DJ played it back through the speakers on the dance floor.

"It sounds good." He decreed.

"Yeah, yeah! You sounded really good!" My friends confirmed enthusiastically.

"You see, I told you your English accent is better than you think." Géraldine added.

I have to say that at the sound of my own voice, a bright halo of self-importance hovered above my head and increased my already buoyant self-esteem by two extra notches at least.

"Here you are," the DJ said, thrusting something into my hand. "That's your pass to get in free, but make sure you bring it with you every time otherwise you will have to pay."

"Thanks," I effused, unable to believe my luck.

Chapter 25

Having thoroughly explored the Maddox, we were now ready to storm the Memphis. When we arrived, a thick crowd was already swarming about the place.

"Why are there so many people here?" I asked intrigued.

"Let's go and find out." Claudette said.

Using her strong masculine shoulders and with Céleste in tow, Claudette plunged into the crowd and jostled her way to the front of the human wave. A few minutes later, she re-emerged all flustered.

"There's Tarzan!" She cried out. "That's why there's so many people."

"Tarzan?" I said, immediately picturing a bronzed body dressed in a loin cloth swinging from tree to tree. "I thought he was dead!"

"No," She continued still breathless with excitement, "Not this one. Look, it's Johnny Weissmuller. He's standing at the bar... over there... Can you see him?"

We craned our necks above the crowd and scanned the human horizon. Soon, I caught sight of a shock of white hair and a tanned face smiling broadly at the crowd, clearly amused by all the attention.

"Johnny Weissmuller?" I muttered. "Never hear of him!"

"Come on," The others urged. "Let's see if we can get a closer look."

Unwilling to push my way through a crowd of determined fans, I stayed back.

"I'll wait for you here."

While my friends were gone, this young blond Adonis accosted me and requested a dance. The only reason why I gave him a second glance was because his face reminded me so much of Johan.

As in the past, we made our introductions on the dance floor. His name was Yves and he was not from Germany but very much from France

192

where he studied politics. Disappointed that he was not German and being totally disinterested in all political matters, I knew from the start that our instant relationship would not go as far as the exit door, but Yves had other ideas, and he was rather persistent too.

A few minutes later, Magali returned from her star-gazing expedition. Tarzan had moved on, ready to swing through another human jungle.

"Thank God you're back!" I muttered under my breath.

"Hey! Who's your friend?" She hailed loudly.

I could have strangled her. Reluctantly, I turned to my escort.

"Er… this is my friend Magali… and this is Yves." I reeled out, completing the introductions swiftly so that Magali and I could return to the dance floor.

"Oh, I'll come with you." Yves suggested, jumping out of his seat.

"Well, actually, we're just going to the toilets." I said.

Yves sat back down again, clearly disappointed.

"Don't worry, I'll come back for you later." I vouched, hoping to make him feel better."

"I'll be waiting." He affirmed, making me feel terribly guilty for trying to avoid him.

"Why did you do that?" Magali asked, somewhat puzzled.

"I'm trying to get rid of him!" I explained.

"Why? He looks all right. He's blond, you like blond men."

"I know, but he's so boring."

"It doesn't matter," she insisted. "It's only for the holidays."

"Oh no! Last time you said that I nearly ended up with a husband! You have him if you're so keen."

"Poor Yves, I feel sorry for him."

"Take him, then!"

Feeling some kind of obligation, I agreed to meet up with Yves one more time before moving on with my posse of Vietnamese friends who always seemed to know where the heart of the action was.

This time it happened to be in the Memphis's very own kitchen.

"What!" Several of us exclaimed.

"Yes," Claudette declared with excitement. "The Memphis is owned by a Vietnamese family!"

"No!" We all blurted out at the same time.

"That's a hell of a coincidence!" Someone opined.

"And guess what!" Claudette continued. "They've invited all of us for a Vietnamese meal."

"Really? That's ever so nice of them… but there's twelve of us."

"They don't mind. They've got a huge kitchen. I've seen it."

"When are we going then?" Géraldine asked.

"Whenever we want but we need to tell them a day in advance."

"Would we go in the evening?"

"Why not," Céleste suggested. "The plan is: we'll dance at the disco and then have a meal afterwards."

"Great idea!"

"Who's going to ask permission to Madame Lefèvre?"

"We'll all go." Claudette decided. "She's not going to say no. As long as she knows where we are, she won't mind."

Madame Lefèvre was indeed the most liberal leader I had ever come across. Retiring to her bed at the same time as the raucous cockerels and braying donkeys, she always handed over the reins of her leadership to Gérard who could never be found, and Didier who was sometimes here, sometimes there, but rarely with us. And if by chance, someone else was willing to take over completely, Madame Lefèvre was quite happy to withdraw her participation in order to concentrate wholly on the well-being of the younger girls.

So, one evening, we all traipsed down to the Memphis, our hair flowing freely in the hot summer breeze, and our bodies bristling with brash confidence in our best disco gear. Skipping down the dirt track, we advanced, lock armed and singing, ready to partake in our first Vietnamese midnight feast.

At around midnight, Claudette came out of the kitchen and began to gather those of us who were still on the dance floor. Somehow, she always took it upon herself to take charge of everything and since most of us wanted our lives made as easy as possible, we willingly followed her leadership. Inside the kitchen, she made the introductions, after which we were invited to sit around the vast kitchen table and given a bowl each with a pair of chopsticks. The Vietnamese women chatted away happily in Vietnamese, giggling and laughing and nodding their heads enthusiastically as if they had just approved of their sons' marriages. A good catch, they'd make, yes a good catch. Upon which four young men appeared from a side door.

"That's my sons." One of the women declared proudly in a strong Vietnamese accent.

"And these two are mine." Another pointed.

"Very nice. Make good husbands!" The first one chuckled.

We all giggled too. Now, the whole extended family was busy bringing a multitude of dishes all containing exquisite Vietnamese delicacies while one of the mothers carried a big dish of plain white rice which had been tipped out onto an enormous plate.

"You want rice? Have rice! Bring bowl here and me put rice in it. Yeah, yeah, you come here with bowl." She said waving about a huge wooden spoon.

As we were tucking into the exotic feast, the DJ came in.

"Is there anything left for me?" He enquired sniffing around the table.

"Yeah, yeah. Plenty. You take bowl over there… No, take bigger one. You hungry boy… You must eat plenty for strong muscles." The mother giggled showing off her own biceps.

As the DJ settled himself on a wooden stool, he began to talk.

"Now, girls. I thought you might be interested to know that next Saturday, we're organising a dancing competition. The prize is 200 pesetas and if you would like to enter, we'll make sure that one of you wins it."

"Really?"

"Wow!"

"How can you make sure that one of us is going to win?"

"Simple. I'm the judge."

"What if someone else is a lot better than any of us?" Géraldine queried.

"I don't think so. I've seen most of you dance and you're good. Besides, you've got plenty of time to practise until then, that's why I'm telling you now."

We all looked at each other, our mouths baying in complete surprise. We could hardly believe our ears.

"I'll leave the form on the table here and before you go, if you could fill in your first name, that'd be great."

Eight of us signed up for the competition. Back at our Spanish abode, all we could talk about was the forthcoming competition and who was most likely to win it. The verdict was unanimous. It had to be Géraldine.

"Anyway," Claudette declared. "Whoever wins it, I think, should share the prize money equally among all the participants."

"Yeah! Yeah!" We all agreed.

"So it's a deal?"

"It's a deal!"

From then on, our daily routine was altered to make time for dance practice. After the beach, instead of going to the shops or idling our time away, we met in the dormitory and practised our dance moves. Gérard provided the portable record player and some records, courtesy of his girlfriend, and Didier acted as 'unanimously appointed judge'.

"Come on, Géraldine! Show us what to do." We begged.

Very obligingly, Géraldine took to the central spot while we watched her move expertly through the various pop songs.

"Wow!" I exclaimed. "I'll never be able to dance like that!"

"Don't worry, Martha. It's easy, just watch me. Come on, have a go!"

"Not on my own!"

"Come on, everybody!" Géraldine shouted. "Everybody on the dance floor!"

Sitting on Chantal's bed, Didier watched us, highly amused.

"You're too stiff!" He hailed at me. "You need to move your hips more."

Concentrating hard on synchronising my movements to the music, I danced towards him and said:

"What? Like that?"

"Yes, that's better; but relax, Martha, you need to be more relaxed..."

After a moment of reflection, he suddenly declared:

"You know, in Morocco, if a woman dances in front of a man, it means that she wants to make love to that man."

Although my first reaction was to burst out laughing, something happened in that instant that I could not quite explain... it was weird and so unexpected. Standing in front of him, I no longer saw a figure of authority but a dashing young man with eyes sparkling with mischief. I smiled back at him but not with my usual bemused, childish grin. It was a smile of connivance, an alluring smile that opened my eyes and made me realise: I've never noticed you before.

Didier got up abruptly, put his arm around my waist and began to dance with me.

"If you want to improve," He breathed gently in my ear, "you need to relax more… Come on, let yourself go and let the music take over."

Relax? I thought. Impossible. No successful warrior could ever allow that to happen. Having fought so many battles for real and in my dreams, I could not possibly run the risk of being caught off-guard.

"Come on… relax." I heard Didier repeat. "Look, you're as stiff as a board."

"But I don't know what you mean by 'relax'," I pleaded.

"All right. Close your eyes, put your head on my shoulder and let me guide your steps."

But instead of closing my eyes, I looked straight into his and whispered:

"What about my arms? What do I do with them?"

Didier looked surprised.

"Have you ever danced with anybody before?"

"Well… er… no… not that close."

He did not reply but simply took my arms and wrapped them up around his waist. Only then was I able to close my eyes and let him take over.

Chapter 26

At last, Saturday night arrived. We were so excited that we wanted to skip dinner to have more time to get ready.

"No, no!" Madame Lefèvre insisted. "I won't allow anyone to skip a meal. Besides, you'll dance all the better with solid food inside you."

"But, Madame, we can grab something there…" Claudette argued.

"Yes, they said we could have food whenever we wanted." Céleste confirmed.

"No, I'd rather you ate here." Madame Lefèvre replied, adamant. "You're going to need all the energy you can get, especially if you want to win."

So, reluctantly, we all sat around the table to wait for our evening meal. Afterwards, we rushed back to the dormitory and helped each other with clothes and make-up.

"Yes, wear your tight jeans," Géraldine was busy advising everybody. "It'll be better to show off your moves."

"Who's got a pair of jeans I can borrow?"

"Where's my T-shirt? Has anyone borrowed my T-shirt?"

"Who's got some black eyeliner?"

"Can I borrow your hair-dryer?"

"Magali, can you help me with my make-up?"

"Hang on. Let me put my mascara on first."

Once satisfied that we all looked totally irresistible, downright gorgeous and ready to conquer the dance floor, we charged *en masse* towards the Memphis.

The place was already packed and the atmosphere sizzling with excitement. The DJ greeted us and asked us what kind of music we preferred.

"Music with lots of rhythm like some reggae, the Osmonds or the Jackson 5." Géraldine replied.

"Have you got 'Jimmy Mack'? I love 'Jimmy Mack'!" I suggested.

"Ok, girls. You've got an hour to warm up, then, when the competition starts, I'll call the names out and when it's your turn, you go right in the middle of the dance floor and you'll have one minute to show what you can do. Okay? So off you go and practise your dance move! *Bonne chance*!"

At the appointed hour, the announcement was made. The DJ stopped the music, announced the start of the competition and, leaving his assistant to take over the electronic console, he made his way to the dance floor armed with a clipboard. Very quickly, a thick crowd of contestants mixed with onlookers gathered around the dance floor. The DJ began to tick names. We watched with indifferent eyes young locals and tourists strut their stuff. Then, it was our turn. I was so nervous that I started shaking. Why on earth was I putting myself through this? I could hardly dance! I shuffled discreetly towards Géraldine to whisper in her ear that I wanted to drop out.

"You can't drop out now!" Géraldine whispered back in my ear. "It's too late to chicken out now!"

Standing two steps away from the dance floor, I watched Chantal, Céleste, Claudette, Claire and Magali go before me. Then the DJ called out my name. I steeled myself, threw my head back and moved in the middle of the dance floor. Straight away, my body stiffened with shyness. My feet seemed to be glued to the same spot. I lifted one, then the other. Was I marching? No, not quite, for I had one redeeming feature: 'rhythm'. Yep, I got rhythm. From the side, I could see the DJ mouthing: "move around more". So I forced myself to move around the dance floor. Was I marching in a circle? Noooo! I got rhythm! After a few excruciating seconds which seemed to last an eternity, it was over. Now, it was Géraldine's turn and thank goodness she came after me for it made her look even better than ever. We cheered loudly and gasped in wonder as she tried new daring moves. In all fairness to the other contestants, Géraldine looked sensational. At the end of the competition, the DJ announced that it would take a few minutes to pick a winner. So our little group gathered together and speculated.

"It's got to be you, Géraldine."

"Yeah!" We all agreed. "You're definitely the best!"

"I'm not sure." Géraldine hesitated. "That Spanish girl… she looked really good."

"Nothing like you, Géraldine! Nothing like you!" We re-assured her.

Our deliberations were interrupted by the DJ returning with the results. Soon, and quite unheard of before in a disco, a deafening silence followed.

"In third place," his voice boomed in the microphone, "we have Carolina! Well done Carolina!"

Immediately, all the heads swivelled around to see who this Carolina girl was, and yes, she was the Spanish girl who looked so good on the dance floor. We applauded graciously.

"In second place, we have Claire! Well done Claire!"

Loud applause and cheers followed.

"And finally, in first place… the winner is… Géraldine!"

Screams, cheers and loud applause greeted the last announcement.

"Come on here, Géraldine, and come and collect your prize! 200 pesetas! Well done Géraldine!"

At the end of the disco, we all gathered into the kitchen to celebrate our premeditated win. Champagne corks popped while we settled down for another midnight feast.

"Come on, Géraldine, show us the prize!" Claudette asked, all excited.

Géraldine produced a white envelop with the cash inside.

"How much is 200 divided by eight?" Claire wanted to know.

"Don't know. Has anyone got a pen?"

"I think it's 25." Céleste quickly calculated.

"Yeah, you're right. It's 25." Claudette confirmed.

Magali and I looked at each other.

"Well, Martha, tomorrow we're going shopping." She decreed.

We both burst out laughing for we knew that 25 pesetas would not even get us the bottom half of a bikini, but at least, it would be enough to pay for a drink or two.

Chapter 27

Once all the excitement of the Memphis win had died down, the calm and nonchalance of the previous days returned and we settled back into our more sedate holiday routine, enjoying the leisurely pace of a country which did not stir before five o'clock in the afternoon.

Gérard was still nowhere to be seen and Didier, who had up until then kept at a safe distance from a bunch of excitable nubile girls, began to mingle more freely among us. On the beach, he organised games which consisted mainly of us chasing him. In the water, he let us use his body as a diving board, allowing us to jump from his muscular thighs, his cupped hands or his strong athletic shoulders.

God, he looked irresistible! I kept sighing in sheer ecstasy, lying on the beach or on my bed. Do Greek gods sometimes have dark hair and brown eyes? I wondered.

After the beach, there was always a rush to see who would get to the shower first as there was only one bathroom on our floor. One afternoon, he challenged me.

"I bet you I can get to the shower before you."

"No, you won't!" I riposted, starting to run.

Didier grabbed me from behind and pushed me aside. As he passed me, I grabbed hold of his shorts and refused to let go.

"You little cheat!" He shouted. "You're going to tear my shorts! Let go of me!"

"What! And let you run ahead?" I said, tightening my grip.

We arrived at the house, both panting and out of breath, scrambled up the stairs and crashed into the bathroom.

"Right, well I got here first, so I'm having my shower first." Didier declared triumphantly.

I closed the door, leant against it and replied defiantly.

"We both arrived at the same time!"

"Okay… Well, you're going to have to leave because I'm about to take my clothes off."

"I'm not leaving." I warned.

"Suit yourself." He said, taking his T-shirt off. "Are you sure you want to stay because I'm about to take my swimming trunks off?"

"You wouldn't dare!"

Wouldn't he? The next thing I knew his swimming trunks were flying off his hands and, in the same manner as waiters in cafés shout their orders, he shouted:

"*Un moniteur à poil, un!*" ("One naked supervisor, one!")

Then, totally ignoring me, he stepped into the shower, turned the water on and began to sing.

Stunned, I just stared. As he smothered his whole body with the smooth white lather in slow sensual moves, I watched his member rise higher and higher until it stood erect high above the tan line of his swimming trunks.

"Oh my God!" I giggled with embarrassment. "I can't believe you're doing this!"

Then, winking at me, he jerked his head and said:

"Would you like to…?"

"What?!!!"

"Well, you'd better be prepared because it's your turn next!"

I screamed and, as I slammed the door behind me, I heard him shout through the walls:

"I'll wash your back if you like!"

Back in the dormitory, the girls returned from the beach in dribs and drabs. At the far end, Magali was sitting on her bed filing her nails.

"So," she started on a plain tone, "you've had your shower then."

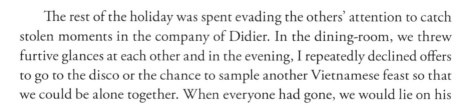

The rest of the holiday was spent evading the others' attention to catch stolen moments in the company of Didier. In the dining-room, we threw furtive glances at each other and in the evening, I repeatedly declined offers to go to the disco or the chance to sample another Vietnamese feast so that we could be alone together. When everyone had gone, we would lie on his bed, talk about his plans for the future and chat about Simone, his fiancée. Sometimes, we would fall into a warm embrace and kiss, neither of us willing or wishing to cross that invisible line. After all, he was a supervisor and I was just one of the girls.

Chapter 28

Back in Paris, I just had time to throw all my laundry in the godmother's washing machine before setting off to a holiday camp in Normandy.

"You haven't put your pants in with my washing, have you? Take them out! I don't want my clothes mixed with your dirty pants!"

The godmother's apartment had now become a sort of transit lounge where I quickly turned around before being off again. She was getting upset and I did not understand why, except that while in Spain, she had sent me a postcard where, for the first time ever, she had written about her feelings towards me.

"Who's that card from?" Magali had enquired.

"The godmother." I stated coldly.

"Let me have a look." She said, grabbing the card before I could stop her. "Oh, look, she's written: *I miss you*. So, you see, she *does* like you."

"Of course she doesn't! She's just bored."

"I like your godmother. She's nice."

At that moment, I remember eyeing Magali as if she were a traitor and decided to ignore her comment.

The godmother, however, was keen to reiterate her point of view.

"It's nice to have you back. Did you get my postcard?"

I looked at her coldly.

"You shouldn't write things you don't mean."

"Like what?"

"Like you missed me."

"But I did and I do miss you."

"You've never missed me before so why now?"

"But I do miss you." She repeated vehemently.

"Why?"

"Because… you're funny… and I like your company."

Was she declaring in her own way that, at last, I was over the ugly duckling phase? Too busy concentrating on her own beauty and that of her friends, was she suddenly noticing me? I was not sure and quite frankly I did not care which prompted Magali to exclaim:

"Martha Bertrand, you're so harsh, you have a heart of stone!"

That may be so, but in the full throes of adolescent fever, I positively did not care. My stubborn streak created conflicts with not just the godmother but with all the figures of authority who were in charge of shaping my destiny. It seemed somewhat odd to me that none of them seemed perspicacious enough to realise that what rankles rebels like me most is not so much that they cannot get what they want but rather that they get what they don't want.

Before leaving for Normandy, however, I made sure I contacted Magali.

"What are you going to do for the month?" I asked.

"I'm going to work in an office in Fécamp."

"Great, that's not too far from where I'll be. You will come and see me, won't you?"

"I hope I can."

"God I hope so!" I said. "Can you imagine… a whole month with nuns… and on my holidays!"

"Yes," Magali laughed. "I can just imagine you… *Sainte Martha*!"

Exhausted by a long boring journey, I did not even react when a nun came to open the strong wooden door of the entrance hall.

"*Bonsoir.*" She greeted cheerfully. "I'm Sister Marie-Ange, and you must be Martha Bertrand."

I eyed her suspiciously and mumbled a greeting in return. What on earth was I doing here, I kept asking myself. This place was so Spartan that it felt like entering a convent or a cloister. I am never going to forgive Madame Chauvineau for this, I grumbled between my clenched teeth.

"I guess you must be pretty tired so I'll take you to your accommodation straight away."

I stared at the nun, startled as if I had just woken up from a dream.

We made our way silently towards a large prefab building, just across the way from the main house, and on the way there, we came across a senior girl.

"Ah," Sister Marie-Ange hailed, "Madeleine! Could you show the new supervisor her room? Have a good night rest, Martha, and I'll see you tomorrow morning at the briefing."

"Good night, Sister." I replied with all the enthusiasm of a dead parrot.

Madeleine took me inside the first dormitory and showed me a cubicle concealed behind a green curtain.

"That's your bedroom." She whispered so as not to wake up the girls.

"Are you one of the supervisors too?" I asked, looking at her rugged features which placed her age anywhere between thirteen and thirty.

"Oh, no," she smiled, looking flattered. "I'm just one of the seniors, but I've been selected to be your helper."

"That's nice," I remarked with a forced smile, already plotting in my head how much I would be able to delegate in order to make my life as easy as possible.

The following morning, I was woken up by the girls stirring in their beds. I looked at the clock: 6.30am. I turned over, pulled the covers over my head and was trying to go back to sleep when a voice called:

"Martha! Martha! You've got to get up. It's 7.30!"

"What?!" I whined. "Why so early? I'm on holiday for goodness sake!"

Madeleine looked at the lifeless pile buried under the covers and instantly knew she had to take action.

"Er... I'll get the girls ready and send them to breakfast."

"Thanks, Madeleine."

A short while later, Madeleine accompanied me to the small refectory. At a glance, I estimated that there were about 50 girls. All the supervisors were sitting together at the table nearest to the door. As I settled myself down, greeting the others in the process, Sister Marie-Ange appeared, bobbing her head cheerfully, and said:

"Good morning, everyone. Now, girls, remember, meeting at 10 o'clock, all right?"

"Where, Sister?"

"Here, in the refectory."

I looked around the table. All the supervisors looked about the same age as me. Had they all been conned, like me, into believing that in order to become a skiing instructor you first had to earn your stripes as a supervisor in a convent, cloister or any other religious institution?

At the meeting, we were all given a diary for the month and a pen to write in our various duties. After completing all the introductions, Sister Marie-Ange proceeded to open the meeting.

"Now," she said, "the first thing we need to organise is who's going to accompany the children to church on Sunday."

"I can do the first one," Marianne volunteered.

"I can do the second one," Solange offered.

"Wonderful!" Sister Marie-Ange exclaimed. "If everything goes as smoothly as this, we shouldn't take too long to go through all the formalities. Now, who's going to do the third one?"

Two rows of blank faces stared back at the nun.

"Martine? Would you like to do the third one?"

"Sorry, Sister, I'm going to my aunt's that weekend."

"What about you, Nicole?"

"I'd love to, Sister, but I can't, it's my cousin's wedding."

"Martha?"

I looked at all the faces staring at me expectantly.

"Me?!!!" I gasped. "I don't go to church!"

Instantly, all the heads turned back towards Sister Marie-Ange to catch her reaction. I looked directly at the nun, expecting some kind of remonstrance or at the very least a stern word to remind me of my duty towards Our Lord. But no, to my complete surprise, nobody reacted.

Very calmly, Sister Marie-Ange took her pen, peered at her diary and declared quite unconcerned:

"Hmm... in that case you'd better have your day off on Sundays then..."

In the past, each trip had been a brand new adventure, an exciting discovery which had opened the flood gates to a powerful wave of delectable sensations. Here, however, in a lost corner of Normandy, I felt totally disinterested, aloof and detached from everything around me. With nuns going about their daily duties in soulless surroundings, the whole set up was a sharp reminder of a ghastly place that I had long ago relegated to the back of my mind. As with invisible ink, the memories of a lost childhood were indelibly etched on a sombre canvas which I had successfully blanked out thanks to my firm resolve. With them out of sight, hence out of mind, I had been able to forget about the whole miserable episode and move on. Now, I found myself forcibly back into the olden days within the perimeters of an eerily familiar frame that was startlingly dull and grey. Surrounded by children with soulful eyes devoid of any spark who went through the motion of each day with the resigned look of doomed children who have only known misery and pain, I felt no pity, only a profound disdain. For one long interminable month, I would have to assume the reviled role of 'supervisor' to the lost children of society, and I seethed with anger, damning adults and cursing through my clenched teeth: 'I'll never forgive you, Chauvinette!'

Still, those brave little girls depended on me to brighten up their days and I felt sufficiently duty bound to put on a brave smile and proceed to lead activities which would be fun for them and less daunting for me.

At least I had my day off to look forward to, except that on Sundays… well, what do you do on a Sunday in the middle of nowhere?

It was customary for all the supervisors to gather in one of the playrooms, once we had put all the children in bed, leaving the helpers in charge. So, I began to make enquiries.

"What is there to do around here?" I enquired.

"We go to town mostly." Solange replied.

"There's no point in going on a Sunday, though. Everything will be closed." I remarked.

"Yes, but there's the market. It's fun going to the market." Mathilde stated.

"Oh yes," Véronique said. "We can buy food for our midnight binges."

"Midnight binges?" I quizzed.

"Yeah," Solange said. "Every now and again, we have a midnight binge, once all the girls are in bed. It's great fun!" She enthused.

I looked at them with a quirky smile. Was this the ultimate thrill I could look forward to during my time here: sharing midnight feasts while listening to the Dark Side of the Moon and scaring each other out of our wits with ghost stories?

"What if Sister Marie-Ange finds out?" I asked.

"Oh, she won't mind, as long as we get on with our duties and we're punctual."

"How do you go to town?" I eventually enquired.

"By bus…" Véronique replied.

"But sometimes we hitchhike." Solange chipped in.

"Hitchhike?" I said.

"Oh yeah, it's really easy around here. The locals are really friendly."

"Can someone come with me, then? I'm scared to go on my own." I pleaded.

"I'll come with you." A friendly voice offered.

"Oh, thanks Mathilde."

So, on Sunday, we took the bus to the local market town. Mathilde, I soon discovered, was a keen gossipmonger and during the whole half-hour journey, she never stopped talking once, raving about the nuns – 'they're really nice, you know' – reeling out a character reference on each of the supervisors and chatting animatedly about Sister Marie-Ange, constantly singing her praises – 'she's the best'. After a while listening to facts and comments about people in whom I did not have the slightest interest, I sat back in my seat, crossed my arms and ogled the landscape without seeing any of it.

Fortunately, I had finally managed to make contact with Magali. Sister Marie-Ange had kindly allowed me to use the phone.

"So," I said, somewhat impatiently. "When can we meet up?"

"What about next Sunday, in Fécamp?" She replied, pre-empting my next question.

"How will I get there?"

"You'll have to take the train."

"Oh God. How am I going to find out the time of trains?"

"Don't worry. I'll find out for you and I'll ring you back."

At last, I thought, I'll be able to break free… for one day at least.

The following Sunday, I took the bus and the train, and reached the industrial town of Fécamp just before eleven o'clock. A stickler for punctuality, Magali was already at the station, waiting for me at the end of the platform.

We greeted each other like long lost friends and kissed.

"Right, well, what have you got planned?" I immediately asked.

"Shall we go for a coffee in a café first…"

"Good idea, I'm starving! I didn't have any breakfast this morning."

"Come on, then. Let's go. We can decide what to do afterwards while we have a bite to eat."

When the waiter came to take our order, I eyed Magali to see if she had any plans to go off with him but after giving him the once over with a cold eye, I guessed she would not be giving him anything beyond our straight forward order. Nope, not today, never on a Sunday, I could almost hear the Greek actress Melina Mercouri rile.

"Have you been to Fécamp before?" She asked.

"No, this is my first time." I replied, not even attempting to hide my lack of enthusiasm for the industrial town.

With nothing else to do, we finally decided to stroll down to the Sunday market. We sauntered nonchalantly around the multitude of stalls. We stopped at one that sold leather goods.

"Come on, my lovelies!" The stallholder hailed.

We both guffawed.

"You like that handbag? You can have it for 100francs! It's pure leather, best quality leather! Well worth the price. Come on here," he said, "smell this. Isn't that a great smell?"

"Yes, but it's too expensive." Magali replied.

"Okay, young lady. Because it's you… and only because it's you, you can have it for 80 francs. Come on, give me 80 francs!" He negotiated jovially.

"I'll give you 50 francs." Magali bartered.

"Come on, my lovely; you must understand, it's the best quality leather! I can't give it to you at that price. I've got a living to make. Come on, 80 francs and that's my last offer."

"No thank you." Magali replied, grabbing my arm and dragging me away from the stand.

"You never had any intention of buying that handbag, did you?" I said.

"I know. I just like to barter." She giggled heartily.

When we saw the stallholders beginning to pack their wares at around one o'clock, Magali and I set about to look for a café for lunch. We left the market square, walked inside the first establishment we came across and sat at a table near the *terrasse*. Scouring the lively clientele, Magali suddenly snagged my arm.

"Oh look, Martha! Isn't that the stallholder at the bar?"

"Is it?" I pondered out loud.

"Come on, let's go and say hello. We might get a drink out of him."

"I don't want to but you go. I'll keep the table."

With youthful aplomb, Magali grabbed the stool right next to the man and smiled sweetly at him.

The man lifted his flat cap to take a better look at the young girl who had just accosted him.

From my seat, I observed Magali, though I averted my eyes from the bar every time her companion turned to look towards our table. As she was talking, Magali raised her hand and pointed:

"That's my friend, Martha."

The man turned his head in my direction. With his greyish hair and rugged features, he looked old enough to be Magali's father.

Suddenly…

"Martha!" Magali hailed to my utter embarrassment. "Come and say hello. Raymond wants to buy us a drink."

Reluctantly, I got up and walked to the bar.

"Come right over here." Raymond insisted, pulling a stool towards me. "Hi, Martha. I'm Raymond. Please to meet you." He smiled while his lecherous eyes roamed all over my body.

"Hi." I replied coldly, mindful not to flare up his basic instinct.

"You want a drink?"

"I'll have a pineapple juice, please."

"You can't have a fruit juice! You need something stronger. I tell you what, here they sell the best calvados in the region. You've got to taste it." Then, turning towards the barman, he hailed: "Patrick! Two calvados for these two demoiselles, please!"

"I can't drink that!" I immediately panicked.

"'Course you can!"

I looked at Magali with pleading eyes.

"Don't worry," she whispered, "you don't have to finish it."

"So, what are your plans for the rest of the day?" Raymond enquired, sipping his calvados. Magali shrugged her shoulders.

"Don't know… Have lunch I suppose."

"I tell you what. Why don't you come home with me and I'll make you a nice lunch…"

After taking two sips of calvados on an empty stomach, I was rapidly turning green.

"I live in a farmhouse, about ten minutes away from here." He continued.

Magali looked at me for an answer.

"I don't want to." I whispered, feeling increasingly worse by the minute.

"But we've got nothing else to do…"

"All right, then, you go if you want and I'll go back to the station." I replied.

"I don't want to go on my own. Come on, you come with me."

"I don't want to." I insisted. "I'm feeling sick."

Magali turned towards the man.

"My friend doesn't want to come."

"I've got to go to the station." I said.

"What time's your train?" Raymond asked.

"I think it's at about three or half past."

"Oh, plenty of time, then. Come on. You come with us and then, I'll take you to the station. How's that?"

"All right…" I conceded, lacking the strength to resist.

We left the bar but not before Raymond had upped our drinks and finished them both.

"Silly to waste such fine calvados." He chuckled.

Once in the street, our escort guided us towards a line of vehicles. I looked at the estate cars in particular, trying to guess which one might be his. As it turned out, none of them were. A few seconds later, we watched him hop into a small rusty truck. Despite my fragile state, we both burst out laughing.

"Well, that's class for you." Magali sniggered. "You jump in first."

"No way!" I said, "I'm not sitting next to him."

"Come on." Magali insisted. "He's not going to bite you."

"No," Raymond quipped. "Your friend is quite right, I don't bite!"

I turned to Magali and said quite firmly:

"You jump in first or I'm not coming."

"All right, all right. I'll sit next to him, then."

Within five minutes, we had left town and the truck was now clattering noisily through the sleepy countryside. At the end of a long straight road, the truck took a left turn and engaged along a dirt track full of muddy potholes. Going with the flow, Magali giggled with each bounce and urged me to join in.

"Come on, Martha. Cheer up!"

After a sharp turn to the right, the contours of a redbrick farmhouse suddenly stood out against the plain landscape of a dull Sunday afternoon.

"Are you married?" Magali asked, as though she intended to propose.

"Have been." Raymond stated plainly. "I live alone now, in that big empty house." He quickly added as if to stop us asking any more questions. "Anyway, let's see what I've got in the fridge."

The kitchen was a huge room with its bare white walls and dark red floor tiles enhancing its cold and harsh atmosphere. The remains of a large loaf of bread lay on the wooden table amid fresh crumbs that had not been dusted away. Near the edge of the table, by the single wicker chair, an enamel carafe of coffee and an empty breakfast bowl still waited to be cleared.

With his arms full of merchandise, Raymond made his way to the room next door.

"Let's go in the dining-room," he invited us. "We'll be more comfy there."

We followed him into this big room cluttered with a large table and chairs and an old sofa and armchairs, threadbare and off-coloured. The tall windows, framed with old grubby curtains, looked onto the yard. I looked at Magali to study her reaction. She did not seem to notice the neglected appearance of the house. Meanwhile, Raymond was busy spreading his selection of food on the table.

"Now, *Mesdemoiselles*, I've got some cheese, pâté, *saucisson*, a piece of quiche fresh from the market and some eggs. Just help yourselves."

"Can we have some plates, please?" Magali asked.

"Oh? You want a plate? They're down there, in the cupboard by the sink."

While she was out of the room, Raymond pulled his chair closer to me and whispered:

"Now... afterwards... if you fancy... you and me..."

As he delivered his cryptic message, he kept jerking his head towards a door opposite the kitchen door.

Feeling sick and revolted by the sight of this old man with grubby hands, I averted my gaze away from him and mumbled:

"I'm not interested."

Magali returned with three plates. I helped myself to a piece of quiche. Raymond waited for us to finish eating, then he beckoned Magali.

"I want to ask you something," he said, leading her towards another room.

A few minutes later, she re-emerged on her own and joined me at the table.

"He wants to 'do it' with you." She confided.

"I don't want to. He makes me feel sick."

"He'll give you 250francs!"

"I've already told him I'm not interested." I decreed.

Magali went back into the other room but returned soon after.

"He'll give you 500francs! Come on, 500francs! That's a lot of money. Even if we split it 50/50, that's 250francs each. Just think what we could do with 250francs!"

"I don't care. Tell him I'm not interested!" I stated adamantly.

Magali disappeared again, for longer this time. Eventually, she returned, sat at the table and said:

"You're not going to believe this. He said he will give you all the takings of the day. That's nearly 2000 francs!"

Despite feeling queasy, I glared at my friend with some determination.

"I am not interested! Why don't you go and do it, then?"

"I would but I don't think he's interested in me."

"Of course he is."

Magali returned to the adjoining room with the final verdict. While they both busied themselves, I looked for something to browse but there was not a single book, magazine or even newspaper in sight, so I proceeded to the kitchen where I explored the empty shelves, the odd assortment of chipped crockery and blackened pots and pans. Outside, I caught sight of a cat. When the mouser spotted me, he froze and glared at me for a few seconds, then scurried away as if scared. With nothing else to explore, I returned to the main room and slumped back into the chair. I looked at my watch. Twenty past two. I wondered how much longer they would be. I was beginning to fret. I had a train to catch.

Finally, Magali re-emerged and came to sit at the table. I immediately raised my hand to shut her up.

"Don't tell me. I don't want to know." I said, turning away from her.

At long last, the moment came for me to leave. I kissed my friend and urged her to ring me.

"Are you sure you're going to be all right on your own… with Raymond." I enquired with genuine concern.

"Of course I am. And yes, I'll give you a call later."

As I climbed into the truck, I suddenly felt nervous. What if Raymond was going to try something on the way? We were travelling alone on a deserted road in the middle of nowhere. Anything could happen. I sat in the truck as far away from Raymond as it was physically possible, practically leaning against the door and clutching the door handle with both hands as if holding on for dear life. I jumped nervously when Raymond suddenly spoke.

"You know… You could have made a lot of money back there… 2000 francs is a lot of money. That's the most I've taken in one day…"

Too scared to even look at him, I kept my eyes firmly fixed on the road with my lips tightly sealed. When we arrived at the station, I jumped out of the truck as if I had just been bitten on the butt by a giant spider. Finally I was free. Standing on the deserted platform, I took a deep breath full of the thick, hot and sticky air that, at that very moment, smelt as sweet as if I had been in the middle of a glorious field surrounded by roses and daffodils. In one instant, the sooty smell that emanated from the hot tarmac dissipated the scent of danger and fear, and I felt able again to stand with my head held up high as I gazed intently at the train tracks that would soon lead me to the safety of a place I absolutely detested.

For my very last assignment as a somewhat obstreperous teenager on a working holiday, I was sent to Belgium. My main task was to wash dishes in a seaside hotel/restaurant. The human sloth was about to work as she never had done before! Fortunately, my dear guardian angels were, yet again, watching over me and they blessed me with the cheerful presence of my skiing buddy who, back in the Alps, had left her indelible mark by being sick all over my brand new ski boots, talking non-stop the minute she awoke and who, each night, had forced me to dangle on the edge of the double bed we had to share as she subconsciously spread her petite frame all over the large mattress.

When I was not busy doing the dishes in the crowded kitchen, while singing loudly old French ditties that my friend had just taught me, or scoffing crème caramels or ice cream Sundaes that my buddy and I found 'resting' in the cold room, I was wrestling with the ice cream machine parked on the pavement, just in front of the hotel.

After three solid weeks of working from seven o'clock in the morning until the last customer had left the restaurant, which could mean anytime between eleven or past midnight, I asked the hotel owner for a day-off. He refused. This made me consider my position. If, as the hotel owner, it was his prerogative to refuse to grant me a break, surely it was my prerogative, as the injured party, to refuse to continue working… which I did. To my surprise, the owner asked, pleaded, begged even for me to go back to work.

"Please…"

"I want a day off."

"Please…"

"Give me a day off."

"You know… my wife… er… she will probably want me to sack you if you don't go back to work."

"Sack me then."

So he did. And, because the management considered my refusal to work as a rebellious act, the owner's wife, who was in charge of the books, did not feel compelled to pay me more than the equivalent of £10 for the whole three weeks I had been slaving.

I ended up finishing the summer working as an au pair for a charming family, some distance away from the seaside resort.

"And don't give her any money!" Madame Chauvineau ordered them firmly. "It's a punishment!"

But they did. Bless them.

Chapter 29

Back in Paris, unbeknown to me, Sister Marie-Cécile had been battling with Madame Chauvineau over my fate again, which had prompted the highly stressed social worker to yell, citing one of my friends' surname: "I'd rather have one hundred Nguyen than **One** Bertrand!"

For the sake of the school community, Sister Marie-Cécile had decreed that my status as a 'boarder' was no longer a viable option.

"…We'll only have her as a day pupil. She's too much of a bad influence on the other girls…"

Quite by chance, Madame Chauvineau found a '*foyer*', a hostel for young women a mere ten minutes away from the school.

This totally unexpected gift of near total independence filled me with absolute joy.

I was now where I had always aspired to be, in the *Baccalaureat* stream hoping to make sense of the profundity of Philosophy mixed with the resourcefulness of analytical accountancy and organisational strategies. At least, the main focus this year would be on the French *Baccalaureat* which was always sat the year before the final exams.

Rimbaud and Verlaine had always intrigued me. I knew next to nothing about their private lives due to the school censors. Thus, the burning question remained unanswered: why was Verlaine languishing in a prison cell? It took a trip to a Welsh university for me to discover the true meaning behind one of Verlaine's most celebrated poems '*Le ciel est par-dessus le toît, si bleu si calme…*'. In the lesson of Literature given back in Paris, Mademoiselle Germaine had firmly framed the poem within the perimeters of common decency, only deigning to reveal that Verlaine had written this particular poem whilst in prison. Mourning his lost youth, he projected the inner turmoil of his tortured soul onto the small patch of clear blue sky which he could just about see through the bars of his prison cell. Unable to understand the cause of Verlaine's agony, we had let it pass over our heads and learnt the poem by heart, reciting the words, oblivious to the profound tragedy of a life sacrificed for love. Later, Rimbaud appeared on the scene with poems declaiming his fascination for the untouchable beauty of death. Hence, the unfortunate '*Ophélie*' glowed under beams of sunrays as her inert diaphanous body surrounded by spring flowers glided majestically through the limpid waters of the shallow river, and the '*Dormeur du Val*', that young soldier looked so devastatingly handsome and serene, asleep against a tree with a red rosette glistening on his breast where a bullet had pierced his heart. At school, like saints and sinners, Verlaine and Rimbaud had never been mentioned in the same breath but in Wales, away from the rigorous censorship of a respectable 'School for Girls', I suddenly discovered that the two had been lovers but the fickle Rimbaud wanted to live his youth like a man in a hurry to die. A free spirit can never be contained and when the insouciant Rimbaud threatened to leave, Verlaine shot him. That was what Mademoiselle Germaine, as head of a respectable Catholic establishment, could not bring herself to reveal. In the days when the whole nation was captivated by the passionate love affair of 'A Man and A Woman', reeled out in cinemas all over France, it seemed quite unthinkable, even improper, to introduce the taboo notion that love can evolve between a man... and another man.

However, she was right to hold back. Children do not need to know everything. They simply would not understand. The poem was beautiful in itself with verses singing to the glory of a lost earthly heaven. For us girls, barely in our teens, the dissection of an obsessive passion would only have spoilt the sheer splendour of words rhyming to heighten the torture and pain of one lonely heart.

Up until now, Mademoiselle Germaine had been the teacher I admired most. Now in the Baccalaureat stream, I learnt that my French teacher was going to be Madame Sinclair.

On that first lesson of Literature, she walked in. Instantly, the class fell silent. She looked imposing but only because she was tall. Her slim graceful silhouette towered over our wooden desk and her shy retiring smile seemed to lift the overriding gloom that hung around the classroom. She was young and exuded with charismatic charm. Her sheer presence was enough to tame the wildest of spirits and the hush that followed every time she entered the classroom had the most profound calming effect on me.

Under her tutelage, I developed a sound knowledge and understanding of literature, skills which, up until then, had been rather limited. Quite by chance, as if the Gods were determined to get the best out of me, I became friends with Sophie, the star of the class who time after time produced the best essays, quoting authors and literary works that nobody else had ever heard of. She even managed to get full marks for one of her essays. On the day the teacher handed it back, the whole class gasped in total disbelief. Someone heckled:

"That's impossible!"

Madame Sinclair responded very calmly.

"I know. It shouldn't be possible but I couldn't fault it. Sophie's essay is as good as if it had been written by a university student. I did hesitate about the mark but in the end, I had to give it the mark it merited."

Unfortunately, Sophie's popularity did not match her literary skills. It all started the previous year when, during a gym lesson, she tried to 'touch up' Virginie who retaliated by slapping her squarely in the face. After that incident, girls became wary of her. What did not help her cause was the fact that Sophie was extremely secretive. We knew nothing about her except that she was good at writing essays. Every time we asked, she would flatly refuse to let us read them. Inevitably, she did not have many friends. In fact, she had no friends at all which is probably why, when I came along, she was quite grateful that someone was willing to talk to her. And we talked, mostly about books. She introduced me to new authors, in particular Boris Vian, a literary rebel living on the margin of society, who had been inspired by Jean-Paul Sartre.

"You must read '*J'irai cracher sur vos tombes*' ('I will go and spit on your graves') though I must warn you it's not an easy read."

I had never read anything as blasphemous as the title implied and I was not sure I wanted to, but I was curious. It was by reading this book that I discovered the aggressive and destructive powers of a rebellious mind and I consciously blocked the brutal and obscene images, the raw anger, the anarchic philosophy and the foul language used to express these.

We met at La Coupole, the famous café where the intellectual elite of post–war France used to thrash out their existentialist ideas. Sophie greeted me with the question:

"What did you think, then?"

"Didn't like it. Too violent for me." I simply stated.

"Maybe you'll like his other one better: *'Automne à Pékin'* ('Autumn in Beijing'). It's not violent at all. The story takes place in a fantasy land and has more to do with symbolism. I think you'll enjoy it more."

I did not enjoy it at all. For a start, the story had nothing to do with the seasons and was not set in Beijing. In fact, it was not even set in China! And what about those symbols Sophie had referred to? What symbols? Did I miss them all? Come to think of it, I did not understand the book at all.

From then on, Sophie and I met regularly after school and always in cafés. Bits by bits, I learnt more about her and a tiny bit about her private life. When she finally revealed that her parents lived not far from the school, I wondered why we did not go there for our little meetings.

"We can't. My parents don't like visitors, my mother especially."

"Why?" I could not help asking.

"I don't know. That's just the way they are."

It was months before she trusted me enough to open up the door of her secret world. The first thing she revealed about herself was that she was an only child. Well, I thought, nothing extraordinary about that. As far as I knew I was an only child too. Then, before she could reveal anything about her parents, she swore me to secrecy which I readily did because I could not wait to find out what the big secret was all about.

"Now, promise you won't say anything," she started, staring at me straight in the face with her big blue eyes.

"My mother is a freelance journalist."

"Ah!" I exclaimed. "That's why you're so good at writing essays."

What I really wanted to say was: 'what was all the big fuss about?' But I did not. I did not want to probe too much in case she would clam up on me.

Now she wanted to introduce me to her parents.

"It's not going to be easy, though. As I said, they don't like visitors but we might be able to catch them on a good day."

We crept up the stairs to the first floor of this modern building, almost as if we were afraid to disturb the peace.

"I've got my key but I'd better ring the bell just to warn my parents that we're here."

After a few seconds, the front door opened… ever so slightly. Through the narrow gap, I saw a pair of eyes scowling back at us.

"Yes?"

"Hi mum, it's me. I've brought my friend Martha… you know… the friend I was telling you about…"

The pair of eyes narrowed to take a better look at me.

"Yes, yes. Pleased to meet you but I'm afraid I can't see you today. I'm too busy."

After this extremely brief encounter, we retreated to a nearby café.

"Sorry about that but I did warn you. I'm sure you'll meet them eventually… one day." Sophie began apologetically.

"Don't worry, I'm sure I will."

However, fate decided otherwise. I never did meet her parents and I never got to read any of Sophie's essays but our friendship continued to thrive through our love of books and through our mutual admiration for one particular teacher: Madame Sinclair.

At senior school, I expected to be intellectually stretched and challenged. I wanted to be inspired if not by the teachers at least by the learning process. I yearned to be encouraged to think independently, form my own opinion and satisfy my intellectual curiosity. Yet, the teaching was little more advanced than that at elementary school. Teachers still expected us to learn pages by heart without us being required to understand, discuss or evaluate a single word of the topics we had to regurgitate the following lesson, and all for the sake of gaining a mark that would end up in our school reports. Refusing to indulge in this pointless exercise, devoid of any intellectual merit, especially when studying Literature, I created a conflict I was desperately keen to avoid with one particular teacher.

On that day she picked my name. I stood up.

"Could you recite…" Madame Sinclair began.

I looked straight at her.

"I haven't learnt it."

Aghast, the whole class turned towards me.

The teacher seemed taken aback.

"Why?"

"I don't know… I haven't learnt it."

"Maybe you didn't have enough time…" She suggested, hoping to give me some excuse to justify my lack of effort.

"No, I had plenty of time."

"Was it perhaps too difficult?" She queried, looking increasingly sympathetic.

"No."

"Or perhaps you didn't understand it…" She stated, trying in vain to rescue me from an impossible situation.

"No… I understood it perfectly."

A long silence loaded with suspense followed. Everyone waited with bated breath for the teacher's reaction. Eventually, Madame Sinclair's eyes fell on her mark book. She seemed to hesitate.

"Very well…" She finally said. "You may sit down."

Despite this little contretemps, she remained my favourite teacher. Meanwhile, rather than devote most of my time studying my main subject which was Accountancy – a complete aberration for any writer, poet or a bohemian soul like mine – I chose to spend all my intellectual energy writing verses and poems.

These were the glory glory days. Even Sister Marie-Cécile had stopped picking on me and rarely ventured into our domain where in the past she had been so unceremoniously booed, preferring to remain in the relative safety of her office tucked away behind the staffroom on the first floor.

Back at the *foyer*, my newly independent life resumed. I met up with old friends and made new ones from Germany, Canada and other countries that I did not even know existed. Nothing noteworthy happened, during my short time there, although… The Sister in charge decided that in order to prepare us for the outside world, we needed to be thoroughly briefed on the cycle of life, just in case we did not know that babies had nothing to do with the 'spontaneous generation' or the well-flogged notion of the 'immaculate conception'.

Sure enough, a short time later, an expert in the matter presented himself at the electronic doors armed with projector, slides and various diagrams. The television room was set up with extra rows of chairs to accommodate preacher and learners. That evening, we took our seats, feeling in a rather frisky mood. The man propped up his projector on the metal pedestal whilst we cheered his every move. He did have some difficulty in calming down a nubile audience whose raucous behaviour matched that of a bunch of women waiting for the Chippendales to strip. However, he did eventually manage to restore some calm. Just as he was about to click on the first slide, a large bastion of thick dark robes swept silently into the back of the room. Everyone turned around. I think I counted at least nine nuns standing like a solid row of prop forwards waiting for the proceedings to begin. Waving her hand with carefully calculated indifference, one of them hailed:

"Don't mind us, just carry on!"

Where on earth had they all come from?

At first, the speaker showed a black and white diagram of the female anatomy: the usual standard upturned triangle with curled-up antennas as depicted in all medical journals that none of us could satisfactorily identify with… even with the use of a mirror… especially with the use of a mirror! Swiftly, the speaker moved on to the male anatomy. A black curvy line delineated the rough shape of a male member in its inert state. Then, without warning, the speaker clicked on to the next slide. Suddenly, a huge diagram of a fully erect member appeared, surrounded by names and numbers. The rather abrupt apparition caused uproar in the room. Shrieks of sustained laughter forced the speaker to delay the proceedings for a while, giving me time to check on something.

"Dom!" I called out. "Turn around and see if the nuns are laughing."

"I can't!" She protested. "I dare not to."

"Come on, quickly." I urged her.

"Well, **you** turn around and see for yourself, then."

So I turned around. Some of the nuns were gripping their chins tightly with one hand. Others were simply standing very straight with their arms firmly folded across their chests, but all without exception were smiling…

or smirking as one of the girls pointed out. At the end of the session, we all stayed behind while the nuns filed quietly out of the room. Then Chantal, a girl from Orléans, turned around towards us and said out loud what every single one of us had been thinking:

"What did they want to know all that stuff for?" she asked, setting off another volley of rippling laughter.

"I mean," she continued unabated, "what business is theirs to know what an erection looks like… As for contraception, what nun needs to know all about contraception?"

We were now howling with laughter, doubled up with pain as our abdominal muscles contracted as they had never done before. Amid this cacophony of side-splitting laughter, a perfectly controlled voice rose and asked:

"Okay, then. Who wants to go to town with me?"

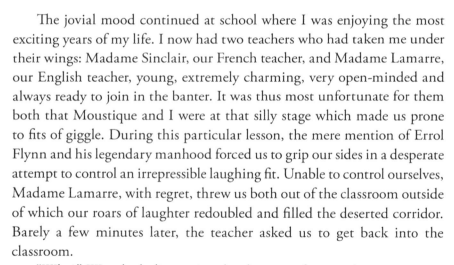

The jovial mood continued at school where I was enjoying the most exciting years of my life. I now had two teachers who had taken me under their wings: Madame Sinclair, our French teacher, and Madame Lamarre, our English teacher, young, extremely charming, very open-minded and always ready to join in the banter. It was thus most unfortunate for them both that Moustique and I were at that silly stage which made us prone to fits of giggle. During this particular lesson, the mere mention of Errol Flynn and his legendary manhood forced us to grip our sides in a desperate attempt to control an irrepressible laughing fit. Unable to control ourselves, Madame Lamarre, with regret, threw us both out of the classroom outside of which our roars of laughter redoubled and filled the deserted corridor. Barely a few minutes later, the teacher asked us to get back into the classroom.

"Why?" We asked, disappointed to have our fun cut short.

"Because you were making more noise outside than you were inside the classroom."

Forget about Errol Flynn. We were there to learn English and our dear teacher would make sure that we did. It was customary for her to give us newspaper clippings for us to translate usually cut out from the Observer, the Times and sometimes the Guardian, but not too often because the latter newspaper was considered leftist and she did not want to get into trouble with the authorities. Anyhow, for that particular lesson, Madame Lamarre had decided that for a change we would study a dialogue to get us familiar with the vernacular. She distributed photocopied sheets depicting a husband and wife in the process of doing some DIY around their home. Unused as we were with spoken English, we struggled to make sense of the situation. Finally, running out of time and patience, Madame Lamarre decided to take the situation in hand and guide us through by explaining each of the scenes.

"Look!" She started. "The man's just hit himself on the thumb with a hammer and he shouts '*Confound it!*' Come on! Use your common sense, what do you think he's shouting?"

'*Confound it?*'

We all looked at each other with blank faces.

"We don't know, Madame."

"Come on, if you hit yourself on the thumb, what would you shout?"

"I'd say *Zut!*"

"Me, I'd say *Mince alors!*"

"Well, me, I say *Mer-de!*" Someone sounded.

The whole class erupted. We joked and laughed for the next five minutes until it was time to take down our homework. After Madame Lamarre had packed her things and left the room, Virginie turned towards the whole class and waving her arms like an orchestra conductor and chortled:

"Now girls, don't forget. From now on if you hurt yourself, remember to shout: '*Confound it!*'"

If Madame Lamarre had been careful to tread cautiously around political grounds, our History teacher, a spinster named Mademoiselle Boucher, had far less political scruples. As she explained during a lesson how the Renault factory in Saint-Cloud had been nationalised after the Second World War as a punishment for having collaborated with the Nazis, she had taken the opportunity to jump to the defence of workers unions, veered towards socialist ideology and ended up touching upon the principles of communism. I do not know how Sister Marie-Cécile got to hear about it but the next thing we knew, Mademoiselle Boucher was sacked, summarily dismissed and thrown out to the wolves. With that kind of dismissal, our poor unfortunate teacher knew that she would never be able to teach again and on several occasions, we spotted her in the café opposite the school pouring her heart out over a glass of red wine while we listened to her embittered plea, sympathising with her and telling her what a good teacher she really was, to which she had replied:

"What good is it to me now? I'm effectively unemployable."

As we stared at her dejected face slumped over her empty glass, I felt pity for the woman, the kind of pity that gnaws at the root of each nerve and snags the heart. It was a painful spectacle to watch but refusing to contemplate her doomed future, we wished her well, convinced her that she would find something else, something better even. She smiled at our misplaced optimism, and then... she disappeared for ever.

Chapter 30

"To leave is to die a little…"

The move to a *foyer* was my first step towards independence. I could come and go as I pleased without having to tell anybody where I was going. At weekends, I was no longer obliged to traipse to the godmother's apartment, with the inevitable result that from then on we rarely saw each other. There was no point. Having droned on for so long how much of a burden I was, I had long considered her a burden too. She occasionally left a message at the foyer's reception begging me to come home because she was having a party and there was no one to help her clear up the dishes afterwards.

It was during one of these impromptu evenings that I finally solved the mystery of my birth. When I arrived at the godmother's apartment, I opened the door and was immediately confronted by a man the size and looks of Napoleon. As soon as he saw me, he exclaimed:

"Qu'est-ce qu'elle ressemble à *Adèle!"* ("Doesn't she look like Adèle!"). The godmother panicked. Very swiftly, she grabbed the bewildered man by the arm and dragged him into her bedroom where they stayed for a good ten minutes. As they re-emerged from the bedroom, the godmother put some music on. An awkward silence froze everyone on the spot and shifty glances swept the stunned faces. Far from being put off by the sudden icy climate, little Napoleon invited me to dance and began to make small talk.

"You're very pretty… I have a son who is six foot tall… I wish you could meet him… you'd like him…"

I know and I knew. As far as I was concerned, nothing more needed to be said. My suspicions had been confirmed by this little man, a colonel in the French Army, whom I had long suspected to be my father. The mystery solved, I did not want to think about it anymore.

As I became more and more detached from the godmother, I relegated her to a part of my life that already belonged to the past. I still hear Martine's reproachful tone echoing in my head:

"Gosh, your poor godmother… you're so harsh with her…"

Then, out of the blue, after months of not communicating, I received a letter from Jack. Could he come and visit me in Paris? I was not ready for this and quite frankly, I wanted him out of the frame and out of my life but unbeknown to me, fate had already decided upon our future.

Right now though, I had to prepare for the French Baccalaureat. In class, Francine and I always sat together. We had met as boarders, discovered that we both loved books and had a similar sense of humour; so we had remained together ever since. What I found so endearing about her was the way she parodied her looks, constantly complaining about her thin lips too close to her nose, her large protruding chin, her small eyes set too close to each other, her skin covered in *baby* freckles – I mean, I'm seventeen for goodness sake - and her hair so limp and lifeless that she compared it to a pack of cooked noodles.

"There's no point in me putting any make-up on," she had once declared with a resigned sigh, "because whenever I do I end up looking like Cleopatra with crossed eyes."

To listen to her, you would have thought that she had been created straight from one of Quasimodo's ribs. But I loved to stare at her when she was busy pointing at her every quirky feature. I wanted to tell her that physical beauty is a distractor of the soul and that, through her crunched-up face, it was easier to see her gentle spirit in total harmony with her beautiful soul. And then one day, she told me something nobody had ever said about me.

"You're lucky because you don't have to bother… you're beautiful… You're so beautiful that you actually glow."

I was stunned.

"I mean it." She insisted. "You glow from within. You have this kind of beauty that makes people notice you. It's nothing to do with the physical… it's more like… actually, I don't know how to describe it."

I stared at her, lost for words.

"For example, when you walk into the classroom, we don't need to turn around, we feel your presence… we know you're there."

"Do you?"

I was intrigued. Having long come to terms with the plain fact that I was the proverbial ugly duckling, the runt of the litter, it seemed very odd and rather peculiar to hear anyone deviate from the blatant truth. But she was, with the difference that I was not prepared to accept it while Francine was not prepared to let me ignore it.

In our idle moments, we often talked about our favourite romantic heroes. Rousseau was one - he had to be - and Chateaubriand, although I did find him somewhat dark, often churning lugubrious thoughts. Then Francine suddenly effused:

"Don't you just love Monsieur Rochester?"

"You mean, Monsieur Rochester from Jane Eyre? Oh, I love him and I love him even more because he doesn't look like a Greek god; I love his rugged features and his manly stance and his straightforwardness… What about Maxime de Winter?"

"Oh I love Maxime de Winter! He's so sophisticated with his dark and mysterious looks and the fact that we never know what he's up to right up to the very end."

The more names we cited, the louder we screamed… with laughter, excitement and awe because we were both transported and swirling into an euphoric spiral of love: from the primitive, instinctive and exclusive to the more sophisticated, spiritual, and universal, from the mutual and fulfilling to the unrequited and destructive. Sometimes we discussed the stronghold of love, so powerful and so devastating that it equated death as in 'Paul and Virginie', 'Romeo and Juliet', 'Tristan and Isolde' and *'Les Enfants Terribles'*… which made me wonder: doesn't love always equate death?

I went to spend the Easter holidays with Jack who had now graduated and lived in a seaside town in Wales where he had a steady job. Sophie came with me because she had fallen in love with one of Jack's friends, Bob the hippy who lived in a derelict bothy in the Welsh hills. But life among the bracken and the odd sheep finally got to him, so he eventually made his way back to town where he settled down with a conventional girl who worked for the Council.

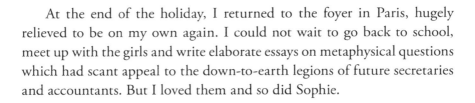

At the end of the holiday, I returned to the foyer in Paris, hugely relieved to be on my own again. I could not wait to go back to school, meet up with the girls and write elaborate essays on metaphysical questions which had scant appeal to the down-to-earth legions of future secretaries and accountants. But I loved them and so did Sophie.

The day of the exam finally came. We were dispatched to various schools and as I made my way to my designated establishment, I felt all my nerves tingling with excitement. I took deep breaths as I walk briskly along the avenue. The sunrays streaming through the clear blue sky and the warm tranquillity and serenity that filled the air reminded me of Verlaine's poem. I felt elated and could not wait to sit at the desk which would have my name on it, line up my pens in the wooden groove and launch into a written rendition of all the poetic notions I had accumulated over the years.

For once, the examiner was a young man. He swiftly distributed the exam papers and promptly gave the signal to begin. During the exam, he tip-toed around the classroom and stopped several times near my desk to peer at my work.

Having completed the grammar section, I quickly moved on to the main part of the paper. As usual, it was a choice between an 'étude de tex*te*' or an essay. I knew before I had even begun that I would opt for the essay as it allowed me more freedom of expression. I read the title: *'Partir, c'est mourir un peu…'* ('to leave is to die a little') Discuss using relevant literary references.

A sudden rush of illustrious names came to the fore and I found myself sifting through poets and authors, poems and novels, sailing away with Pierre Loti's mariners and Lamartine's sailors, bewailing separated lovers and the inexorable end that most of them chose: death. The ideas came thick and fast and I hurriedly scribbled down a draft before writing the final version with my fountain pen, slanting the letters more than usual in order to give the written work that extra romantic feel.

The stratagem clearly worked because when the results came, just before the end of term, I could not believe my mark. 16/20.

"That's impossible!" I exclaimed. I looked at the front of the envelop again to make sure it had my name on it. The biggest surprise, however, was to discover that Sophie's mark was identical to mine. I suddenly found myself on a par with the super brain of the class, a feat I had never thought possible, and once again I donned my superior airs, resumed my triumphant march and looked down with sheer insolence at Sister Marie-Cécile's discomfiture. I wanted to brag and tell her that I was right up there floating on cloud nine in the company of angels; and in that triumphant moment I felt as if my feet would never touch the ground again.

Alas they did, much sooner than I expected, for something happened that made me crash back down to earth. On my subsequent visit to Madame Chauvineau to give her my astonishing result, I learnt that Sister Marie-Cécile adamantly refused to have me back and this time, her decision proved to be final. I froze in a state of shock mixed with anger and frustration while at the same time feeling overwhelmed by a sense of betrayal and revulsion, immediately followed by profound sadness. What made it worse was that at no time did Sister Marie-Cécile pluck up the courage to tell me face to face *why* I was being expelled, and just when my teachers had finally succeeded in taming the little rebel, I was firmly shown to the door. Everyone was in shock. The atmosphere in the staffroom became heated as teachers argued for or against me, and friends who happened to pass the staffroom during those heated exchanges diligently reported to me what they had overheard. But Sister Marie-Cécile would not be swayed, so the teachers *en block* wrote a petition to try and save me, but to no avail. Overnight, I had become a *cause célèbre* but as in most cases, the *cause célèbre* ends up a victim and that was something I had vouched never to be. Neither a saint nor a martyr be. So I accepted my fate stoically and made the most of my final days at school.

As the end approached, I became acutely aware that I was about to lose my earthly heaven and my school friends. I would no longer be transported into the heady swirl of pupils and teachers rushing to their classes. I would miss the hustle and bustle of steamy corridors, their musty smell rising from damp wooden floors, the intellectual exchanges with teachers and friends and the excitement of learning different subjects. Thrown out at the mercy of a cold alien world, who would I have to discuss my favourite authors and poets?

I never went on holiday again with my mischievous friend, Marie-France. Moustique had long disappeared in the Parisian rush-hours. Martine took her Baccalaureat in Accountancy. She is probably a successful accountant somewhere in Paris. Magali accompanied me to the station on my way to England, neither of us aware that we would never see each other again. Francine and Yvette stayed on to complete their final year of the Baccalaureat. As for the godmother, she remained on the inaccessible eighth floor of her apartment in the suburb of Paris surrounded with all kinds of paints and varnishes she needed for her nails and canvases.

But worse of all, I never went back to Germany.

Alone in Paris, there was only one thing left for me to do. Fly away and start another adventure somewhere new, somewhere perhaps even more exciting, make new friends and start all over again just like I had had to do when I left the orphanage. But in my heart of heart I knew this would not be possible because forced to face the painful reality, I could not help asking myself: would I ever find again the same cluster of loyal friends like Moustique, Francine, Yvette, Sophie and Martine or devoted and caring adults like Mademoiselle Germaine, Madame Sinclair, Madame Dubernet, Monsieur Grivard and Madame Lamarre?

Would I ever experience again the mutual admiration, the same glorious adulation, the scripted and unscripted cerebral challenges or simply the sheer joy of being in their company? Leaving so abruptly and so unexpectedly the place where I had spent the happiest years of my life was like receiving the final *coup de grâce*, the ceremonial slaughter that would end for ever those wild and carefree adolescent years.

This is why, dear friends, '*to leave is to die a little...*', and more... much more.

THE END

Lightning Source UK Ltd.
Milton Keynes UK
UKOW04f0554120118
315995UK00001B/69/P